The Pedagogy of Self-Authorship

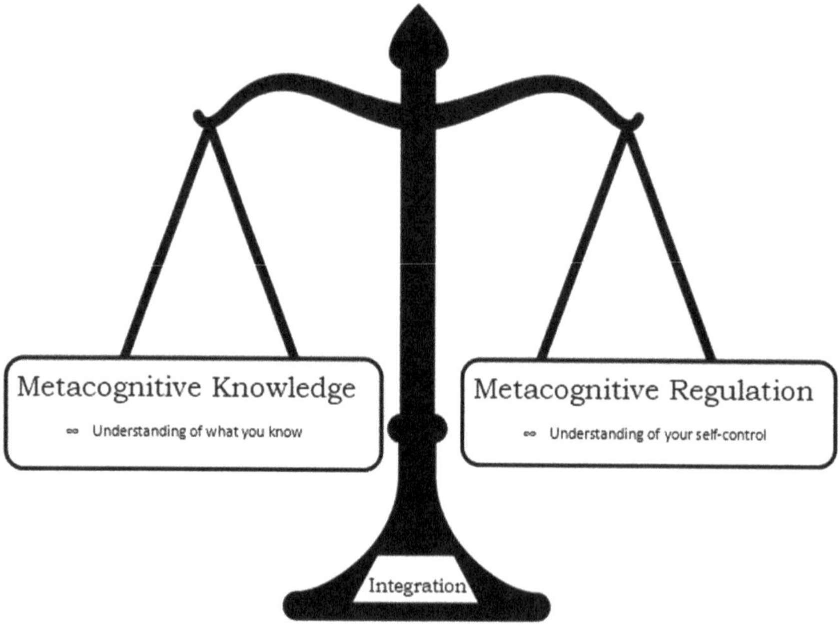
Metacognitive Knowledge
∞ Understanding of what you know
Metacognitive Regulation
∞ Understanding of your self-control
Integration

Philip R. Hulbig

The Pedagogy of Self-Authorship

The Neurocognitive Impact of Science and Metacognition

Springer

Philip R. Hulbig
Program for the Advancement of Learning
Lesley University
Cambridge, MA, USA

ISBN 978-3-031-41435-0 ISBN 978-3-031-41436-7 (eBook)
https://doi.org/10.1007/978-3-031-41436-7

This Springer imprint is published by the registered company Springer Nature Switzerland AG
The registered company address is: Gewerbestrasse 11, 6330 Cham, Switzerland

Paper in this product is recyclable.

To my wife Laurene whose love and support
has kept me hopeful
and working towards my highest goals.

In loving memory of my father who did not
live to see me finish this work.

You are the inspiration for this work and
greatly missed.

Contents

List of Figures

List of Tables

Part I
Knowledge

Chapter 1
Purpose

The last century saw a very clear demographic shift as millions were pulled out of poverty, and chief among the reasons for this economic growth was ever widening access to education (Pinker, 2018). The growing number of educated people has had profound effects on the world, increasing the number of breathtaking discoveries and the ability to mass distribute innovations that have changed the way we work. It has produced a sharp rise in standards of living for many and brought hope to many more that the lives of their children will be better than their own.

For decades, this relationship between education and standard of living has been clear. Children in regions of the world that lack basic public education often dream of going to school. It's an experience they seem to intuitively know would provide them with knowledge and skills to positively change their lives, if only they had the opportunity. However, in the parts of the world where students do have compulsory public education, there is a ubiquitous and growing challenge. Students are becoming harder to reach.

In one sense, schools have fallen victim to their own success. As time has gone by, there has been a shift from small one room rural schoolhouses to ever larger and complex industrial buildings capable of educating hundreds of students. In some respects, these developments in education mimic the growing industrialization of society itself. Efficiencies to support mass production were adapted for the job of mass education. But these efficiencies had their own weaknesses and also brought into the field certain attitudes of the world of business that have changed the practice of education profoundly.

Education has a history that extends deeply into our cultural past. To some evolutionary biologists (Laland et al., 2010; Morrison & Miller, 2018), the ability to be educated is an essential feature of humans as a species. It is thought that the oldest cave paintings in France's Lascaux cave system were used in rituals to teach young hunters their craft (Maier, 2021). So even here, at education's earliest stages, there is a relationship between education and the production of goods and services for the community. This economic relationship is only part of the story. It does not reveal the whole relationship between these artifacts and their creators, but our present

P. R. Hulbig, *The Pedagogy of Self-Authorship*,
https://doi.org/10.1007/978-3-031-41436-7_1

knowledge of cognition and learning suggests that the subjective experience of the individuals involved in this teaching experience would have been just as important as the products of the hunt itself. The veteran hunter's, or perhaps the tribal shaman's, knowledge about how the young hunters would experience the cave would help them support the self-regulatory abilities of the young hunters and craft an experience designed to maximize their learning.

From the subjective perspective of the teacher and the student, what is occurring is incremental and interactive. In the case of the young hunter, the experience is about gaining the skills necessary to be a productive and valued member of the community. In the case of his shaman teacher, it would be about integrating what they know about the hunt and what they know about their student to craft an experience. To successfully teach the hunting skills, the shaman would need to carefully consider the student's reactions and behaviors to determine their level of development and effectively address personal factors that may affect the student's learning and motivation. With this knowledge, interactions and experiences are crafted to promote the learning and development of the skills. Both the skills and the steps in the process of development were integrated to produce an individual capable of hunting at their highest level for the good of themselves and the community.

The caves of Lascaux were crafted to help young hunters learn practical hunting skills. This is evidenced by the fact the large cave paintings of bison and other animals had clear markings at critical anatomical locations for hunting a real life bison (Maier, 2021). Moreover, it is believed that these ritualized hunting lessons were held in the darkness of caves to invoke feelings of fear that the young hunters would need to learn to regulate if they were to achieve success hunting the megafauna of their day (Medina-Alcaide et al., 2021).

However, one can imagine another shift in perspective when it came time for the young hunter to join the actual hunt. Here the young hunters actual performance becomes the focus. Here his skill working in the moment, together with the other hunters of the tribe becomes paramount. His ability to support the other hunters and be supported for the greater success of the hunt will now be judged and evaluated by the tribal community. If their developmental level of hunting knowledge is commensurate with the actual hunting task, then their actions would produce tangible results for the tribe during the hunt. Ultimately, their success or failure would reflect on their social value to the group, and on the group's general fitness for survival, but also reflect on how the young hunter would come to value themselves. So, while their social standing would rise or fall based on the objective results of their behavior, their behaviors would have also been underpinned by their ability to muster the confidence and motivation needed for effective participation.

While the objective reality of their success or failure on the hunt would determine their social standing, it would be the hunter's own ability to identify their own personal strengths and weaknesses and push their own development in ways that would ultimately determine their value. This is a kind of knowledge that is different from knowing where to strike a bison. It is a knowledge of how one's abilities can be improved through practice and effort. It is a mindset based on the assumption that they have the ability to improve, an assumption that experience, social support, and their own internal dialogue can enhance.

Tribes that understood this underlying developmental reality would produce more effective hunters, and more of them. This is because these tribes would possess specific knowledge of how to support the other members of their tribe to reach ever higher levels of personal skill, productivity, and success. The ability to support and motivate others for the common good would have been a distinct kind of procedural knowledge, separate from hunting and gathering, that could have been part of the shared knowledge of the community, and perhaps was even codified in rituals like those used for hunting in Lascaux.

This dichotomy within human learning became more pronounced as societies developed agriculture and cities. Notions of developmental knowledge began to become decoupled from the valued products this knowledge could produce. The development of skills necessary for survival of the community were replaced by specialized skills. Communal knowledge would lose its perceived value in the face of the new value produced by possessing proprietary knowledge of narrow skill sets required for the production of products. The value of specialized knowledge would eventually come to overshadow the collective responsibility of the community to tend to the developmental capacities of all its members.

While the advent of money made it easier for those in the community to reward individuals for their contributions, it also supported social stratification and subjugation in ways not possible in a hunter gatherer community. The development of skills became viewed as an economic activity, seeing the situation more through the lens of what it produced and less through the lens of the process it took to get there. Economies of specialized workers developed, with each performing a designated service necessary for the city to function, but without individuals really knowing or understanding what or how those others did what they did. City life and specialization would have produced a more episodic experiential reality for people than the more integrated natural experiences of communal living experienced by tribal hunter gatherers. Interestingly, this system would have been more taxing on an individual's self-regulation as deep seated neurological instincts of tribalism found in all primates (Sapolsky, 2017) would have been more acutely and routinely activated in city dwellers, as individuals with different backgrounds, means of survival and levels of prestige would have had more opportunities to come in contact with each other and have conflicts. This would have required more robust methods of teaching self-regulation. This would have been a job that naturally fell upon families, and was probably supported through community rituals that evolved into the centralized religious authority that came to rule early city states.

This would have further supported the growing disconnect between the development of skills and the skills of self-regulation needed to achieve those skills. The invention of slavery exacerbated this problem as it not only obscured the relationship between output and the developmental skills needed to produce the output, but actively sought to destroy the development of those enslaved. Slavery's notions of manpower, gained through acts of subjugation and obedience, began to replace the notion of supporting the development of knowledge.[1]

Developmental education became the domain of elites, who unlike the rest of the society were afforded time to develop their thinking. Often these were self-reflective practices and philosophies that prepared them to assume the leadership positions of their societies. This division in education supported highly stratified societies with little to no social mobility. Essentially, those with the most access to both developmental and skill-focused education became the dynamic and thriving elite, while an ever more subjugated population received little to no support in their developmental education, outside of the skills that were developed within families, or shared within their religious communities. For most, a caring family member may have been their only hope, as finding a person who had both the time and the willingness to build and support a self-reflective, developmental mindset would have been rare for those born into the lower strata of society. Worse than this would be the various nefarious forces both natural, like the sudden death of caretakers, or socially imposed, like the social brutality that evolved to keep a developmental mindset from ever forming in the minds of those they oppressed (Miller, 1999). This tragic fact is evidenced by early manuals on how to keep slaves (Toner, 2014) and manage peasants (Vanhaute, 2021). These manuals outlined practices expressly designed to inflict levels of trauma that could effectively prevent any future cognitive development from occurring, all in the name of ensuring passivity and obedience.

Were it not for the reorganizing impact of pandemics on societies (Diamond, 1998), and the invention of the scientific method, the majority of mankind would still be as it was in the Middle Ages. The power of the scientific method on the collective consciousness cannot be overstated. It represents a simple heuristic, which can be learned and applied by anyone to solve problems as a natural part of the problem-solving process. The hypothesis contained in this book is that this scientific heuristic, while historically identified with the study and control of the physical world, can also be applied to the mental world, and has been applied this way since its inception. However, for much of the history of the scientific method, people did not fully realize its relationship to their generation and development of self-regulatory abilities. They conceptualized the process of becoming a scientist or 'enlightened' in terms of an end product. They did not see that at the foundations of their enlightenment was an increasing ability for the self-regulation and behavioral control necessary to organize experiments and achieve scientific aspirations.

This enlightened way of thinking enabled some members of society to break out of their social cast, and also challenge long-established ways of doing things. It is no coincidence that the first modern formulations of the approaches of science were by European philosophers like Bacon and Descartes only after the invention of

---

[1] The relationship between innovation, and the support or suppression of developmental education is clearly reflected in the Technological development of Ancient Rome. Its agricultural production was almost exclusively run by slaves, and over Rome's 2000 year history it made few innovations in agriculture. But in fields not dominated by slaves, like engineering, politics and war, fields where elites received both a strong developmental and skills based education, Rome demonstrated tremendous growth and advancement over its history.

the printing press. For this reason, it is important to think of the Western European Enlightenment as part of a metacognitive expansion of the common intellect. Just the very notion that there was a method that could be used to produce an idea about the truth of the world compelled ever larger numbers of individuals to contemplate their own problem-solving methods. Just knowing that there was a problem-solving method probably led to more people using a problem-solving method rather than the superstitious or ritualized behaviors of the past. This is not to say that systems of oppression did not remain firmly intact during this period, but they were now powerfully challenged by 'reason'. This led to revolutionary reforms that offered more opportunities to more people, breaking traditions and excuses for oppression, and offering practical solutions and ideas derived through using a scientific heuristic.

Systems of oppression really started to break down in the nineteenth-twentieth centuries (Jackson, 2003; Freire, 2018). During this time it was found that to produce a truly modern society, a population must have a basic level of education. While this idea was first used to build a threatening Prussian-style war machine, later Americans, like Mann (1855), realized such a system could be used to build the broad level of basic skills needed to support the businesses that were modernizing quickly. Slaves would not be able to reliably support this kind of economy. Factory jobs required an ability to follow more complex directions, communicate effectively, and work for the common good of the business. In other words, those in positions of power were again forced to consider the communal interests and developmental needs of the masses if they were to successfully produce goods for the community. This is why public schools of this time focused on developing reading, writing, and mathematical skills, while imposing inordinately harsh levels of discipline on those who did not conform to norms.

Early public schools were there to support the factories. The economic success of the factory system was able to offer an alternative to the agrarian lifestyle of the yeoman farmer a generation earlier. It produced a new kind of elite. This was an industrialist elite with the wealth and capability of supporting the workers in their factories as well as a whole new class of people who would work indirectly for the factories by providing valuable support services. However, these elites, unlike the aristocrats of the past, required an ever more skilled labor force capable of producing ever more complex products.

In many ways, the modern development of industrial society, with its recurring spurts of boom and bust, is mirrored in cycles of reform seen in education. Modern innovation required skills like writing and mathematics, skills that required an organized approach to their teaching and a level of self-regulation to access. As the need for an ever more skilled population was addressed by education, ever more expansive educational movements vied to provide the educational innovations needed to support the new and developing needs of industrial production. As time passed, cycles of innovation, improved educational access, and efficiency produced a society that required a higher level of education, not simply just to function at their jobs, but to enjoy the complex fruits of advanced industrial production.

Pragmatic reformers like Dewey (1903) realized in a world of growing authoritarianism, education and free thought were critical for a healthy democracy. Thanks to his efforts and those of other educational reformers, the twentieth century produced a curriculum for the average public school student in America that would have included not only reading, writing and mathematics but also science, social studies and history. Students were afforded unprecedented opportunities for group sports and athletics. They were afforded opportunities to produce art, participate in theater, and develop other creative outlets like poetry. Even courses that were at one time the hallmark of an elite education, like philosophy, were offered in high schools across the country as reform movements cyclically rose to the challenges presented by an expansive approach to mass education.

Lipman (1988), whose most influential work *Philosophy Goes to School* outlined an approach to philosophical discussions with children to build critical thinking and ethical reasoning skills through the use of philosophical inquiry. In this book, Lipman describes how he and his colleagues at the Institute for the Advancement of Philosophy for Children developed the approach and implemented it in schools across the United States. Lipman argued that philosophical inquiry would help children develop thinking skills, empathy, and a deeper sense of social responsibility. Lipman's research and work on teaching thinking and philosophy to children has influenced the development of many similar programs around the world.

For the first time in American history, swaths of the population were receiving an education that addressed both the skills they would need to become economically successful in the society, and also the needs of their developmental education. This can be evidenced by the acceptance of institutions of learning fostering developmentally informed teaching practices in primary schools and the widespread implementation of developmental education programs like kindergartens.

Moreover, the average family structure, which had for so long been the only source of developmental education for much of the population, was more stable than it had ever been for most Americans. For example, African Americans, who in earlier centuries would have had their families ripped apart by slave masters and peddlers in an attempt to deny them the opportunity to develop the complex supportive knowledge of how to promote self-regulation, now had the opportunity to develop this knowledge in their own community. This freedom afforded the African American community the stability to build supportive family structures, capable of facing the continued social and structural racism of the day. This social stability produced a generation of African Americans capable of the Herculean feats of self-regulation demonstrated during the protest movements that eventually led to the Civil Rights Act of 1968.

Public education at this time was not perfect. There were always some students left behind, usually due to economic, ethnic, or neurological reasons. However, each year the number of students left behind decreased as a share of the population. Civil rights legislation and special education programs made gains in both providing access to resources and innovations to support that access. But then something happened. American schools stopped making gains.

The number of students demonstrating advancement on standardized tests plateaued (NAEP 2022). This remained the case through the '80s, '90s and 2000s. By the late 2000s, for the first time in the history of American public schools, the overall number of students reaching basic academic proficiency began to decrease. This retraction has escalated to a point of crisis due to the worldwide pandemic (Mervosh, 2022).

For the first time since its inception, the statistical trend for students finishing their public education in America showed that the population would be less prepared academically than earlier generations (National Assessment of Education, 2022), and entering into a job market that will require a highly specialized skill set. The age of factories requiring ever growing manpower have passed and with it the expanding definition of what is required from a basic education. Computers, and soon a new generation of robots, have begun to replace human workers. Most of the jobs Americans historically would have been doing back in the 1970s, the last time student test scores in math were this low, are now overwhelmingly done by computers.

More than this, colleges (Cheng, 2022) and businesses (Hansen, 2021) have both noted that they are dealing with more students who are less prepared to meet the academic and economic needs of the advanced postmodern world that they inhabit. Perhaps more alarming is the building evidence that students are entering this system even less emotionally prepared than ever before. In a mixed methods investigation I (Hulbig, 2021) conducted asking kindergarten and first grade teachers to describe the behavioral presentation of their students, I received many statements like these from teachers across the country:

> Behavior has seemingly gotten worse in the 5 years I have taught. I am seeing a lot more students with high emotional, behavior and developmental needs.
>
> Lack of support with high incidences of aggressive behavior has led to less educational potential and thus more issues with behavior. (13 years of teaching experience)
>
> I have had kindergarten students who have been a physical danger to both me and to my students. (26 year teaching experience)
>
> I have years of experience so I am able to do it. Without my experience, my job would be virtually impossible. (Hulbig, 2021)

What is most alarming is that these were perceptions just before the outbreak of the COVID-19 pandemic and forced worldwide shutdown of educational institutions. There have been other concerning trends that suggest that it may be more difficult for the academic scores of students in public education to bounce back to their pre-pandemic plateaus. This is because just as more complex, socially and behaviorally involved students are arriving in the school systems, more veteran teachers are leaving, and the effects of burnout for those who remain is reaching crisis proportions (Fig. 1.1).

So while it may be tempting to scapegoat the present problems of the education system on the pandemic, the fact is COVID-19 only exposed faults, weaknesses, and broader social trends that have remained unaddressed. Educational leaders and politicians became complacent, viewing the years of plateaued test scores as, perhaps, just the way it is, an accurate reflection of those who are more and less capable of responding to education, an expression of the bell shaped curve. We now know based on the success of other countries in educating their populations that these scores were

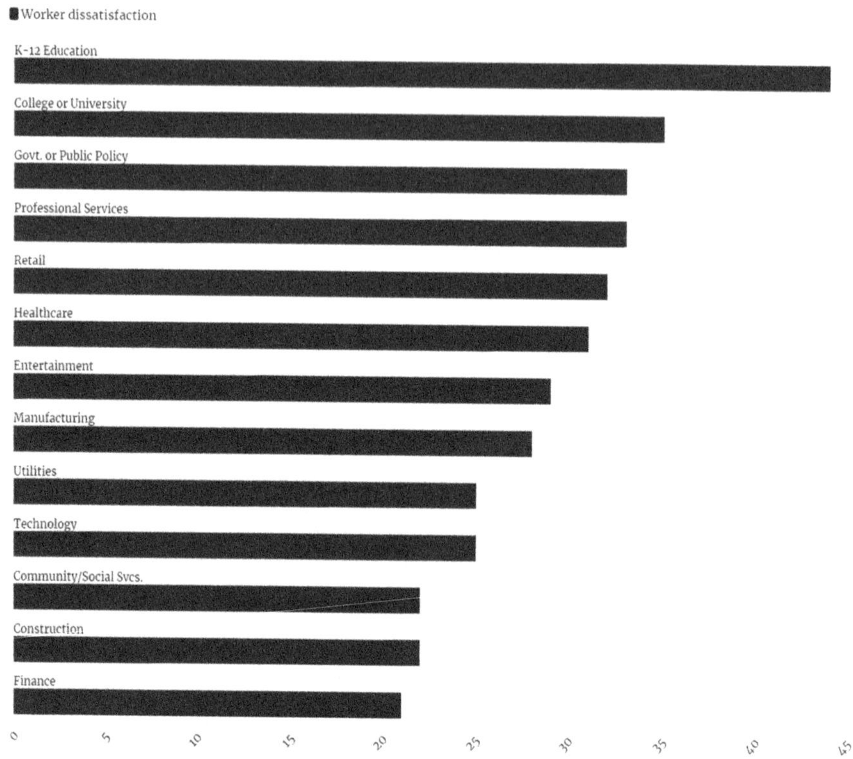

Fig. 1.1 US teacher satisfaction and burnout. *Note:* Gallup survey of percentage of US full-time worker dissatisfaction conducted March 14, 2022

more a representation of the implicit bias many inside and outside education feel about human capacity. They are a representation of what they believed was possible from those neglected demographics that were allowed to fail to show progress because their matrix for success was considered beyond the capacity of the school to teach. For example, in the case of the neurologically divergent, it is expected that a number will fail due to personal flaws that cannot be compensated for.

This willingness to allow and even expect failure is the result of the business-oriented attitude that has swamped American education. This is an attitude that sees an education as a commodity and feels it is a waste to spend time on those who don't deserve or can't afford to pay for it. From a business perspective, the ability to learn is a luxury that not all students can mentally and monetarily afford. Rather than building an education system capable of leaving no child behind, we have allowed our business sensibility to systematically leave behind the same demographics, and even use their past failures as a rationale to accept more failure, rather than realizing that what is really missing is a robust developmental education in the ways they can use their strengths and grow their skills and ability.

The reason developmental education is not a central feature of American education is not because we do not know how to deploy it. There are countless examples of similar school systems succeeding where others fail (Altshuler, 2003; Lipsitz, 2019, Perez, 2008). When researchers have gone out to investigate these anomalous school systems, their success always has to do with systematic efforts to build connections and a culture of support among students and faculty. This focus, when successful, also generally produces high levels of academic rigor and productivity.

Of course, wealthier schools are often able to best implement routines, programs, and other mechanisms to build these academic cultures of support. But I believe there is another factor at play, a factor that explains why even some poverty-stricken schools have been able to achieve academically rigorous cultures of learning in their schools. The deeper underlying factor in these cases is a willingness of the school and community to give students' developmental learning as prominent a role as skills-based education. These are both schools and communities that have found a way to commit to both forms of education.

Children in wealthy communities often have their developmental needs met and encouraged by parents who have the time and financial means to address these needs. Wealthier parents can afford to address their children's needs personally or through the hiring of surrogate professionals, and most often do both. Children from poorer communities often come from fractured families who are under tremendous financial and social pressures. These pressures affect their ability to have basic developmental needs met, let alone encouraged, fostered, and grown.

Money can enable districts to buy specialized programs or hire better-trained teachers. However, if students lack developmental understanding of their own learning and behavior, they will fail to regulate themselves, even if they are learning in well-funded schools, with well-credentialed teachers. What is developmental education and what are the best ways to approach it?

In this book the answer to this question is traced back, through educational routines and psychological theories, to its most primary neurological and information processes and functions. It presents an educational approach designed to reconnect modern and rapidly evolving educational technology with those ancient educational practices of self-knowledge and self-development that were at one time only deemed necessary for elites, but are now critical to the general education of an ever-widening population to support the postmodern economic activities critical for maintaining the advanced information-driven societies we currently inhabit.

The last 50 years in American public education have borne witness to a declining efficiency in the business modeled, skill-based education system. These systems are failing because self-developmental learning, which at one time would have occurred in an extended family or community, has collapsed. Sexism at one time prevented women from seeking any role other than the developmental education of their children. Women should be encouraged and supported to grow and develop in all ways they are able to grow and develop, but someone must be there to provide their children with the same support that will afford them the developmental education they need. This role can be taken on by fathers as readily as mothers. In fact, studies by the Pew Research Center have identified increasing numbers of stay at home dads taking on this vital role once reserved for women (Livingston, 2018).

However, increasingly both parents must work just to afford housing and basic utilities. The ability of families to balance household costs with the developmental needs of their children has become harder as the cost of basic needs like housing, health care, petroleum, and food have risen, forcing many parents to sacrifice more of their time with their children to make ends meet. This problem is amplified by the fact that the majority of students coming to schools these days are coming from single-parent homes, or moving through the turmoil of divorce.

In the early '70s, professionals warned about expanding numbers of unsupervised latchkey children (Venter & Rambau, 2011), so called because their parents were still at work when they arrived home from school, leaving them largely to socialize themselves. Today, this problem of students who fend for themselves while their parents are at work has not only increased, but also represents an inter-generational challenge to child rearing. This is because what is lost is not just the time parents could have spent with their child. There is a loss of stored family knowledge about how to approach developmental education when parents are not around to teach it. This is because much of the knowledge of self-regulation is conditional and not well-transferred abstractly. Learning self-regulation requires a direct and embodied approach, meaning an interaction must occur between teacher and student to both transfer and receive the knowledge.

These are the skills related to the actual physical and psychological nature of performance. They are more experiential than the abstract skills commonly accepted as part of good parenting. Family structures have historically been the last bastions of storage for this kind of developmental education across populations. And as generations of parents lose contact with this knowledge, the collective readiness for the usual skills-based education expected from students declines.

While the family has historically been the storehouse for this knowledge, it does not mean that individuals from outside the family cannot take up the slack, and they have. In many ways, this is what our best schools are doing, but the onslaught of factors that impair or prevent developmental learning from happening are going to require a new community, society, and worldwide commitment to developmental education. New factors that are affecting our ability to provide developmental education to students are arising everyday due to our ever expanding technological abilities.

Just as families and schools' capacity to provide the developmental education received in the past has come under real pressure, technology has changed the way we interact. Computers, smartphones, and the like allow parents to provide their children with hours of passive entertainment rather than hours of rough and tumble interactions that defined childhood in the past. Some of this online entertainment does include powerful academic or even important self-regulatory information. But concern is mounting that without real world experience and the support of a vested other person, all these devices are providing is an escape from the real world engagement needed to learn and sustain self-regulation.

It is my sincere hope that the information contained in this book will elucidate what I believe to be the underlying neural psychological phenomena underpinning developmental education—metacognition, or the ability to reflect and expand upon one's own learning. More than this I hope to show how weaknesses that impact an individual's ability to receive a developmental education can be addressed pedagogically through a metacognitive approach to problem solving that puts the tools of effective developmental and skills-based learning into the hands of the student. Empowering them to take charge of their own learning and their own development to achieve a self-authorship ability and personal transformation can only be achieved with the support of a community dedicated to the development and learning of its members.

1.1 Introduction

We live in two universes. One that extends as far as we can see, extending into space and infinitely beyond. It is the universe before our eyes. The other lives behind the eyes. It is a universe that is equally expansive, but in a much different way, expanding into an infinite realm of ideas and possibilities. That we have the ability to observe ourselves shifting between these distinct modes of processing is surprising (Nelson & Narnse, 1994), but perhaps even more surprising is that we have this ability to direct and control our function in each of these mental universes to lesser and greater extents. The definition of metacognition is succinct. It's generally described as the ability to think about one's thinking, or as Flavell (1979) described it, "cognitions about cognitions" (p. 906). It is a description of a property of the mind that can be identified through the brain's neurological processes (Allen et al., 2017; Fernandez-Duque et al., 2000; Peterson et al., 1999; Shimamura, 2000;) and the individual's developmental behaviors (Kegan, 1996; Nelson, 1996; Sapolsky, 2017; Valiant, 1993), opening it up to scientific investigation.

The definition of metacognition is elegant in its simplicity, but it is also practical in ways that open vistas on an evolving phenomenological complexity that straddles both sides of the Cartesian model of the universe. The brilliance of Flavell's model was to see that metacognition was a process of integrating thinking and action. Rather than trying to place one over the other, metacognition was a singular phenomena with sub-components like knowledge, regulation, or goal/task understanding. It provided theoretical support that made it possible to identify specific metacognitive skills, like feelings of knowing, judgments of learning, and other skills of metamemory, which have been studied as part of the process of learning and are localizable neurological skills in the brain that develop over an individual's lifetime (Ghetti & Fandakova, 2020). More than this, metacognition has changed the way educators approach their craft as teachers, promoting the study of specific techniques (Meher et al., 2021) and strategies that could enhance learning (Radovan, 2019; Woolfolk, 2016).

Educationally focused research has consistently found metacognition playing a fundamental neuropsychological role in the processes of learning and problem solving (Hulbig, 2021; Shimamura, 2000; Schraw et al., 2006; Quigley et al., 2019). Because of this, metacognitive elements are deeply embedded into many effective education practices (Dunlosky & Metcalfe, 2009; Schmitt & Newby, 1986). This, in turn, has led educational policymakers in the European Union and the OECD to advocate for greater acceptance of metacognitive practices that teach students how to learn about their learning (Radovan, 2019).

Beyond its role in improving a student's academic function, personal practices that promote an individual's metacognitive development can lead to educational transformations (Mezirow, 1975, 1991) as personal habits of self-directed learning develop into an ability for self-authorship (Kegan, 1982, 1996) over the course of one's life. The transformational qualities of a metacognitive education have been less studied than the impact of metacognitive strategies on specific areas of study (Desoete & De Craene, 2019; Schraw et al., 2006), educational routines (Dunlosky & Metcalfe, 2009; Vandenbroucke et al., 2018), or even metacognition's neurological components (Fernandez-Duque et al., 2000; Fleming et al., 2014; Wong et al., 2018). However, the self-transformative aspects of metacognition hold the hope that widely implemented educational approaches can be developed to positively address different ways of knowing, different ways of learning, and differing levels of personal productivity.

As discoveries in neuroplasticity make their way into the metacognitive practices of individuals, new and powerful approaches to self-regulation will be discovered, capable of bringing both physical and psychological healing to a vast array of conditions. These approaches will produce real and measurable effects, as well as subjective feelings of self-control and motivation in those who practice them. Metacognitive knowledge of this order will enhance self-regulation at the individual level in a way that could ultimately affect regulation at the communal and societal levels. For example, if an individual discovers a technique that improves their performance, that knowledge could be broadly disseminated. Modern communication technologies will make knowledge that at one time would have only supported the individual who discovered it, and perhaps those engaged in learning relationships with them, to be scaled up in a way that could ultimately support many others as it is shared across social media and the internet. Inversely, in classic human fashion, it can also be imagined that a community that lacks, or has been denied, this knowledge of how to learn about their learning could be marginalized by the larger society, a competing social class, or abusive individual to justify their prejudice, segregation, or repression, recreating the intellectual caste systems of the past that have historically divided people into groups of haves and have nots.

The passage of time also affects metacognitive knowledge and regulation in interesting ways that can shift based on developmental factors. Temporal factors of timing can be very powerful. It is well known that what may make sense in the short term may make decidedly less sense as the time horizon is extended. Knowledge of one's self is not immune to this effect. The person we believe ourselves to be is affected by the time horizon we are capable of conceptualizing. Different patterns become apparent as a personal timeline is extended, producing differing perceptions of events. Literally, the same events in a person's life can be integrated into their self-conception in different ways based on the temporal lens the events are viewed through. At every level, the processes of the brain are predictive (Seth, 2021) and constructive (Eagleman, 2020; Hoffman, 2000). An individual's interpretation of these self-generated predictions and constructions ultimately becomes the core feature of the cognitions that drive a person to act and determine their level of resilience.

The idea of a conceptual lens is very important when thinking metacognitively. The act of self-regulation always occurs in an immediate moment of subjective awareness. But the ability to step back, disengage with subjective experience momentarily, contemplate, and plan our actions can change the way we act the moment we re-engage. The metacognitive literature suggests that this integration process of our perceptual reality uses knowledge to produce evermore sophisticated actions. To capture this integrative aspect of metacognition, and the expansive developmental nature of transformational learning, this book presents its various themes on the subject through three lenses: *objective*, *subjective,* and *interpersonal*.

The goal of this introduction is to prepare the reader for the unique research model used here to capture data about the transformative learning experience. It presents a transformational learning experience from a student, teacher, and researcher's perspective. Part of what makes this work unique is that I am the writer, the researcher, and the student/subject whose transformative learning experience is going to be presented. I am a teacher who has spent my career working to promote the educational transformation described. I have investigated the science and interviewed the professors from the program whose educational pedagogy made the transformation described in this text possible. From this, a theory of metacognition is presented that, because of this unique integrative metacognitive methodology, is grounded in personal experience, research, and experimentation.

This book will present the research that is core to a strong abstract understanding of the subject of metacognition from a rich diversity of scientific fields and specialties, as well as sharing second- and first-person perspectives on the craft of teaching, learning, and transformation. These different forms of data and perspective are presented to support you, the reader, in your understanding and analysis of the phenomena, and provide valuable background information about transformation, insight into the student–teacher interactions that produce these transformations, and a strong theoretical grounding to further support your understanding of why transformational learning occurs.

1.2 Forms of Discourse and Data

The juxtaposition of first-person and third-person formats/perspectives is a purposeful way of representing both the data and a level of methodological process that is rarely reflected in scientific treatments of this subject. It is an attempt to represent, and stimulate, the methods of metacognitive thinking that integrate these differing modes of thinking. How the brain is capable of integrating various perspectives, models, and modes of thinking is not yet well understood. This question is described as the binding problem (Feldman, 2013; Isbister et al., 2018; Vroomen & Keetels, 2010) of neuropsychology.

The binding problem is a rather philosophical question. Physiological investigations into the phenomenon involve the integration of information coming into the brain. Different sensory inputs arrive in the brain at different times and are processed at different rates, and yet are experienced as occurring simultaneously (Feldman, 2013). Neurological binding has yet to receive a strong explanation, but binding information into a functional whole is also a distinct challenge for the field of computation, where it is not clear if computational solutions to the problem would inform neurological solutions. Presently, it has proven very hard for computers to make simple identifications that the human brain is able to make using relatively few sensory inputs. These differences have been made more apparent in recent *DishBrain* experiments using in vitro neural networks of living human nerve cells that demonstrate much stronger stimulus–response learning not seen in silicone-based computer systems performing the same task (Kagan, 2022).

The human experience of sensory perceptual binding demonstrates an implicit understanding of which sensory relationships meaningfully bind together to form higher-order organizations and meanings. Even the most powerful artificial intelligence programs start with hand-programmed solutions and are not a natural developmental process. While some programmers (Bäck & Schwefel, 1993; Kannappan et al., 2015) have devised very powerful programs that do have the capacity to evolve, as of the time of the writing of this book these programs have all required sometimes tremendous amounts of human programming and reprogramming (Yampolskiy, 2018). Metacognition's role in conscious integrative thinking suggests it may be part of a deeply seated cognitive process that plays a role in 'binding' the neurocognitively distinct ways of knowing that exist within and between individuals.

Metacognitive analysis integrates perspectives. The three core perspectives of cognition integrated are represented in the ways we can express ourselves in writing. First is the intra-personal subjective perspective, which is represented in this piece narratively, in first person. The second is still intrapersonal, but is more abstract. It is the objective/abstract perspective, written in the third person mode of academic writing and represented here through a deep review of the literature and analysis in the final chapter. The third perspective is produced through interactions with another person, and is more about managing the movement between first and third person perspectives during conversation. This interpersonal understanding is represented through interviews of eight professors from the PAL program. Interestingly, conversational modes of learning were found to be significantly related to metacognitive learning. Aspects of perspective shifting, from first person to third person, allow a qualitative experience to be cognitively integrated with abstract goals and desires.[2]

[2] Subjective perspective is a first person, largely qualitative perspective that holds primary the experiences, feelings, and perceptions of the mind of the individual. Objective perspective is a third person, largely quantitative perspective that holds primary the abstract, intelligible, and cognitive processes of the mind that perceive relationships which transcend experience, revealing conceptual patterns. There are many representations of this perceptual shifting from first person to third person in communication, language, and writing, but it is also represented in artwork, or even video games

This has been done to induce a level of metacognitive awareness that is demonstrative of the study's main conclusions and provide a full picture of the phenomena.

Changes in the narrative format here are intended to signal to the reader important shifts in perceptual stance, requiring readers to be active in their reading, connecting objective, subjective, and interconnected understandings that are not always possible to represent overtly in a text without distracting from the core message. From a writer's perspective, this is a curious feature of the subtle limitations of both first- and third-person descriptive approaches. The subjective, first-person perspective is able to capture subtle details, particularly motivational and emotional details that are not easily represented objectively. Inversely, the objective third-person perspective is able to link ideas and express connections more clearly and concisely, but only at the expense of removing many of the specific, and possibly obscuring, details of the subjective mode.

The subjective perspective can obscure objective connections precisely because of its ability to convey emotional and motivational data. For example, I find it difficult to talk about my early schooling from a first-person perspective without presenting the school's position negatively. This is because, from my subjective viewpoint, particularly at that time, my experiences were overwhelmingly negative. However, I caution the reader to refrain from simplifying the complexity of the narrative. Details in the narrative connect powerfully to later insights and educational issues in a broader context. Many connections remain embedded in the text and were not further elucidated to remain focused on the book's central themes of metacognition, the development of transformative self-authorship, and metacognitive pedagogy.

The reasons behind the school's actions were examples of connections not fully elucidated in the personal narrative. The school's perspective could have simply been that they were responding to the relevant facts of the situation. School personnel used their subjective experience, training, and knowledge about learning and human potential to both determine and justify their actions. Just as my limited personal experience colored my interpretation of events, so did theirs. As the writer, I have taken great care to honestly present what I remember about growing up as a "special education" student in the public schools. However, my perspective was produced by a lived response to the school's decisions and actions. So, while the school's reasons for acting must be inferred, the forces that compelled their actions are important in that they develop a deeper understanding of the data presented. For this reason, the reader is encouraged to think about how this integration of third-person abstract understanding with first-person embodied understanding produces the choices and courses of action that are realized and performed by the individual.

---

where you can play either behind the eyes of the character in first person, or from the third person view, looking down on the character as an object in the field of game play.

1.3 Forming a Theory of Mind

First-person descriptions invite the reader into a more personal understanding of an individual's theory of mind. A theory of mind is an internal, cognitive heuristic used by individuals to explain their behavior and predict the behaviors of others (Gallagher & Frith, 2003; Premack & Woodruff, 1978, Seth, 2021). In the narrative investigation of my metacognitive development, the high school made certain predictions and treated me in certain ways, not because they had nefarious intentions, but more likely because they had seen students like me before. They had seen what happened to students who presented with my educational profile. Professionally, they defined a specific learning disability as a permanent, neurobiological fixture of my being. From a practical perspective, they believed that if you could not read, write, or do the math, your options in life would be limited. Moreover, their ability to address the academic challenges of individual students, particularly neurologically atypical students, was also limited. Their decisions were often proclaimed out of practicality and with an intent to be realistic about the situation.

1.4 Social Replication

A theory of mind, while developing within the mind of the individual, also has the earlier discussed property that, while developed by an individual, can be replicated across a culture like a meme (Spitzberg, 2014), producing the social mechanisms of its justification. Part of the reason I struggled to learn to read and write during my formative years of schooling was I also believed in the fixed and permanent nature of my Specific Learning Disability (SLD). Learning was harder for me, writing seemed impossible. Subjectively, I had bought into the common limiting perspective that there were only so many hours in a day. Why would I want to spend my limited time in a classroom where I was constantly reminded of my academic weakness, my lower educational prospects, and the general hopelessness of my situation. Why try (Corrigan et al., 2009)? It seemed more sensible to put my limited time into doing other things besides school.

The goofing around in class and skipping school that I engaged in as a response to my situation, however, would be the very things administrators would later point to as the data points that both predicted and justified their actions. Actions that, when viewed from the third-person perspective, can be seen as promoting the behavior they were seeking to limit. This is how the culture within an institution can play a role in the broader social problem of marginalization. Often, institutions inadvertently produce the very social conditions that reinforce student limitations and social stigma (Corrigan et al., 2009; Corrigan, & Rao, 2012; Kieling et al., 2011; Vogel et al., 2013). Rather than help students in developing their competency, implicit bias, administrative roadblocks, and ingroup and outgroup politics prevent educators from being fully present for their students. This is a problem that can occur even as the institution produces mission statements and policy strategies to address these problems.

1.5 Repairing the Damage

In their interviews, the professors of PAL described their often-herculean struggles to undo the ingrained beliefs of inadequacy and limitation held by their students. Such beliefs are all too easily adopted by anxious students, who are most likely to experience failure. Students for whom failure has become a regular and recurring feature of their education often find themselves living out roles that were predicted by school personnel or parents, and yet desired by no one, least of all the student. When this kind of experience is described in first-person detail, an emotional landscape comes into view that can more properly inform other more objective vantage points.

The eight professors interviewed for this study used their own uniquely personal theories of mind, and approached the education of their students differently from one another, while retaining certain universal features. For example, the limitations identified as learning disabilities in the earlier paradigms, by these professors' theory of mind, were confronted as "problems to solve" (Subject B). Over the 50 years that the PAL program has been in place at Curry College, its professors have been enabling neurologically diverse students to demonstrate the capacity for success at this advanced level of education and imbued them with the capacity to become self-directed self-authors of their own lives.

As a student, I was somewhat surprised when I first learned about metacognition. Thinking about thinking and the reflective practices of metacognition seemed obvious and ubiquitous. Despite the intimidating sound of the word, the idea hardly seemed like anything special. However, after years of practice and research into the subject, I believe that metacognition only appears easy and obvious because it is a fundamental feature of our learning. I invite the reader to contemplate this culmination of a lifetime's work thinking about how one builds greater levels of self-regulation in themselves and the students they are teaching. I encourage the reader to try to construct a Learning Conversation (Adelizzi & Goss, 1995; Fox, 2010; Harri-Augstein & Thomas, 1991; Pennini, 2006) with their students and contemplate the role metacognitive instruction has to play in the development of educational transformation in all students.

1.6 How I Got Here

Here I will introduce you to where my interest in metacognition, the Program for Advancement of Learning (PAL), and Dr. Webb came from. I have had a transformative experience. This transformation has been the result of being identified as a student with a specific learning difference as a child, and how I was able to recover from the educational trauma of that experience because of PAL's metacognitive instructional approach. Here I present that story in my own words. My intent, as briefly described in the previous chapter, was to capture the first-person phenomenological aspects of metacognitive development, from student to adult, and integrate them with the insights gained from interviewing the professors teaching in the program that made such an impact.

I have come to realize I must clearly situate myself inside this research if I am going to express the intricate and, at times, fragile relationship between experience, understanding, development, and transformation. The narrative reflection of my formative experiences and personal metacognitive insights presented here were coded and analyzed alongside the case study data collected from the eight PAL professors, whose insights form the core of the data reviewed in subsequent chapters. The narratives presented across this work are a chance for you, the reader, to look within the researcher. Likewise, as the researcher, this approach has enabled me to deeply connect my experience to my research. I believe this approach brings a level of authenticity and uniqueness of perspective to this study, which will deepen understanding of the study's objective elements and insights.

My educational path to this point has not been typical. As an elementary school student placed on an Individualized Education Program (IEP)[3] *during kindergarten screening, I was unaware that there was anything wrong. When I was being pulled out of class for all kinds of related services like speech and language, occupational therapy, and phonics, I just figured that everybody was being pulled out of class as well. I had no idea that while I was being pulled from the mainstream classroom to do Orton-Gillingham,*[4] *which I hated, the rest of the class was doing history or science, two of my favorite subjects.*

I should have been tipped off that I was not learning like everyone else because of things like the Reading Race in fourth grade. My teacher had this big chart with everyone's name on it, which snaked around the whole classroom. For every page of a chapter book you read, you would get a sticker. By the end of the year, sticker lines would run all the way around the room, wall to wall to wall, until they ended up back at the start/finish line. I remember I was one of two students that did not get enough stars to get off the starting wall. In fact, that really wasn't a fair comparison either, since the other student was a girl who had a heart condition and was constantly taken out of class for medical reasons. I can't remember ever missing a day that year. But I forget things, and like other aspects of my learning disability, sometimes I am not aware that I have forgotten.

---

[3] An Individualized Education Program (IEP) is a legal document that identifies a student's disability and outlines the approaches and supports used to address the student's specific learning needs. Only about 23% of students are identified as SLD as early as I was (https://www.ncld.org/wp-content/uploads/2014/11/2014-State-of-LD.pdf).

[4] Orton-Gillingham is a direct, explicit, multisensory, structured, sequential, diagnostic, and prescriptive way to address reading, writing, and spelling to students with SLD in the domain of language function. Methods of direct phonics instruction, such as Orton-Gillingham, have been shown to be among the most important interventions for students with reading and writing impairments.

It was not until junior high school that I really noticed there were some big differences between the other students and me. It all happened in a rather traumatic fashion. I had been assigned the meanest teacher in the whole sixth grade, Mr. Barnett. This was not unusual. I would always get the strict teacher if there was one teaching in that grade, and Mr. Barnett was legendary. He said one of the scariest things I had ever heard from a teacher up to that point. He said it in kind of a rage, but I can't for the life of me remember what I did to provoke him. He said, "You think you're funny, don't you Mr. Hulbig! Big funny man MR. HULBIG!" He called everyone Mr. or Miss., particularly when angry. "Well it won't be so funny in junior high.... because that's when you'll find there is not as much time to play around because there is no recess!".

No recess! I remember being stunned by this. Recess was pretty much what I built my day around in elementary school. Recess was the only class I was kind of good at. So I panicked all summer. I double checked with anybody who might know the truth that there was no recess in junior high. Ironically, school finally arrived, and my new schedule listed a double block of "recess study." Like a wish fulfilled. I was vindicated! Mr. Barnett had been wrong. I started tapping on the kid next to me.

"Hey, got recess?"

"No."

"Ha! Ha! Well I do!"

Yes, I was that obnoxious, and worse. It is not something anyone wants to admit to, but to be an adult survivor of special education, it is part of your history and makeup that you must contend with. I believe you must come to terms with it. In this situation, however, I received my comeuppance as somebody finally read my own schedule to me, "That doesn't say recess, you idiot," they scoffed, "it says resource. You're in the retard room.[5]*"*

I think that was also the first time I heard the term "retard room" used in context, but it still did not mean anything to me until I arrived. Sure enough, when I showed up to the tiny partitioned cluster of rooms for study, there were 'retarded' kids there, and I was there with them. That was when it hit me. Something **was** *really wrong with me.*

However, before I go any further with this story, I would like to say, as a teacher, I now have tremendous appreciation for Mr. Barnett and his skill and artistry as a teacher. He had a great 'schtick'. Schtick is one thing not generally taught in schools of education, and sadly is less appreciated, and sometimes poorly deployed. But every good teacher learns to develop a schtick that improves the interactive power of their teaching. Mr. Barnett's schtick was perfectly devised for maximum impact on sixth grade students, particularly hyperactive boys like myself. His role was that of an unflappable and disciplined teacher with a tinge of military drill sergeant. He would show up for class in a military-issued green button-down shirt buttoned to the top, and a pair of Dickies often tucked into a pair of jet black ankle high

[5] I believe it is important to point out here that I learned, decades later, that I was among the charter members of this program. At this time, this pull out model of special education had been in place for about a year at the school. So not only was I new to this program, but so was everyone else.

combat boots. When things would get chaotic, he would start barking orders like the class was his platoon coming unglued under surprise enemy attack. Discipline was key. Every student had an essential job in his class. Mr. Barnett stressed their responsibility to not only do their job, but to do it well. Everything was also highly regimented, and even though my capacity to perform his regimented routine was not the best, I learned a lot. I never felt bad or ostracized because Mr. Barnett had this great way of getting students to come back and try again until you didn't fail at it, or at least you didn't seem to fail so badly, and could walk away feeling like you learned something. For all the strictness he projected through his schtick, he would see and acknowledge your learning in a way that would empower and encourage your growth.

My junior high special education class, on the other hand, was a daily exercise in fear and humiliation that I was unprepared for. This was' back in 1982, just before most schools began to group special education students with their intellectual development in mind. At this time, however, public school resource rooms housed everyone on an IEP, regardless of their disabilities. Since I did not know about clinical diagnoses like ADHD, autism, dyslexia, Down's syndrome, muscular dystrophy, or bipolar disorder, and I had not yet been exposed to the idea of metacognition, my 12-year-old mind needed some way to categorize what I was experiencing. All these different students in this class; what was my placement? At that time, I only had two categories, 'stupid' or 'crazy'. I knew I wasn't crazy, so I figured I was there because I was stupid. By this time, my difficulty with written language went way beyond most other students. I was about the worst speller in my resource class, a fact other students always pointed out for self-esteem reasons of their own.

In my general education classes, I simply could not do what the other students did. The teacher would ask for an essay and I could barely write a paragraph, and my best paragraphs still looked like hell. It didn't stop there. I could not erase without tearing the paper apart, leaving big splotches all over the paper. It seemed I could do nothing neatly. If I made a model airplane, I would drown it in glue, and I applied paint so thick it always ran, making it look like a mangled mess. Everything I touched, I ruined.

These episodes were not great for my self-esteem. In junior high, my classes started to be divided by level. Soon my good, goal-driven, mainstream friends from elementary school were tracked away from me and into the higher level classes. This left me in lower level classes that were overloaded with students who simply did not care.

This reality was never specifically addressed, for self-esteem reasons, because at the time the prevailing belief was that if a student with a learning disability realized what was really wrong with them, the hit to their self-esteem would be such that they would never recover. However, by this time, my segregation from those students who I believed were more worthy than me was clear. There were very few students in my classes who were interested in learning, and most were engaged in a radical defense of their self-esteem. In response, I developed coping strategies to help me get around the social awkwardness of being a dumb kid.

I probably did the least amount of reading and writing I had ever done during junior high. The intervention strategy used by my special education teachers made it easy to get away with. The less it looked like I could do, the less they would hold me to, and if I held out long enough, even those expectations would evaporate. Over time, this became a self-destructive feedback loop. It also justified my earlier assumption that I was "stupid" not "crazy". However, it is funny, in a way, because as I look back on it now, I put so much effort into being "stupid" it ***was*** *"crazy"!*

1.7 Paradox and Choice

There is a paradox at the heart of the human ability to learn. It is the ability to both identify, or perceive, boundary conditions, or final terminal states, and then transcend those boundaries or reframe those terminal states as part of a larger process or state. It is a special quality of human cognition that is able to transcend our tools, even the tools of our thought, like mathematics (Gödel, 1992). It is one of only a small handful of cognitive skills that cannot be simulated by a computer and it is not even clear how one would even begin to program a level of proto-understanding (Penrose, 1989, 1994) into one. However, what is even more curious is the common assumption that human cognitive function, when given enough time to accumulate knowledge, develop nuanced abilities, and allocate resources, equipped humans to solve the problems that confront them. This is a tremendous amount of confidence in a neurocognitive process that is not yet well understood. The whole conundrum is made even more confusing when you realize that this process that is not yet well understood is the ability to understand itself.

It has been proposed by Duetch (2011) that perhaps humans are a special kind of computational beast endowed with a special universal problem-solving capacity not unlike a Turing Machine.[6] That humans are in fact a kind of beast-machine with a brain that is using a not yet understood computational process. If humans are endowed with an underlying universal problem-solving ability, that would go a long way toward explaining why we generally perceive the world in terms of problems. Why do we immediately begin identifying and organizing perceptions into a format that can promote problem-solving? This would also explain human restlessness, but it would also present another paradox. If we were able to identify and make sense of the underlying processes of understanding we were using, we would be able to use that knowledge to assist ourselves, and others, in their understanding of understanding.

[6] A Turing Machine is sometimes called a universal computer because it is not just able to solve certain kinds of computations, but it is actually able to solve all computational problems given enough time and resources. Deutsch's idea stems from the fact that Turing style computers process in a binary two dimensional fashion, and from this two dimensional approach produces a system that can solve all classes of computational problems. Deutsch proposes that quantum computation, that uses a four dimensional qubit, likely has an analogous process using four bits, and would be able to universally solve other classes of problems, not just computational ones.

However, if there is an underlying capacity that produces understanding, why should we even expect to be able to know what it is?

In the field of linguistics, Chomsky (1959, 1999) described a human ability to transcend the meanings of the words presented. This ability to apprehend the full meaning of what was being communicated occurred even when that meaning was intentionally obscure. Popper (2012) described the plight of an open society as being largely a story of oppressors finding new ways to oppress, and then its champions finding ways to transcend the new oppression. In economics, Adam Smith (1937) was among the earliest to discuss how human knowledge of an economic process changes economic behavior. This ability of humans to see the same old patterns and understand them in a new way that forever changes their behavior has been well-documented in psychology (Jarvis, 2004; Kaufman, 2021; Kegen,1996; Valliant, 1993) mathematics (Gödel, 1992; Perose, 1989, 1994) and information processing (Hofstadter, 1979; Kelly, 1995).

While there has been considerable research demonstrating how our conscious perceptual experience may be an evolutionary fabrication of our senses (Dennet, 2017; Hoffman et al., 2015) or perhaps a hallucinatory overlay (Seth, 2021), neurological and educational investigations suggest humans in fact do possess capacities that irrefutably allow for a level of monitoring, control, and behavioral choice that make a certain level of free will possible. So even as researchers like the venerable Sapolski (2017) lament over what appears to be an ever-receding capacity for free will in the universe, what seems to be happening is our understanding about the form of the actual choice space of humans, its kinds and conditions, which support or inhibit the actual choices we are capable of, is being revealed through methodical scientific investigation. How the choice space of humans functions may represent among the most important subjects relative to understanding, self- regulation, development, and transformation.

When one contemplates all the factors and possible micro-disturbances, starting with those caused by imperfect protein production, hormones, or other molecules, through to large-scale internal cellular- and organ-level impacts that could occur, particularly those that impact brain function, on through physical trauma, historical, and developmental experience, as well as all the cultural, political, and environmental constraints on our choices, it may seem there is not much space for the free will to make choices at all. The experiences of individuals like Yeonmi Park (https://www.yeonmi.com/) growing up in North Korea suggest that humans can even be raised in conditions where the environment can arrest the development of the conception of free will, or even the development of the self-reflective thinking needed to resist subjugation.

However, one interesting thing about stories like Yeonmi Park's is that they tell us about what it is like to be raised without the concept of free will, and how those living conditions prevent the development of the ability to perceive subjugation, ultimately they chose to flee those conditions and describe them for others. This is an expression of the most important quality of choice. Even those who wish to argue the point that humans have no free will must concede they have personally made a choice to study and engage in the debate about the subject, rather than choosing any number of other behaviors. However, armed with only this meager level of free choice, the nature of knowledge seems to suggest that once made aware of a skill, you can begin a process of learning and improving that skill.

The ability to self-regulate and choose the correct behavior is central to our processes of education. If children did not believe they could change their behavior to please adults, and teachers did not believe they could affect student behavior with their lessons, education as presently constructed would have failed to ever get off the ground. So while it is clear that humans have a much smaller choice space than we would perhaps like to believe, the fact that there is a choice space should be a call for deeper investigation. The ability to think about choices, or possibly just having the knowledge that a choice is possible, demonstrates that something akin to the concept of free will exists and this opens the possibility of individuals gaining greater control over this power through understanding the constraints on their ability to control and direct learning and development (Hulbig, 2021).

References

Adelizzi, J. U., & Goss, D. B. (Eds.). (1995). *A closer look: Perspectives and reflections on college students with learning disabilities*. Curry College.

Allen, M., Glen, J. C., Müllensiefen, D., Schwarzkopf, D. S., Fardo, F., Frank, D., Callaghan, M. F., & Rees, G. (2017). Metacognitive ability correlates with hippocampal and prefrontal microstructure. *NeuroImage, 149*, 415–423. https://doi.org/10.1016/j.neuroimage.2017.01.060

Altshuler, S. J. (2003). From barriers to successful collaboration: Public schools and child welfare working together. *Social work, 48*(1), 52–63.

Bäck, T., & Schwefel, H. P. (1993). An overview of evolutionary algorithms for parameter optimization. *Evolutionary Computation, 1*(1), 1–23.

Cheng, Y. C. (2022). *School effectiveness and school-based management: A mechanism for development*. Taylor & Francis.

Chomsky, N. (1959). A review of BF Skinner's Verbal Behavior. *Language, 35*(1), 26–58.

Chomsky, N., & Kenstowicz, M. (1999). *Derivation by phase*. An Annotated Syntax Reader, MIT Press, 482.

Corrigan, P. W., Larson, J. E., & Ruesch, N. (2009). Self-stigma and the "why try" effect: Impact on life goals and evidence-based practices. *World Psychiatry, 8*(2), 75–81. https://onlinelibrary.wiley.com; https://doi.org/10.1002/j.2051-5545.2009.tb00218.x

Corrigan, P. W., & Rao, D. (2012). On the self-stigma of mental illness: Stages, disclosure, and strategies for change. *The Canadian Journal of Psychiatry, 57*(8), 464–469. https://journals.sagepub.com; https://doi.org/10.1177/070674371205700804

Dennett, D. C. (2017). *Consciousness explained*. Little, Brown Book Group.

Desoete, A., & De Craene, B. (2019). Metacognition and mathematics education: An overview. *ZDM*, 1–11.

Deutsch, D. (2011). *The beginning of infinity: Explanations that transform the world*. Penguin Books

Dewey, J. (1903). Democracy in education. *The Elementary School Teacher, 4*(4), 193–204.

Diamond, J. M. (1998). *Guns, germs and steel: A short history of everybody for the last 13,000 years*. Random House.

Dunlosky, J., & Metcalfe, J. (2009). *Metacognition*. SAGE.

Eagleman, D. (2020). *Livewired: The inside story of the ever-changing brain*. Canongate Books.

Feldman, J. (2013). The neural binding problem(s). *Cognitive Neurodynamics, 7*(1), 1–11.

Fernandez-Duque, D., Baird, J. A., & Posner, M. I. (2000). Executive attention and metacognitive regulation. *Consciousness and Cognition, 9*(2), 288–307.

Flavell, J. H. (1979). Metacognition and cognitive monitoring: A new area of cognitive development. *American Psychologist, 34*(10), 906–911. https://doi.org/10.1037/0003-066X.34.10.906

Fleming, S. M., Ryu, J., Golfinos, J. G., & Blackmon, K. E. (2014). Domain-specific impairment in metacognitive accuracy following anterior prefrontal lesions. *Brain, 137*(10), 2811–2822.

Fox, L. (Ed.) (2010). *Changing lives through metacognitive relationships: LD/ADHD and college success.* Curry College.

Freire, P. (2018). Pedagogy of the oppressed. Bloomsbury Publishing USA. (Original work published in 1968).

Gallagher, H. L., & Frith, C. D. (2003). Functional imaging of 'theory of mind'. *Trends in Cognitive Sciences*, 7(2), 77–83.

Ghetti, S., & Fandakova, Y. (2020). Neural development of memory and metamemory in childhood and adolescence: Toward an integrative model of the development of episodic recollection. *Annual Review of Developmental Psychology, 2*, 365–388.

Gödel, K. (1992). *On formally undecidable propositions of Principia Mathematica and related Systems.* Courier Corporation.

Hansen, M. (2021). The U.S. education system isn't giving students what employers need, Harvard Buisness Review, https://hbr.org/2021/05/the-u-s-education-system-isnt-giving-students-what-employers-need

Harri-Augstein, E. S., & Thomas, L. (1991). *Learning conversations: The self organized learning way to personal and organizational growth.* Routledge.

Hoffman, D. D. (2000). *Visual intelligence: How we create what we see.* WW Norton & Company.

Hoffman, D. D., Singh, M., & Prakash, C. (2015). The interface theory of perception. *Psychonomic Bulletin & Review, 22*, 1480–1506.

Hofstadter, D. (1979). *Gödel, Escher, Bach: An eternal golden braid*. New York: Basic Books.

Hulbig, P. R. (2021). Fundamental Principles of Metacognition: A Qualitative Study of Metacognition, Pedagogy and Transformation. Lesley University. https://www.proquest.com/openview/31dce8c293a0439393ad856023e3dac0/1?pqorigsite=gscholar&cbl=18750&diss=y

Isbister, J. B., Eguchi, A., Ahmad, N., Galeazzi, J. M., Buckley, M. J., & Stringer, S. (2018). A new approach to solving the feature-binding problem in primate vision. *Interface Focus, 8*(4), 20180021.

Jackson, V. (2003). In our own voice: African-American stories of oppression, survival and recovery. *Off Our Backs, 33*(7/8), 19–21.

Jarvis, P. (2004). *Adult education and lifelong learning: Theory and practice.* Routledge.

Kannappan, K., Spector, L., Sipper, M., Helmuth, T., Cava, W. L., Wisdom, J., & Bernstein, O. (2015). Analyzing a decade of human-competitive ("humie") winners: What can we learn?. *Genetic Programming Theory and Practice XII*, 149–166.

Kaufman, S. B. (2021). *Transcend: The new science of self-actualization.* Penguin.

Kegan, R. (1982). *The evolving self: Problem and process in human development.* Harvard University Press.

Kegan, R. (1996). *In over our heads: The mental demands of modern life.* Harvard University Press.

Kelly, K. (1995). *Out of control: The new biology of machines, social systems, and the economic world*. Reading, Mass.: Addison-Wesley.

Kieling, C., Baker-Henningham, H., Belfer, M., Conti, G., Ertem, I., Omigbodun, O., ... & Rahman, A. (2011). Child and adolescent mental health worldwide: Evidence for action. *The Lancet, 378*(9801), 1515–1525. Retrieved from http://news.medlive.cn/uploadfile/2011/1018/20111018031042509.pdf

Laland, K. N., Odling-Smee, J., & Myles, S. (2010). How culture shaped the human genome: Bringing genetics and the human sciences together. *Nature Reviews Genetics, 11*(2), 137–148.

Livingston, E. M., Siegel, L. S., & Ribary, U. (2018). Developmental dyslexia: Emotional impact and consequences. *Australian Journal of Learning Difficulties, 23*(2), 107–135.

Lipman, M. (1988). *Philosophy goes to school.* Temple University Press.
Lipsitz, J. (2019). *Successful schools for young adolescents.* Routledge.
Maier, G. J. (2021). Lascaux Cave, Part four: Evidence of hunting strategies identified in paleolithic cave art. *Journal of Transpersonal Psychology, 53*(1), 81–98.
Medina-Alcaide, M. Á., Garate, D., Intxaurbe, I., Sanchidrián, J. L., Rivero, O., Ferrier, C., ... & Líbano, I. (2021). The conquest of the dark spaces: An experimental approach to lighting systems in Paleolithic caves. *PLoS One, 16*(6), e0250497.
Meher, V., Baral, R., & Bhuyan, S. (2021). A meta-analysis on the effectiveness of metacognitive strategies and interventions in teaching and learning process. *i-Manager's Journal on Educational Psychology, 14*(4), 47.
Mervosh, S. (2022). *The pandemic erased two decades of progress in math and reading.* The New York Times.
Mezirow, J. (1975). *Education for perspective transformation: Women's reentry programs in community colleges.* Center for Adult Education Teachers College, Columbia University.
Mezirow, J. (1991). *Transformative dimensions of adult learning.* Jossey-Bass.
Morrison, D. M., & Miller, K. B. (2018). Teaching and learning in the pleistocene: A biocultural account of human pedagogy and its implications for AIED. *International Journal of Artificial Intelligence in Education, 28*(3), 439–469.
National Assessment of Educational Progress NAEP (2022) 2020 and 2022 long-term trends Reading and math assessments. US Dept. of Education
National Assessment of Educational. (2022). 2020 and 2022 long-term trends reading and math assessments. *US Department of Education.* https://www.nationsreportcard.gov/
Nelson, T. O. (1996). Consciousness and metacognition. *American Psychologist, 51*(2), 102–116. https://doi.org/10.1037/0003-066X.51.2.102
Nelson, T. O., & Narens, L. (1994). Why investigate metacognition. *Metacognition: Knowing About Knowing, 13*, 1–25.
Pennini, S. W. (2006). *College students with learning disabilities: A case study* [Doctoral dissertation, Lesley]. https://digitalcommons.lesley.edu/education_dissertations/77
Penrose, R. (1989). *The emperor's new mind: Concerning computers, minds, and the laws ofphysics.* Oxford U. Press.
Penrose, R. (1994). *Shadows of the mind* (Vol. 4). Oxford University Press.
Perez, M., & Socias, M. (2008). Highly successful schools: what do they do differently and at what cost?. *Education Finance and Policy, 3*(1), 109–129.
Peterson, B. S., Skudlarski, P., Gatenby, J. C., Zhang, H., Anderson, A. W., & Gore, J. C. (1999). An fMRI study of Stroop word-color interference: Evidence for cingulate subregions subserving multiple distributed attentional systems. *Biological Psychiatry, 45*(10), 1237–1258.
Pinker, S. (2018). *Enlightenment now: The case for reason, science, humanism, and progress.* Penguin Random House.
Premack, D. & Woodruff, G. (1978). Does the chimpanzee have a theory of mind? *Behavioral and Brain Sciences, 4*, 515–526.
Quigley, A., Mujis, D., & Stinger, E. (2019) Metacognition and self-regulated learning: Guidance Report. *Education Endowment Foundation.* Retrieved March 3, 2019 from https://educationendowmentfoundation.org.uk/tools/guidance-reports/metacognition-and-self-regulated-learning/
Radovan, M. (2019). Cognitive and metacognitive aspects of key competency "learning to learn". *Pedagogika, 133*(1), 28–42. https://www.ceeol.com/search/article-detail?id=805934
Sapolsky, R. M. (2017). *Behave: The biology of humans at our best and worst.* Penguin.
Seth, A. (2021). *Being you: A new science of consciousness.* Penguin.
Schmitt, M. C., & Newby, T. J. (1986). Metacognition: Relevance to instructional designing. *Journal of Instructional Development, 9*(4), 29–33. https://doi.org/10.1007/BF02908316
Schraw, G., Crippen, K. J., & Hartley (2006). Promoting self-regulation in science education: Metacognition as part of a broader perspective on learning. *Research in Science Education, 36*, 111–139. https://doi.org/10.1007/s11165-005-3917-8

Shimamura, A. P. (2000). *Toward a cognitive neuroscience of metacognition.* https://doi.org/10.1006/ccog.2000.0450

Smith, A. (1937). The wealth of nations [1776] (Vol. 11937). https://orbit.texthelp.com/?file=https://bxscience.edu/ourpages/auto/2018/10/23/54894030/Adam%20Smith%20Excerpt%20Student%20%20copy%20_1_.pdf

Spitzberg, B. H. (2014). Toward a model of meme diffusion (M3D). *Communication Theory, 24*(3), 311–339.

Toner, J. (2014). *The Roman guide to slave management:* A treatise by nobleman Marcus Sidonius Falx. Abrams.

Vaillant, G. E. (1993). *The wisdom of the ego.* Harvard University Press.

Vandenbroucke, L., Spilt, J., Verschueren, K., Piccinin, C., & Baeyens, D. (2018). The classroom as a developmental context for cognitive development: A meta-analysis on the importance of teacher–student interactions for children's executive *functions. Review of Educational Research, 88*(1), 125–164. https://doi.org/10.3102/0034654317743200

Vanhaute, E. (2021). *Peasants in world history.* Routledge.

Venter, E., & Rambau, E. (2011). The effect of a latchkey situation on a child's educational success. *South African Journal of Education, 31*(3), 345–356.

Vogel, D. L., Bitman, R. L., Hammer, J. H., & Wade, N. G. (2013). Is stigma internalized? The longitudinal impact of public stigma on self-stigma. *Journal of counseling psychology, 60*(2), 311.

Vroomen, J., & Keetels, M. (2010). Perception of intersensory synchrony: A tutorial review. *Attention, Perception, & Psychophysics, 72*(4), 871–884.

Woolfolk, A. (2016). *Educational psychology.* Boston, MA: Pearson Education Limited.

Wong, S., Balleine, B. W., & Kumfor, F. (2018). A new framework for conceptualizing symptoms in frontotemporal dementia: From animal models to the clinic. *Brain, 141*(8), 2245–2254. https://doi.org/10.1093/brain/awy123

Yampolskiy, R. V. (2018). Why we do not evolve software? Analysis of evolutionary algorithms. *Evolutionary Bioinformatics*, 14, 1176934318815906.

Chapter 2
Psychobiology

The psychobiology of metacognition is a vast field of investigation despite being rarely conclusively demonstrated in many species (Basile et al., 2009; Kornell, 2014; Sutton & Shettleworth, 2008). The modern conception of metacognition was originally defined by Flavell (1979) as a process of learning to learn that integrated aspects of knowledge about learning and knowledge about behaviors. Nelson (1996) later proposed that metacognition was produced as a result of an interaction between two distinct conscious states, a subjective externally focused conscious state and an abstract internally focused state. Interactions between these internally and externally directed states of consciousness produce the intentional goal-driven behavior that is the hallmark of metacognitive thinking, and also open the concept to be scientifically observed and tested (Dunlosky & Metcalfe, 2009; Flavell, 1979; Nelson, 1996; Metcalfe et al., 1994). This conceptualization also makes it possible to identify aspects of metacognitive thinking from artifacts found in the archeological record (Falk, 2012; Nielsen et al., 2020; Roper, 1969; Vyshedskiy, 2014).

Educational research has shown metacognition to be incredibly important to learning and teaching (Dunlosky & Metcalfe, 2009; Dweck, 2013, 2017; Hattie, 2012; Mancini et al., 1991; Pace, 1991; Price, 1991; Weinert, 1987). Research also indicates that metacognitive skills can, and need to, be taught for students to fully understand and use them (Hulbig, 2021; Pintrich, 2002; Tanner, 2012). Neurological investigations appear to show that metacognition is more than an educational routine to improve self-understanding, but rather an inherent quality of the process of cognition itself. For this reason, research into metacognition and executive function have proceeded on several distinctly different tracks (Mazzoni & Nelson, 1999; Nelson & Narens, 1994). One track is neuroscientists focusing on the relationship between executive control, brain regions, and behavior using adults in laboratory settings. Another track would be psychologists working in clinical settings. Perhaps the largest track is educational metacognitive researchers, who focus on the learning of children in naturalistic settings. However, new tracks of investigation into metacognition are now being conducted in a diversity of fields such as computation, information processing, and evolutionary biology. The expanding interest in the concept of

P. R. Hulbig, *The Pedagogy of Self-Authorship*,
https://doi.org/10.1007/978-3-031-41436-7_2

metacognition across scientific domains suggests a convergence in our understanding of the phenomena in a very fundamental way.

2.1 Historical Perspective

In his influential and paradigmatic article *Metacognition and Cognitive Monitoring*, Flavell (1979) first described metacognition as "thinking about thinking" or "cognition about cognition" (p. 906). However, the idea of using self-knowledge to promote human development and understanding is an ancient idea. Over three thousand years ago, the phrase "Know thyself and thou shall know the universe and God" was carved on the Temple of Apollo at Delphi in ancient Greece and was attributed to Socrates by Plato in his *Dialogues* (Hamilton, 1961; Vyshedskiy, 2014). However, the phrase is also attributable to Imhotep and the Egyptian Book of the Dead, which states, "Name yourself in your heart and know who you are" (Ellis, 2009, p xxxviii).

Literary and metaphorical evidence of metacognitive thinking is ubiquitously demonstrated across ancient societies and is reflected in the historical record of mental synthesis collected by Vyshedskiy (2014). In China, the practice was identified by Lao Tzu in the 33rd verse of the Tao, "Knowing others is intelligence; knowing yourself is true wisdom. Mastering others is strength; mastering yourself is true power (Mitchell, 1988)." Some of the earliest expressions of the idea of an interaction between a subjective/experiential self and an objective/contemplative self that can regulate achievement of higher and more developed behavior are expressed metaphorically in the Hindu Rigvadaś Parable of the Body and Soul:

> Two birds with fair wings, inseparable companions; Have found refuge in the same sheltering tree. One incessantly eats from the fig tree; the other, not eating, just looks on. (De Nicolás, 2003, p. 66)

These ancient references to the metacognitive practice of knowing oneself seems to point to a much deeper understanding of the learning process than would be expected from primitive cultures. This may be the result of the modern shift to compulsory public education, as discussed in the purpose of this book. Modern systems of mass education shifted the focus of instruction from discourse to discipline, with an emphasis on the identification of economically useful skills in a population over the development of an individual's skills and talents, as was seen in more ancient times. Freire (2018) describes this modern style of education in his book *Pedagogy of the Oppressed* as the banking model of education, and has suggested that what has come to be seen as education is more a mechanism of state and cultural control. It seems that ancient cultures may have had a far more sophisticated concept of learning than has been appreciated. Unfortunately, much of this knowledge was lost by later modern cultures and religions that sought to promote greater social cohesion over the needs of individuals, and the impacts of modern advances on our collective memory.

In fact, memory is an excellent example of how self-regulatory knowledge is lost. At one time the ability to memorize and recall information was central to learning. It was standard for students to learn the use of mnemonic devices to assist their memory using cognitively generated strategies like rhymes, rules of thumb, phrases, diagrams, and acronyms. One mnemonic device, credited to the Greek poet Simonides of Ceos in 500 BC, was called the Memory Palace and was taught ubiquitously during the rise of Greco-Roman culture. It was found that connecting information to internal visualizations of well-known locations, like the various rooms of one's home, would powerfully support memory.

Today there is a newfound appreciation for the Memory Palace technique because the reasons for its effectiveness are well described by what we have learned about the neuropsychology of memory. However, before Foer (2012) wrote his seminal book *Moonwalking with Einstein* this technique had been largely forgotten, surviving only in small cohorts of individuals looking to gain advantage in memory competitions. For the rest of the population, the use of mnemonic techniques has been thoroughly replaced by tools like notepads and smart phones that function like prosthetics for memory. One can see a similar phenomena now happening with the physical act of writing, as word processing and speech-to-text programs render obsolete old techniques like shorthand and cursive The advent of new technologies like ChatGPT, DeepMind, and Google Brain are going to produce similar effects on the process of composition in various creative endeavors in the future (Fig. 2.1).

The idea that understanding one's own cognitive faculties can have a beneficial impact on one's learning and development is not even a recently rediscovered idea. William James in 1890 made one of the earliest references in modern western psychology to the self-observing power of the brain. Dewey (1997, 2007), the great American teacher and philosopher, placed self-reflection as the most crucial component of both learning and a healthy democracy. Modern investigations of metacognition did not start until 1965, when J. T. Hart completed the first research on memory

Fig. 2.1 Know thyself. *Note* From excavations in the convent of San Gregorio, Via Appia, Rome, Italy (The artist is unknown. Public domain)

and the feeling-of-knowing, considered to be one of the first modern studies of a metacognitive skill (Harten, 2014).

The study of the influence of conscious, self-reflective, metacognitive thinking on behavior was overshadowed for much of the twentieth century by the dominance of Skinner's (2011) behaviorist conception of the mind as a black box. This form of radical behaviorism saw consciousness as epiphenomenal and believed it to have minimal to no impact on real human action. Behaviors were seen as the result of conditioning. However, by the time Flavell (1979) wrote his seminal work on metacognition, behaviorism 's dominance was beginning to wane, as its adherents failed to demonstrate their claims conclusively (Chomsky, 1959; Harzem, 2004; Virués-Ortega, 2006). This set the stage for deeper neurocognitive investigations into human learning and development using paradigms that more fully appreciate the role of conscious thought and behavioral choice.

Metacognition's unique relationship to consciousness makes it an important methodological and investigational concept in this domain. It provides an experimental framework capable of probing the neurological relationship of not just conscious cognition, but also behavior, and its relationship to discrete tasks of memory and performance. By more clearly defining thoughts about thoughts to include the integration of knowledge and regulation in the form of conscious monitoring and control opened up the study of metacognition to a true diversity of fields (Mazzoni & Nelson, 1999; Nelson et al., 1994).

2.2 Psychological and Developmental Perspectives

Subjective, introspective, cognitive, and psychological approaches to understanding the mind occupy a rich and unique research space that is increasingly becoming accessible to neurobiological investigations. Increasingly, the interdisciplinary blending of neurophysiological and psychological understandings are producing nuanced theories and new avenues of investigation, which in turn are producing new and more effective intervention. Today, many disorders of the mind are most effectively treated with combination therapies involving physiological, biological, often chemical, and psycho-cognitive interventions (Busch & Sandberg, 2012; Picardi & Gaetano, 2014; Vitiello, 2009).

The practice of psychology has been inherently based on self-reflective principles since Freud's identification that subconscious elements were powerful, and often hidden, drivers of human behavior. Freud identified several subconscious and conscious defense mechanisms that were later enumerated by his daughter Anna Freud in 1936 (Lipot, 1956). Vaillant (1993) identified a developmental difference between the various psychological defenses, placing them on a continuum from mature to immature. Mature psychological defenses allowed for the holding of two opposing ideas without distortion, whereas less mature defenses involved a distortion of perceptual experience when confronted with the same information. This ability to hold opposing ideas requires the development of a meta understanding of the situation that allows for a more accurate perception of the event, and an ability to withstand the emotional discomfort needed to execute positive solutions to difficult problems. Less mature thinkers do not possess this meta understanding, and instead distort their reflection of events to fit established cognitive paradigms. Frequently, these distortions support the individual in avoiding conflicting situations, issues, or ideas that do not fit into their present conceptual schema of the world. Vaillant (1993) identified a psychologist's chief role as helping patients identify distortions in their perception and develop more mature coping mechanisms (Table 2.1).

Interestingly, it was found that hemispheric neglect patients who have had stroke damage to their right hemisphere often suffer the loss of their ability to interpret novel situations (Corballis, 2003; Ramachandran et al., 1998). Because of this they can no longer adequately process the reality of their own paralysis, and simply neglect, or fail to realize there is anything wrong with them on the left side of their body. In these patients, when their linguistic left hemisphere remains intact, the patient is able

Table 2.1 Valiant's psychological defense mechanisms

Developmental level	Defense mechanism	Definition
Mature defenses	Suppression	Postponing gratification
	Altruism	Doing for others over the self
	Sublimation	Channeling or harnessing of emotional energy toward a higher goal
	Anticipation	Realistic planning for the future
	Humor	The ability to see life as funny. The highest of defenses according to Freud
Intermediate defenses	Reaction formation	A distortion of the value of a feeling or idea to make it seem more or less important than it really is
	Repression	Hiding one's true thoughts and emotions from the mind
	Displacement	A detachment from thought and emotion
	Isolation/intellectualization	A detachment from emotion using the intellect
Immature defenses	Dissociation	Neurotic denial of reality
	Projection	When the object is turned into subject
	Passive aggression	Self sabotage of ideas or individuals to avoid an issue
	Hypochondria	Sublimation of psychological pain into physical pain
	Fantasy	Creation of an artificial world
	Acting out	Total loss of behavioral control

Note: Vaillant (1993) identified that less mature defenses involve a distortion of experience or a manipulation of perceptual input, whereas mature defenses involve new modes of processing perception that enable productive action to create excuses for the situation, which has been demonstrated by Ramachandran et al. (1998) to follow the Freudian patterns of the psychological defense mechanisms, suggesting that psychological defense mechanisms are somehow both neurological and developmental in structure.

Erikson (1997) saw development as the resolution of internal personal conflicts that occurred at different times over the course of the human lifespan. His idea was that an internal crisis triggers a degree of self-learning, which in turn leads to more and more sophisticated cognitive conceptions, and the development of behavior that effectively addresses the conflict. Similar ideas of conflict triggering learning and higher levels of development were identified by Jarvis (2004) as central to adult education. Self-directed learning in adults is generally thought to begin with a difficult encounter, experience, or conflict that cannot be easily accommodated or assimilated by the learner (Jarvis, 2004; Merriam et al., 2007). Through metacognitive reflection and self-questioning, personal beliefs can be dissociated from, allowing the formation of new, more developed beliefs (Iordanou, 2016).

In his book *In Over Our Heads,* Kegan (1996) described the psychological development of consciousness using terms similar to descriptions of metacognitive consciousness put forth by Nelson (1996), and notions of understanding put forth by physicists and mathematician (Penrose 1989, 1994). Kegan (1982, 1996) described a shift between subjective consciousness and objective consciousness. Objective consciousness contains objective elements of our knowing that we can reflect on. The subjective level of consciousness refers to elements of our knowing we identify with, or are subjectively embedded within. The interplay of these types of consciousness, one that is able to embody itself in the moment and one that is able to reflect on both the self and the moment, produces a clearer understanding of one's self as a cognitive object and part of the larger system of interactions.

Kegan (1996) identified that the ability to integrate subjective and objective levels of conscious perspective leads to higher order conscious states and healthier, more productive behavior. These findings have further been supported by research into the development of epistemological perspective (Kuhn et al., 2000). However, the development of these more advanced ways of knowing in adulthood do not follow the linear chronological course seen in the cognitive development of children.

Kegan (1982, 1996) found that it was relatively uncommon for adults to reach the highest levels of development. These levels are described as *Self-authorship,* where an individual is able to understand and direct their own personal development, and *Self-transformation,* where an individual comes to understand their ability to direct the development of their culture and society. Kuhu et al. (2000) found that the highest levels of epistemological development, which involve advanced evaluative approaches to knowledge, were likewise rare, and may require more than just time or education to attain.

2.3 Development of the Self

Psychologists and theoretical cognitive scientists have puzzled over what forces drive this process of development in humans. This has been an investigation historically rife with expressions of racism, prejudice, and tribalism, often being expressed through the lens of an innate superiority of those members of the correct in-group. There are countless examples of religions or political factions dictating standards of proper human development that in reality produced examples of heinous repression. From the ancient Spartans who would enroll their male children, which were first deemed healthy enough to live by a council of elders, in brutal schools of combat called *Agoge*, to modern fundamentalist religious movements that excommunicate or withhold psychological or medical treatments from children they believe are not chosen because of a physical or neurological difference (Linton, 1999; Maxwell, 2020).

Turn of the century scientific beliefs like Craniometry (Scientific Racism, 2023), Polygenism, and interpretations of Darwinian evolution as survival of the fittest (Hofstadter, 1992) were all, in a sense, scientific theories looking for markers of the developmental superiority of one group over another. While these theories have all collapsed under their own asininity and destructive impact, the desire to dehumanize those who have developed differently continues to be expressed as a science in many quarters. The primary reason for this, to use Valiant's model, is the modern world struggles to maturely hold the two ideas that all humans have value despite their differences, together at the same time. This is because it is difficult to see a developmental change, particularly when it occurs slowly over time, and particularly when change has not yet occurred. Another reason for this repeated hostility toward out-group members may simply be that we are looking at an underlying trait common to primates (Sapolsky, 2017). However, an additional underlying factor that holds us back may also be that we do not have a theory that answers the question: *What are the universal drivers of human development?*

Most theories of development fall into the category of nature or nurture. Meaning development is either an inborn feature of a person's genetic heritage or the result of some process of learning that is nurtured through interaction. At this stage, it is clear that both nature and nurture are part of the answer. The certainty of a predetermined genetic destiny has had to succumb to the uncertainty introduced by epigenetics, social engineering, and the dogged motivation of individuals. All of these factors and more can play a role in human development.

One unitary feature of human development, regardless of nature or nurture, is that it is expressed through a conscious internal narrative called the self. The form of the self seems to emerge from the interplay of partly autonomous neural networks working together in ways that attempt to bring order to our experiences (Dennett, 1992). However, the self is more than an inner monologue, narrating the events of our lives. It is a construct of emotions, feelings, beliefs, experiences, and sensations that forms a core, cognitive "center of gravity" (Shibolet, 2019, p. 30), and supports our mental acrobatics. An active narrative we are forever returning to edit.

Our sense of self, from an embodied perspective, is a structure of abstract mental representations that support a mode of interpreting and engaging with corporeal experience (Ricoeur, 1984; Shibolet, 2019). The self is the essential structure that we both literally and cognitively build all our lives. Neuroscientist Seth (2021) has proposed that the core feature of the self is prediction, and ultimately all aspects of both our sensory perceptions and internal objective experience are predicted into being. We construct our perceptual experience from our predictions. Predictions that are repeatedly shown to be accurate become seamlessly integrated into the construction. The state of being that is predicted by your sensory experience becomes the self that dictates your behavior, personality, goals, aspirations, and development.

2.4 Evolutionary Perspective

Rudimentary examples of metacognition have been seen in other species (Hampton, 2009) ranging from rats (Foote & Crystal, 2007; Templer, 2019) to dolphins (Smith et al., 1998), with chimpanzees demonstrating the strongest sense of metacognition (Beran et al., 2015). However, even rudimentary metacognitive behaviors are a rare adaption and have failed to be conclusively demonstrated in other species, such as the pigeon (Sutton & Shettleworth, 2008), and even other primates, like the Capuchin monkey (Basile et al., 2009). Moreover, while there is no evidence that any animal is capable of the systematic metacognitive reasoning seen in humans (Kornell, 2014), evolutionary evidence for the advanced development of metacognitive ability seen in humans is beginning to be uncovered.

New technologies will continue to push our understanding of the minds of other species. For example, a procedure called Neuropixel can record the whole brain activity of small, genetically engineered animals like fish and mice (Abbot, 2020) that were bred to express a molecule that fluoresces when their neurons fire. The technology is able to image thousands of individual neurons interacting in real-time. One study (Marques et al., 2020) of zebrafish larvae found three neuron groups: one that remained activated during hunting, one that remained activated during exploration, and a third that activated as the fish switched states. The changes in activation triggered by the third state were not always related to hunger (Marques et al., 2020), and may be evidence that even at early evolutionary stages of development, there are neuronal systems engaged in mediating choice making, which may be the possible neurocognitive forerunners of the metacognitive capacities seen in more complex organisms.

2.5 Neurological Perspectives

Metacognitive methodologies have played an important role in the study of the brain and mind. The conceptual framework of metacognitive research first laid out by Flavell (1979), and then later delineations by Nelson (1996), have enabled certain activities of conscious cognition to be better studied scientifically. Thanks to modern imaging technologies such as functional magnetic resonance imaging (fMRI), positron emission tomography (PET), and single-photon emission computerized tomography (SPECT), complex representations of the brain's different regions have been created, and their involvement in various kinds of cognitions have been inferred (Gerhard et al., 2011), providing new ways to conceptualize what is occurring in the brain. Metacognition's unique relationship to consciousness and behavior has always made it an important methodological and investigational construct in the domain of psychology. But now with the advent of advanced imaging technologies, we can do experiments into the functional interconnectedness of the brain and mind.

How the physical organ of the brain is able to achieve metacognitive monitoring and metacognitive control is of strong interest to researchers. Developing a deeper, more nuanced neurological conception of metacognition holds the hope of producing new interventions that could improve human learning, development, productivity, and mental health. Thanks to the accumulating evidence gained from brain imaging techniques, large-scale atlases of brain areas and their functions have been produced to facilitate research (Domingos, 2015; Iqbal et al., 2018; Zeng et al., 2016). Possibly the most ambitious imaging initiative is the Human Connectome Project. Sponsored by the National Institutes of Health, its goal is to build a "network map" of the brain's physical connections (Gerhard et al., 2011). This map of the anatomical and functional connectivity of a healthy human brain has already led to some amazing visualizations of the brain, and could lead to important research breakthroughs in the future.

2.5.1 *Frontal Lobe*

No one area of the brain has been localized as the center of metacognitive activity. However, in many studies (Allen et al., 2017; Badre et al., 2010; D'esposito et al., 1995; Fernandez-Duque et al., 2000,; Fleming et al., 2012; Jonides et al., 1993; Petrides et al., 1993), the frontal cortex has been found to play a major role. Before the wide use of fMRI, this area of the brain was implicated through impairments of executive function caused by damage to the frontal cortex called dysexecutive syndrome (Baddeley & Wilson, 1988). fMRI investigations further have been able to provide very detailed and nuanced investigations of the various areas involved in several metacognitive skills. For example, using a similar methodological structure to Heart's 1965 experiment, feeling-of-knowing (FOK) judgments have been correlated with frontal areas using fMRI (Fernandez-Duque et al., 2000).

The brain seems to function back to front (Medina, 2011; Swanson, 2003). Sensory input pours into the hindbrain through the spinal cord and then into midbrain structures of the limbic system that are largely responsible for pairing sensory input with an emotional level of arousal. Even the sensory data from the eyes, in the front of our head, is first processed in the occipital lobe in the back. The processing of sensory experience is moved forward through higher and more frontal brain regions like the parietal lobe and somatosensory areas. The frontal lobes are the last areas of the brain to process. It is believed that as the neurological traces of thought move from the hindbrain to the forebrain, the complexity of those thought traces increase as ever more refined details are added from localized brain regions specializing in specific forms of processing.

What emerges from the frontal lobes is a unified conscious thought, which is able to metacognitively apprehend itself. It's not just providing an awareness that you can learn, but an awareness of the awareness that makes learning possible. This allows planning and behavioral modulation based on abstract meta-features not directly apparent in the experience. This causes the frontal lobe to use tremendous amounts of energy and activate high numbers of genes related to metabolic energy consumption (Sapolsky, 2017).

The morphology, function, and connectivity of frontal areas of the brain have been repeatedly related to self-reflective metacognitive thinking (Allen et al., 2017; Baddeley & Wilson, 1988; Fleming et al., 2012; Macmillan & Lena, 2010). However, closer examination reveals that the prefrontal cortex (PFC) is a functionally very diverse area. Primate studies confirm the PFCs involvement in social behavior by showing that the greater sociability of a species, the larger the PFC and corresponding gray matter (Sapolsky, 2017).

Moreover, it cannot be said that metacognitive function is only correlated with the frontal lobe. Midbrain and parietal areas have also been shown to play a strong role in metacognitive processing. As neurological investigation has intensified, it has revealed that rather than a localized brain region being responsible for metacognition, there are, in fact, many areas involved across various brain regions.

2.5.2 Hind and Midbrain Structures

Since hind and midbrain structures are among the first areas of the brain to process incoming sensory information, it may be assumed that what goes on in these regions should have very little to do with metacognition. However, much of what the midbrain engages in lays the groundwork for later more advanced cognitive tasks, and it is not clear if these aspects should be considered neurologically separate from the act of metacognition. Some researchers have questioned if some aspects of metacognition are subconscious (Brown, 1980; Stajkovic et al., 2006), meaning that some of metacognition's constituent parts operate outside of conscious control. As discussed, several aspects of executive function seem to be performed by the brain before conscious awareness is brought to bear. If there are subconscious aspects of metacognition, they will likely be related to midbrain and intra-brain structures, since these structures are most associated with arousal, attention, and emotional function (Goleman, 2006).

The hindbrain is at the base of the spine. Because of its location, it is sometimes called the brainstem. It is responsible for the regulation of subconscious autonomic bodily functions like digestion, heart rate, and breathing. Though the hindbrain is not considered related to metacognitive function because its functions generally occur outside of conscious regulation, some degree of conscious regulation can be brought to bear on these autonomic functions.

On top of the hindbrain sits the midbrain. The midbrain is primarily responsible for processing emotional information (Swanson, 2003). All sensory input into the brain passes through this area, where it is emotionally processed. This processing takes place in two dimensions. The first dimension is whether the input is a positive or negative experience. The second dimension is the experienced emotional intensity. These emotional aspects drive the attentional processes of the brain by both directing attention and determining the level of emotional arousal behind behavioral responses (Tyng et al., 2017; Goleman, 2006; Foa & Kozak, 1986; Kleinginna & Kleinginna, 1981).

As information enters the brain, it has two characteristics: an emotional variance, experienced as either a positive or negative feeling, and an emotional intensity experienced as a level of energy (Kleinginna & Kleinginna, 1981). Emotional intensity can be best imagined as an energy level that ranges from 1/very slight, to 10/unignorable and intense (Goleman, 2006). Attention is generally driven toward information of higher emotional intensity (Foa & Kleinginna & Kleinginna, 1981; Kozak, 1986). Though ostensibly a subconscious process, it is one of the first points in processing where the brain makes an abstract judgment about a sensory input. This judgment of emotional variances will dictate the level and manner of the neurological processing that follows (Tyng et al., 2017). For example, in a classroom lecture, the professor will likely garner most of your attention both because of the emotional value placed on her role in the classroom, and the information she is imparting. However, if you have a sick parent or child at home, you will find your attention moving to thoughts of them, because they command a higher emotional value than the professor, even though they may not be there in the classroom at that moment.

Moreover, if there were an explosion outside of the classroom, your attention would be immediately drawn to this potential threat and you would experience a corresponding emotional surge of energy, preparing you for action. This is called an acute-stress response or the fight-or-flight response, first described by James (1890) and Carl Lang in the 1880s. During these events, a midbrain structure called the amygdala compels action that is driven by the desire for self-preservation. A cascade of neurotransmitters, such as norepinephrine and epinephrine, increase heart rate, dilate pupils, and constrict blood vessels in the outer extremities, all to prepare the individual for the physical demands of a life-threatening event (Goleman, 2006; Foa & Kozak, 1986; Kleinginna & Kleinginna, 1981). This response is only limited by the more metacognitively regulating frontal areas of the brain, exerting control and regulation. However, this regulation occurs only after this stress response action has been triggered. This level of emotional control and regulation seems to be strongly developmental, and can have a powerfully negative impact on behavior if regulated poorly (Tyng et al., 2017). It also demonstrates a relationship between conscious and autonomic control, affecting how an individual responds to their own interoceptive feelings and experiences of information, which can impact further neurological response (Sapolsky, 2017).

Part of the reason for this is that the midbrain seems only capable of associative thinking (Goleman, 2006; Tyng et al., 2017), Deeper discrimination is a property of higher areas of the brain that are not activated until after the emotional midbrain processes information. For example, my wife has ophidiophobia, and is deathly afraid of snakes. When she sees one, she has an emotional stress response, even when viewing a snake in an advertisement or TV show. One time while we were walking through the woods, I noticed someone had thrown about 20 feet of rope into a bush off the side of the path. My reaction to this was disgust over the litter left in the woods. My wife, on the other hand, never really saw the rope. The information never made it to her frontal lobes where higher levels of discrimination are processed. Instead, the information got as far as her midbrain, which detected the qualities of long, skinny, and in a bush, and immediately associated it with a snake. As a result, she began screaming and running in the opposite direction, before the more detailed discrimination was made. This reaction is sometimes called an emotional hijacking (Goleman, 2006) because it results in the midbrain hijacking control away from the frontal lobes. This can result in a host of emotional behavior, where the individual may end up saying and doing things without really thinking through their actions, essentially because the areas of the brain that are responsible for thinking have been bypassed by the midbrain.

It has been found that emotional regulation can powerfully affect learning (Tyng et al., 2017), and mental health (Aldao & Schweizer, 2010). Even the simple positive–negative emotional variance initiated by the midbrain can have strong downstream effects on learning. Studies of this variance have been central to the studies of mindset. For example, Dweck (2008, 2017) found that students who view their ability to learn positively performed better than students who viewed their ability to learn negatively. This simple variance in the confidence one places on their own learning has been shown to be more predictive of a student's school performance than grades (Dweck, 2017).

Regulating emotional intensity during learning plays an even bigger role in the learning process (Tyng et al., 2017). It has been shown that as the emotional intensity of a situation increases, the ability to command control over one's attention also decreases, while neurological access to working memory and other higher-level thinking processes become impaired (Gabel & McAuley, 2018). Increasingly, it is being shown that optimal learning occurs in a balanced emotional state, one that is not too overly aroused and emotionally reactive, but not too under-aroused, bored, or disinterested. Students who can best manage this emotional regulation tend to perform better than students who do not. Increasingly, it has been found that difficulties regulating the stress and anxiety associated with learning are involved with the developmental symptomatology of learning disabilities (Bonifacci et al., 2016;

Gabel & McAuley, 2018; Thakkar et al., 2016). It is well known that there is a neurochemical interaction that occurs between emotion and memory (Phelps, 2004). When students make mistakes, it produces an emotional response, which in turn provokes the release of neurotrophic compounds that support memory, which in turn primes the brain to better remember events that subsequently follow the mistake (Roediger & Finn, 2009). It has been hypothesized that, in students with learning disabilities, this natural learning process associated with making mistakes is distorted by an education system that provides more shame than support, leading to a feedback cycle that only reinforces emotional memories of failure rather than useful memories that would aid problem solving (Gabel & McAuley, 2018).

2.5.3 Stress

So much stress comes from the manner through which we reason. If we attribute our overbearing stress to forces outside of us, we anxiously withdraw from the world. If it is placed internally, we collapse depressingly into ourselves. Metacognition offers a way to avoid being locked into maladaptive behavior at either end of this continuum.

Active metacognition appears to be a very personal form of scientific method involving hypothesizing about one's situation, planning and executing a response, and then reflecting on the outcome. Its products are developmental and gradual changes in the patterns of one's thinking and behavior. Its development depends on the proper function and integration of a myriad of cognitive processes. However, its conscious implementation opens up the possibility that an individual will notice when something is amiss with any of these processes, making adaptation to personal weaknesses possible. This, I believe, is the evolutionary explanation for metacognition. It seems to be an extension of the human ability to observe the external environment and detect ways in which it can be modified.

There also seems to be a force of human cognition that seeks to maintain stability, which is ingrained in the neurological processes of the brain. This biologically driven process seeks to retain/maintain thoughts and behaviors through habituation and produce a level of cognitive stability where it becomes possible for a developmental process like metacognition to occur. Cognitive stability provides a mental environment where the kinds of insights and behavioral changes that metacognition makes possible can occur. It is somewhat paradoxical in this way, because metacognition is a kind of willful disturbance of the very cognitive stability that is necessary for it to occur, and yet it makes maintaining stability over longer periods of time more possible.

I know that I engage in metacognition personally to bring stability to my environment, both internal and external. Often, what I am trying to bring to bear is a predictable future for myself, one where I will not be caught off guard by events or one where I will be able to execute a task with a high degree of precision. However, everyone has different levels of stability that they can maintain, and different levels of instability they endure. My disability makes a certain level of organizing very difficult and confusing for me, but I also believe I can endure higher levels of instability than most. I sometimes wonder if my inability to manage stability has promoted my ability to endure high levels of instability, or if it was the reverse? Did my high tolerance for instability impair my ability to manage stability? Though I can't be positive where these tendencies came from, I am sure my high tolerance for instability has served me well in my professional career, and my understanding of my degree of tolerance has given me the confidence and fortitude to undertake a career path that someone with a lower tolerance to instability probably would find unbearable. However, I also believe it is a specific kind of cognitive stability that metacognition produces that runs counter to the kind of uncontrolled cognitive instability that leads to mental illness and disability.

2.5.4 Caudate Nucleus

One area of the midbrain that has been implicated in subconscious metacognitive processing is the caudate nucleus. This area of the brain is thought to regulate attentional arousal in much the same way a water faucet regulates the flow of water through a garden hose (Hallowell & Ratey, 2011). fMRI and SPECT studies have demonstrated that blood flow to the caudate increases as the intellectual demands of a task increase, and inversely, decreases as demands decrease. Similar to other autonomic functions in the brain, these changes are generally not initiated consciously, but rather as a result of stimuli. So, when we are confronted by a challenge or problem that requires focused attention, blood flows into the caudate, increasing available glucose and the flow of thought. When we need to relax or get some rest, blood flow decreases to the caudate, slowing the flow of thoughts. The caudate is one of the areas implicated in Attention Deficit Hyperactivity Disorder (ADHD) because it is the target of most stimulant attentional medications. Moreover, neuroimaging has shown that individuals with ADHD demonstrate lower blood flow to this region than normal subjects when given an attention-focusing task (Amen & Carmichael, 1997).

While midbrain structures like the caudate seem to perform their function outside of consciousness, it has been demonstrated that conscious awareness can still be brought to bear in their regulation. For example, it has been demonstrated that individuals can use metacognitive executive function to project and maintain their attention to varying degrees (Astle & Scerif, 2011) in a process called endogenous attention. It has also been shown that individuals can use environmental modifications to regulate attention control, such as playing certain kinds of music (Jefferies et al., 2008). By becoming consciously aware of how certain experiences and environments can enhance or impact attention, individuals can purposely choose to develop behaviors or place themselves in situations that improve this innate and subconscious capacity for attention (Fig. 2.2).

Many of the brain's autonomic functions have also been shown to fall under some influence of conscious control, even the highly autonomic processes of the hindbrain (Swanson, 2003). The simplest demonstration of this would be breathing, which is

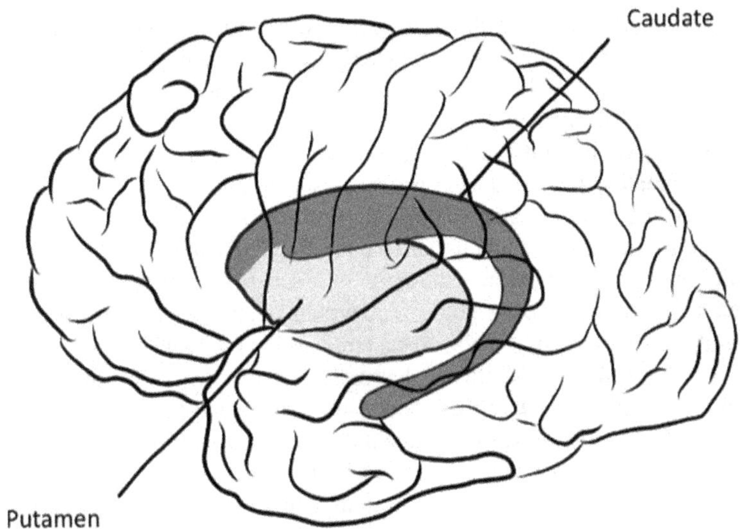

Fig. 2.2 Caudate nucleus *Note:* Mid-brain location of Caudate[1]

controlled unconsciously by the brain stem. However, at any moment we can move our conscious awareness to our breath to regulate its flow. We can even stop our breathing when needed in situations like swimming. Interestingly, full conscious control of this vital neuro-biological cognitive function is never fully granted. If one attempts to hold their breath, past a certain point the hindbrain compels its resumption through a building perceptual pressure, or in extreme cases, literally shutting down consciousness altogether. This leads the individual to pass out so that normal breathing can resume undeterred by conscious interference. Moreover, it seems that this kind of hindbrain control is not driven by a strictly nonconscious monitoring of oxygen levels, as would be suspected (Stratton et al., 2001).

The hindbrain and frontal lobes are not the only brain regions capable of overriding normal control of breathing protocols. Midbrain structures can also seize control of breathing functions in instances of high emotional intensity (Deakin, 1991; Stratton et al., 2001). In situations the midbrain evaluates as too dangerous to suspend conscious behavior, it will override the hindbrain response, even when oxygen levels are dangerously low. This has led to many tragic deaths from a condition called positional asphyxia. Positional asphyxia generally occurs in institutional mental health settings when a patient or client falls into a state of acute stress response and must be restrained in order to maintain safety. Often, because of mental health issues, they

[1] I would like to point out that the following images of the brain are drawn by my own shaky hand using a wonderful instructional book called the *Human Brain Coloring Workbook* by Kapil Gupta (1999) I believe this book was an invaluable tool in supporting my learning of the neurological processes of the brain, and strongly this way on interacting with the data when trying to comprehend neurobiology

perceive the intervention as a threat to their life. This leads to the classic fight-or-flight escalation. These are often terrifyingly physical events. Rather than passing out, these individuals will continue to fight, scream, and threaten. Although their blood oxygen has dropped to dangerously low levels, these individuals will fight on. When these individuals are maintained in restraint positions that restrict their ability to take full breaths, such as during prone floor restraints, deaths from suffocation can occur, even before the usual warning signs of suffocation, because the midbrains stress response has bypassed them (Chan et al., 1997; Deakin, 1991).

While conscious modulation of the autonomic functions of the mid- and hindbrain, like breathing, may seem to have little to do with metacognition, at its heart metacognition is about an awareness of how to best manage and modulate other neurological functions to maximize the ability to learn. As we learn more about learning, we find that to maximize our learning potential we must manage and modulate both the external and internal learning environment. Internal somatic states such as levels of sleep, emotion, and fatigue can powerfully affect learning (Palmer, 2013). Our ability to modulate these states is an imperative component of maximizing our capacity to learn. Plus, such conscious modulations of autonomic functions may be demonstrations of a more elementary component of the broader phenomena. It may be that the mid- and hindbrain areas are more involved in specific kinds of metacognition than presently appreciated, albeit in a less conscious way.

2.5.5 Hippocampus

Improvements in resolution capabilities and techniques, such as parallel magnetic resonance imaging (pMRI), have increased the ability of MRI and fMRI to produce highly detailed investigations into the deep structures of the brain. Investigations using this kind of multi-parameter mapping have revealed that there is a strong relationship between memory, hippocampal microstructure, and perceptual metacognition (Allen et al., 2017). Historically, memory has been considered to be the source of how the known self comes to be known (James, 1890). By "known" I mean a stable, mentally manipulatable memory of an idea that can be recalled and used to demonstrate understanding. Memory allows individuals to not only look back and evaluate experience, but also remember goals and objectives for the future.

Midbrain structures like the hippocampus have repeatedly been found to be related to memory function. Most recently, morphological differences in hippocampal size have been identified in London taxi cab drivers. These drivers must memorize London's entire street layout to secure their licenses. This daunting cognitive task leaves these cabbies with a larger-than-average hippocampus (Maguire et al., 2000). Similar results were found to occur in language acquisition (Sluming et al., 2002) and learning to play an instrument (Gaser & Schlaug, 2003). What has been underappreciated in these studies is the role that metacognitive knowledge and regulation have played in this process, fostering this unique relationship between the understanding

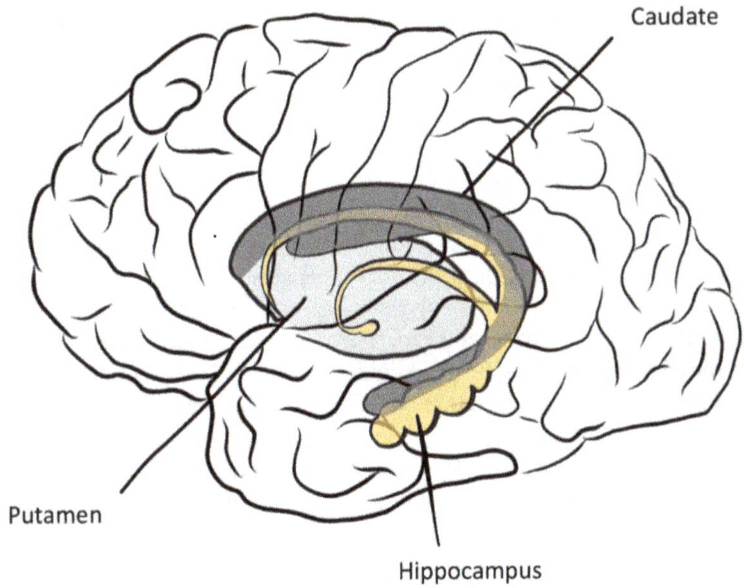

Fig. 2.3 Hippocampus. *Note* Midbrain structures of Hippocampus, Putamen and Caudate

and directing of one's learning, and the physical and structural makeup of one's brain itself (Fig. 2.3).

More recent investigations of the microstructure of the hippocampus (Allen et al., 2017) have found important relationships between this brain region and metacognitive ability. These results suggest that hippocampal, memory-related systems may be very important to perceptual metacognition. A broader question to raise would be, are these processes part of the conscious metacognitive memory regulation, or part of an underlying, subconscious memory network that supports metacognitive function?

2.5.6 Metamemory

To distinguish aspects of subconscious memory processes from the conscious memory processes most associated with high-level metacognition, researchers have introduced the concept of metamemory (Flavell & Wellman, 1975). Metamemory is the ability to monitor and predict memory capacity. Metamemory involves conscious awareness of a felt capacity. Neurological imaging studies further validate this conception by showing strong neurological conductivity between memory related hippocampal structures and the executive areas that organize and regulate behavior in the frontal and prefrontal cortex (Allen et al., 2017).

Metamemory has been studied through simple predictions of memory performance (Yussen & Levy, 1975). For example, Hart (1965) was the first to investigate what has become known as the feeling-of-knowing (FOK) by having subjects assess feelings of confidence that they do, in fact, have something stored in memory, but cannot accurately recall it at the time of questioning. This was achieved by asking subjects how sure they felt they could identify the answer to a question they could not earlier answer if now presented with a short list of possible answers. MRI (Craig, 2009; Kikyo et al., 2002) and lesion studies (Schnyer et al., 2004) of FOK have identified deep prefrontal regions of the brain being involved in such tasks.

Methodological elaborations of the metamemory conceptualization have been quite fruitful and have led to several experimental designs that have yielded valuable insights into the structural and behavioral qualities of the brain. For example, fundamental methodological investigations of judgments of learning (JOL) (Nelson & Narens, 1990), time allotment and selection of mnemonic study strategies (Brown & Smiley, 1978), ease-of-learning (EOL) (Nelson & Narens, 1990), time spent in memory search (Lachman & Lachman, 1980), and go-no-go studies have provided investigational models that transfer well into neuroimaging studies (Cabeza & Nyberg, 2000; Craig, 2009). The success of the metamemory conceptualization has also produced a unique problem, as the variety of research methods used to measure the various manifestations of metamemory have produced a diversity of definitions for a common phenomenon. This inability to settle upon a common language for certain phenomena related to metamemory has contributed to confusion and inconsistent results across the literature (Fernandez-Duque et al., 2000).

2.5.7 Corpus Callosum

As one moves up and forward from midbrain structures one comes to a thick band of neural connections that enable communication between the two hemispheres of the neocortex and frontal lobes called the corpus callosum. The corpus callosum plays a wide role in facilitating neuronal communication across the brain and has been shown to play a large role in our capacity for both verbal memory and encoding abstract, semantic meanings (Kozlovskiy et al., 2012). This is particularly important to the study of metacognition, as it has been shown that we have considerably better memory for things we have associated a meaning to and stored using semantic encoding, rather than repetitive rote memorization (Foer, 2012). We can choose to employ memory strategies, like memory palace, that exploit this neurological predisposition.

Neuroimaging studies have identified morphological size differences in the corpus callosum that can be correlated to individual differences in cognitive function. Differences in the size and shape of the corpus callosum have been found in dyslexics, particularly in the posterior midbody of the corpus callosum (von Plessen et al., 2002). In fact, malformations of the corpus callosum are among the most common congenital brain malformations observed in human beings (Dobyns, 1996).

Interestingly, such morphological differences in the corpus callosum may also result from how individuals process information, and their tendency to use certain kinds of thinking over others. Much of the brain's thinking is lateralized to one hemisphere over the other. For example, most language skills are lateralized in the left hemisphere, and most visio-spatial processing skills are processed on the right (Sperry, 1968). There is evidence that some neurological disabilities result from poor interhemispheric integration. Damage to this left-brain right-brain communication network produces striking neurological conditions that will be delved into more deeply later.

The corpus callosum is also one of several areas of the brain that are affected by habits of learning. It has been shown that behaviors that induce interhemispheric communication promote significant morphological differences in the size and shape of the corpus callosum. Such morphological differences have been detected in musicians (Gaser & Schlaug, 2003; Levitin, 2006) and individuals that are ambidextrous or left-handed (Witelson, 1985). Though probably less involved in the conscious regulation of thought processes involved in metacognition, the corpus callosum is certainly significantly involved in the vast neuronal communication networks involved in higher-order thinking.

2.5.8 Anterior Cingulate

One of the internal structures of the frontal lobe, which resides just outside the midbrain, that has been shown to have definitive involvement in metacognition is an area of the brain surrounding the frontal part of the corpus callosum called the anterior cingulate (AC). Initial studies by Bench et al. in 1993 using PET scans identified this area of the frontal lobe's involvement in attentional control during a Stroop task. This task, which uses a field of words denoting different colors, has subjects identify the color of a written word rather than reading the word naming the color. This task can provoke a measurable state of cognitive interference when the relationship in meaning between ink color and written word is incongruous. Such incongruities between perceptions and meanings produce a measurable delay in response time, called semantic interference. Further fMRI investigations by Peterson et al. (1999) using this construct identified that the anterior cingulate activates a distributed attention network that is arranged spatially, depending on the specific attentional demands of the task.

Studies have shown a close relationship between the size and activation of regions in the AC with metacognitive ability (Allen et al., 2017; Fleming et al., 2014; McCurdy et al., 2013). The work of Peterson et al. (1999) and others like Carter et al. (1998) who used a letter pattern detection model have demonstrated that the AC activates most strongly when the test subject is confronted with competing stimuli that require a shift in attentional demands. It has been suggested (Carter et al., 1998) that the AC is involved in error monitoring and detection (Fig. 2.4).

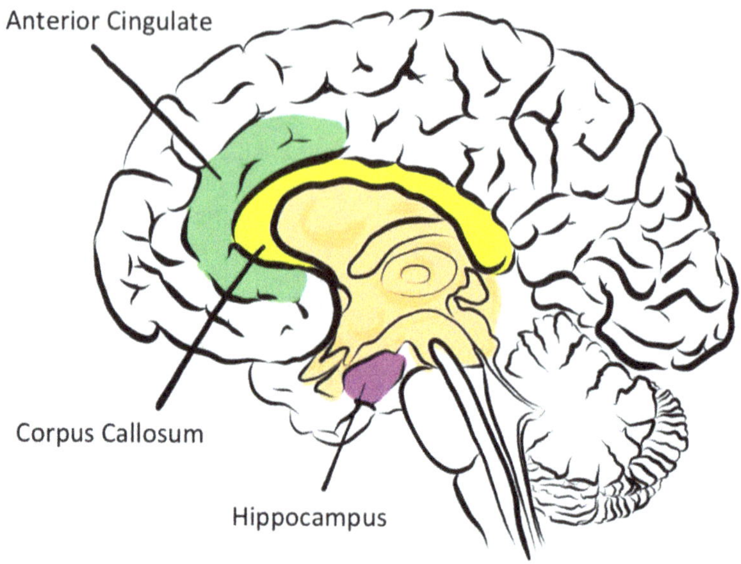

Fig. 2.4 Anterior cingulate

However, our understanding of the relationship between the AC and error monitoring and detection is not settled. It has been observed by Carter et al. (1998) that the activity in these brain regions seems to increase because of the response competition seen in the Stroop task, and occurs during both correct and incorrect responses. This suggests that rather than errors themselves, the AC activates when it detects conditions where errors are likely to occur (Allen et al., 2017). Plus, the AC is not the only region of the brain associated with activation during these kinds of semantic interference tasks (Allen et al., 2017; Fleming et al., 2014; McCurdy et al., 2013). Certain areas of the parietal lobes called the precuneus show significant activation. This area, like the AC, is between midbrain structures and the outer layers of the cerebral cortex. Connections between parietal and prefrontal areas show considerable involvement in episodic memory and reflective self-awareness.

2.5.9 Parietal Lobes

Outside of the frontal lobes, parietal areas are perhaps the most associated with metacognitive and self-regulatory functions. According to the parieto-frontal integration theory of intelligence (P-FIT), it is the neural connections between these two regions that provide the best explanation of where intelligence resides in the brain (Haier et al., 2009). The parietal area has been implicated in specific learning disabilities, such as dyslexia (Catani & Jones, 2005; Eckert, 2004), dysgraphia (Catani & Jones, 2005), and dyscalculia (Von Aster & Shalev, 2007). Damage to areas within this region can produce impairments ranging from the ability to perform specific complex movements, called Apraxia, to impairments in the ability to recognize or discriminate qualities in the sensory field, called Agnosia. Often, localized damage to the parietal can produce fascinatingly specific kinds of deficits. Perhaps most relevant to the study of metacognition is the condition of Anosognosia, or what is sometimes called hemispheric neglect, a condition in which a person suffers from paralysis due to their injury but seems to be unaware of the disability's existence.

One reason researchers have been able to identify many parietal functions is that it is a part of the brain that is easily accessible compared to internal areas like the midbrain. This has enabled researchers to apply electrical stimulation to specific parietal brain regions, which frequently produce noticeable changes in cognitive and perceptual experience (Calvin & Ojemann, 2010). During brain surgery for severe epilepsy, for example, the patient is awake, while the surgeon applies localized electric current to the physical surfaces of the brain and asks/observes changes correlating with that area of the brain. This is to ensure that the surgeon does not damage regions of the brain involved in important functions of daily living. Through this process, researchers have thoroughly mapped the motor area by stimulating the brain and identifying corresponding body movements (Penfield & Boldrey, 1937), and the sensory areas by stimulating the brain and identifying corresponding sensations reported by the patient (Woolsey et al., 1979) (Fig. 2.5).

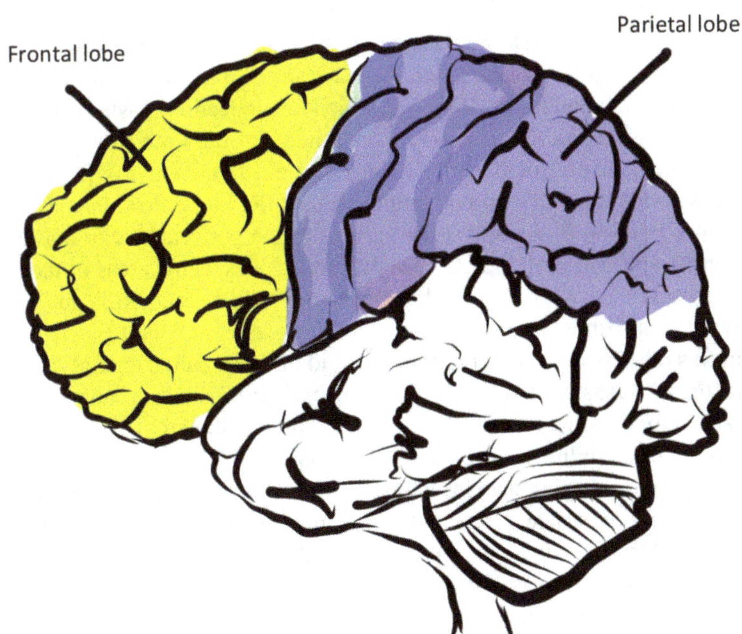

Fig. 2.5 Parietal lobe

Many of the brain's most impressive feats of abstract thinking are involved in the parietal. It has been implicated in the understanding of metaphors (Ramachandran & Hubbard, 2003), directing spatio-visual attention toward salient features in the environment (Seghier, 2012), visuospatial working memory (Todd & Marois, 2004), arithmetic fact retrieval (Dehaene et al., 1999), and symbolic numerical information processing (Cantlon et al., 2006). The parietal is also strongly associated with various types of social skills. An area called the inferior parietal lobule was found to be involved in the perception of emotions in facial stimuli (Radua et al., 2010). This is consistent with earlier work identifying a parietal role in interpreting the intent of others (Grafton, 2006).

However, the ability of these techniques to fully localize these functions is not clear cut. For example, while early investigation seemed to identify the angular gyrus as responsible for creating metaphors (Ramachandran & Hubbard, 2003), later investigations found the angular gyrus was actually less involved in creating metaphors, and it was that conceptual metaphors were activating the somatosensory cortex in the parietal operculum (Lacey et al. 2012). A similar shift has occurred in our understanding of the relationship between formation of, and the access/response to, semantic linguistic expression seen in Warnicke's area (Milberg & Blumstein, 1981).

Generally speaking, the parietal role seems to be in distinguishing specific contextual details (Wagner et al., 2005). The subjective recollection hypothesis (Yazar et al., 2012) explains the parietal's role as one of retrieving contextual details and organizing multi-sensory information stored throughout the brain and likely also supports feelings of confidence in judgments about the accuracy of a memory. Further evidence for this pathway is found in the cingulum, which is a collection of white matter fibers that allow for communication between components of the limbic system, parietal, primary sensory, and prefrontal cortex (Mountcastle, 1984; Pandya & Barnes, 1987).

Along with intraoperative brain mapping and fMRI blood flow data, anatomical data has also been used to connect the parietal to the performance or mastery of a specific task (Sluming et al., 2002). Size differences in specific areas of the parietal have been correlated with improved performance of different skills and abilities. Perhaps the most famous example of this was discovered in Albert Einstein's brain. Einstein was missing much of a pronounced fold of tissue called the Sylvian fissure. So rather than the usual folds and sulci found in this region, Einstein had a surprisingly plump and smooth parietal operculum region, which is thought to be related to his tremendous spatial abilities (Witelson et al., 1999).

Presently, neuroimaging data investigating intelligence indicates that the parietal sub areas of the extrastriate cortex and fusiform gyrus contribute to the recognition of categories of things that are emotionally salient imagery and elaboration of visual input, in much the same way Wernicke's area organizes syntactic auditory input in a meaningful way (Deary et al., 2010). It is thought that information is then moved through the supramarginal, superior parietal, and angular gyri where it is processed for structural symbolism, abstraction, and elaboration. Then these parietal regions interact with parts of the frontal lobe as a working memory network capable of holding different pieces of information in memory so it can be compared to different possible task responses. (Deary et al., 2010). It may be that conscious metacognitive monitoring occurs between the frontal and parietal cortex, as they exchange information to coordinate their activities. It has been found that this decision circuit between frontal and parietal cortex is most active during free-choice decision-making tasks (Pesaran et al., 2008) that require a high level of conscious metacognitive thinking.

2.6 Working Memory and Inhibition

As stated earlier, the frontal regions of the cerebral cortex seem to play the largest role in metacognition. Of the numerous regions of the frontal lobe, imaging studies have identified the prefrontal cortex (PFC) as having specific involvement in self-regulation, judgment, planning, and conscious behavior. This conception is evidenced by data collected from behavioral, electrophysiological, and blood-flow techniques. (Allen et al., 2017; Badre et al., 2010, Fleming et al., 2012; D'esposito et al., 1995) The general consensus view is that PFC is crucial for integrating thought and behavior.

A fundamental component of cognitive neuro-processing is the ability to hold an idea, object, or experience in one's mind and shift one's cognitive perspective. This ability to hold ideas in our mind while we solve problems is called working memory. It has been shown that efficient working memory depends on regions in the prefrontal cortex (Jonides et al., 1993; Petrides et al., 1993).

PFC shows increased activation during mental tasks that make greater demands on attention (Shimamura, 2000). For example, one fMRI study asked subjects to perform a judgment task (e.g., monitoring each time a type of vegetable is presented) and a visuospatial task (e.g., mental rotation) found significant prefrontal activation when both tasks were performed simultaneously rather than separately (D'esposito et al., 1995). Presently, there are two competing conceptualizations for what is occurring in the frontal lobes during these kinds of experiments. One group of conceptualizations centers around the idea that the brain is involved in making ever more accurate associations related to contextual features (Cohen & Servan-Schreiber, 1992; Kimberg & Farah, 1993). The other sees the brain as inhibiting the expression of superfluous or irrelevant information processing (Fernandez-Duque et al., 2000; Knight et al., 1999; Shimamura, 2000) (Fig. 2.6).

One computational model (Grossberg, 1999) proposes that executive control is maintained by exercising both selective and inhibitory control. In this model task-relevant information is enhanced in working memory by a top-down neural mechanism that also inhibits reaction to similar but irrelevant information. Research (Aron et al., 2014) has revealed the existence of both inhibitory and excitatory prefrontal control of distributed neural activity in posterior brain regions. It seems that the cognitive capacities of the prefrontal cortex are bi-directional and exert regulatory influence on numerous cortical, limbic, and subcortical regions (Friedman & Goldman-Rakic, 1994).

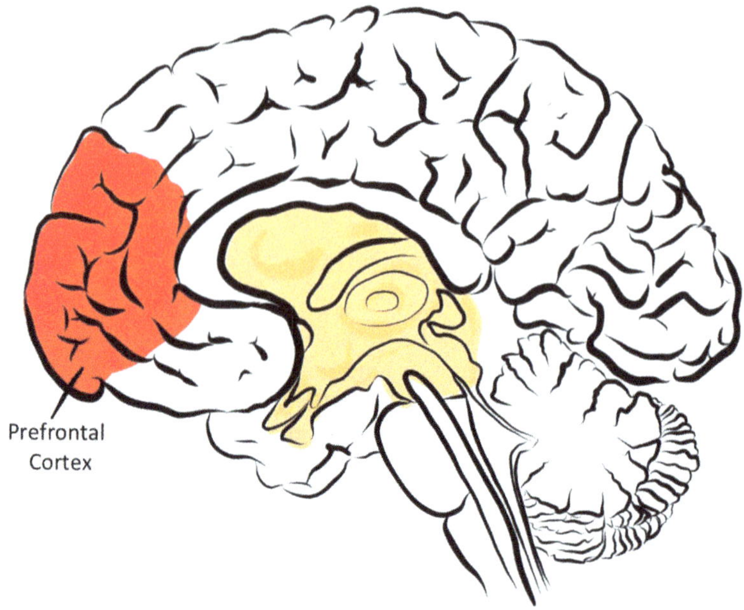

Fig. 2.6 Prefrontal cortex

Neurophysiological insult to the PFC generally produces problems with inhibitory control (Knight et al., 1989; Yamaguchi & Knight, 1990, 1991), particularly in relation to sensory information processing. PFC damage has been correlated to difficulty in both sustained attention and selectively focusing (Woods & Knight, 1986), as well as the impaired detection of novel events (Knight, 1984, 1997). In fact, the study of brain lesions offers yet another lens through which to approach and expand our understanding of metacognition and neurology.

2.7 Implications of Brain Lesions

Specific functions of brain regions can be inferred through changes in behavior produced by damage or purposely lesioning the brain through surgical procedures. The loss or damage of specific areas of the brain has been strongly implicated in very specific disturbances of metacognitive function. For example, Phineas Gage, one of the first well-recorded cases of brain lesion, and possibly the first documented case of dysexecutive syndrome, suffered an accident that destroyed his left frontal lobe, definitively changing his personality and impairing his ability to self-regulate (Macmillan & Lena, 2010). Losses of self-regulation and self-awareness are common features of many brain lesion studies. It has been found that patients with frontal lobe damage generally perseverate on previously rewarded tasks and fail to recognize the full implications of shifts when the relevant dimension of a task changes, as in the Wisconsin Card Sorting Test (Owen et al., 1993), which tests a subject's ability to shift from one cognitive strategy to another. This is achieved by having participants match cards without being told what qualities constitute a match, but telling them whether a particular match is right or wrong. Studies using this kind of test suggest another role of the frontal cortex is the ability to shift mental sets from a previously successful or dominant set to a new set (Shamura, 2000).

Wernicke's aphasia generally occurs as the result of an occlusion in the left middle cerebral artery, producing a lesion in the posterior superior temporal gyrus (Brookshire, 2007). Damage to this area of the brain leaves subjects unable to produce intelligible speech despite an intact ability to form words and syntactic structure. These individuals seem to lack the ability to perceive the intelligibility of their own language or self-reflect on their understanding of what has been asked of them. So, while their ability to construct words and sentences remains intact, they do not seem to be aware of the distortions in meaning presented in their manner of speech and are remarkable because of their ability to engage in conversations with others without acknowledging deeper semantic connections to their language. This stands in stark contrast to Broca's aphasiatics, who can no longer correctly form the words necessary for fluent speech and are deeply aware of their expressive shortcomings. For this reason, Wernicke's and Broca's aphasia seem to implicate separate and specific localized language functions related to the ability to produce language, and the metacognitive awareness of the meanings their language produces.

Lesion studies of the brain often demonstrate impairments of metacognitive awareness similar to what is seen in Wernicke's patients. In these cases, the lesion produces more than just a simple inability to perform a given task, it obliterates the individual's ability to perceive or be consciously aware that there is a problem. As described earlier, damage to the right parietal lobe can produce a syndrome called anosognosia, or hemispheric neglect, where an individual fails to attend to, or even notice, that their injury has caused the left side of their body to become paralyzed (Mesulam, 1981; Kertesz & Dobrolowski, 1981; Hier et al., 1983; Stein & Volpe, 1983). Interestingly, this lack of self-awareness extends through the individual's whole perceptual field. In a famous study, Ramachandran (1997) used a mirror angled to reflect what was occurring on a patient´s neglected left field of vision. After informing and confirming that the subject understood that they were looking into a mirrored reflection, the subject was asked to grab a pen next to them on the left and reflected in the mirror. Remarkably, rather than turning to the left and grabbing the pen, subjects would attempt to reach for the reflection. When asked to explain why they were unable to grab the pen, the subjects would reply, "The real pen is inside the mirror," or, on another occasion: "The pen is behind the darn mirror," (Ramachandran, 2004, p. 35) (Fig. 2.7).

Interestingly, other kinds of lesions to the parietal lobe produce visual deficits, but not a loss in the individual's awareness of the deficit. For example, damage to the medial temporal area affects an individual's ability to perceive the speed and direction of something moving, but not their awareness of their perceptual loss (Ramachandran, 2004). These individuals are frightfully aware of their deficit, despite possessing

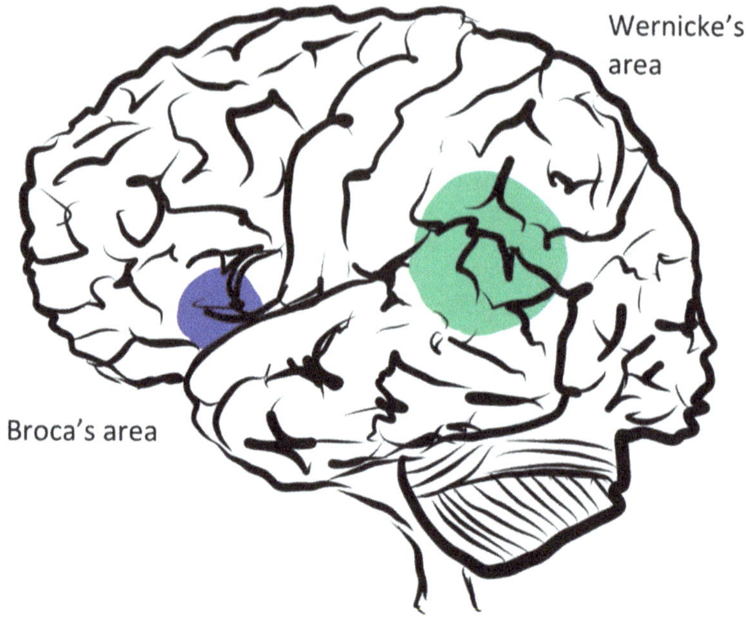

Fig. 2.7 Language areas. *Note* Broca's and Wernicke's areas of language function

vision that is functionally normal in all other ways. It seems that only certain kinds of brain damage come with corresponding damage to self-perceptual awareness, as seen in these neglect or Wernicke's patients, that leave individuals unaware of their deficits. However, while it is clear that damage to some brain regions affects the performance of a neurocognitive skill, and others the perception of that skill's performance, the cognitive interactions that produce these differences should be a focus of future neuro-metacognitive investigation.

Memory is another cognitive skill,[2] that engenders this elusive quality of performance perception. Memory is a cognitive skill that has long been studied because of its ability to offer a window into the workings of the mind. Hart (1965) demonstrated that despite being unable to clearly remember if an answer to a question was right or wrong, most people can fairly accurately determine if an answer is right or wrong by accessing a metacognitive feeling about what they know. Another example of this ability to monitor our memory quality is the fact that nearly 1 in 8 Americans over the age of 60 report that they have noticed a decline in their memory (Alzheimer's Association, 2016). Under normal circumstances, most people possess a metacognitive awareness described as metamemory (Pannu & Kaszniak, 2005) that allows them

[2] I have spent considerable time going back and forth as to what to call memory here. Is memory a feature or attribute of cognition? Or is it more of a developable skill of cognition? I have decided to come down on the side of calling memory a skill because it is inherently developable, and when memory is described as an attribute it infers that there is less room for modification and improvement, which is clearly not the case (see Foer, 2012).

to assess the qualities of their own memories. However, brain lesion patients like Henry Gustav Molaison (HM), who had most of his hippocampus removed during a bilateral medial temporal lobectomy to control his seizure activity, demonstrated an inability to form new long-term memories, but maintained a relatively intact short-term and working memory (Baddeley et al., 2009; Corkin, 2002). HM was able to remember information over short intervals of time, but he would subsequently forget whatever had just happened when his attention was drawn to a new situation, or there was a shift that refocused his working memory. Interestingly, though HM was consciously unable to form new memories, he was able to demonstrate motoric, muscle memory and spatial learning through repetitively playing a new piece on the piano (Corkin, 2002). Essentially, HM could be taught to play new music, despite never remembering that he had been taught.

Damage to other limbic structures can have a dramatic impact on social behavior, like what is seen in Kluver-Bucy syndrome, which produces a range of aggressive and sexual behaviors. Damaged limbic structures like the amygdala can lead to a decline in such aggressive behaviors. Inversely, repeated exposure to fear or traumatic stimuli can lead to an enlargement of the amygdala seen in patients with PTSD, producing hypersensitivity and increased aggression (Gilboa et al., 2004). Functional conductivity of the prefrontal cortex and amygdala in PTSD seem to indicate this region's connection to violence are the result of learning (Sapolsky, 2017). The connections between limbic brain and frontal lobes are involved deeply with our emotional responses to others. For some, damage to this pathway produces an inability to change strategies in an economic game when it becomes clear the other player is taking advantage, called "pathological altruism" (Oakley et al., 2011). Pathological altruists present with a similar inability to detect angry facial expressions seen in other disorders that affect social judgment, like Urbach-Wiethe disease.

Brain damage is rarely clean or exact. Often, brain damage leads to skill deficits that are only partially obscured to awareness. For example, Young et al. (1990) identified a woman who suffered a right middle cerebral artery subarachnoid hemorrhage, leaving her unaware of her deficit in face recognition. However, she was aware that she had other deficits in other domains, such as memory, motor function, and vision. It has been a general assumption of neurologists that if damage were more exact, specific areas of localized brain function would appear. However, while it may be tempting to attribute haphazard destruction of brain matter caused by stroke or injury to nonuniform presentation and symptomatology of brain lesions, surgical ablation studies, where lesion damage can be very tightly controlled, seem to add more questions than they answer.

2.7.1 Surgical Ablation

For ethical reasons, ablation studies are usually carried out in animals. Analysis must be inferential when considering metacognition in these studies, since not all species demonstrate metacognitive aptitude (Sutton & Shettleworth, 2008) and no species can demonstrate human levels of metacognitive sophistication (Kornell, 2014). However, such studies can be highly selective and specific about the brain regions being studied (Teuber, 1955) and have served to identify the role of specific brain areas, like motor areas or the prefrontal cortex (Jacobsen, 1935). What is interesting is that even with the ability to make exactingly specific brain lesions, there is little evidence of this specificity producing a correspondingly pure expression of a lost skill (Lashley, 1950). In fact, it has been demonstrated that control of complex motor patterns can find a way through lesioned connections between neurons (Lashley, 1950), indicating that there is some kind of neural executive function mechanism regulating this phenomenon.

Ablation studies have found behavioral habit formation among the brain's most highly conserved abilities. Lashley indicated that "Even combined destruction of the prefrontal, parietal, occipital and temporal areas, exclusive of the primary sensory cortex, does not prevent habit formation, although preexisting habits are lost and their reformation is greatly retarded" (Lashley, 1950, pp. 12–13). Observed behavior related to habit formation could be a highly ingrained stimulus response mechanism, or it could represent a primitive manifestation of self-regulation. How one answers this question has tremendous functional and philosophical implications.

Not only do specific brain lesions fail to produce cases of pure localization of function, it is equally difficult to identify if observed effects represent a genuine total loss of a neurocognitive skill or a disruption of the brain's organization (Lashley, 1950). In other words, it is nearly impossible to rule out that a given presentation is the result of a loss of a functional unit in the brain or the disruption of a more peripheral yet fundamental process in the network. For example, further studies of Wernicke's aphasics have shown they are unable to group words in relation to shared categories or features (Zurif et al., 1974) and tie words to affective and situational data (Zurif, 1974). So, rather than a loss of semantic expression, Warnicke's aphasics may lack the ability to access semantic information for linguistic use or interpretation (Milberg & Blumstein, 1981). Perhaps they are suffering a disruption in brain organization rather than an actual loss of a skill.

2.7.2 Split Brain and Alien Hand Syndrome

Of the few surgical ablation-related studies performed on humans, most are performed on epileptics to remove the source of their seizures. Only those epileptics with the most dire symptomatology ever received a complete callosotomy, or severing of the corpus callosum, to prevent their seizure activity from crossing between hemispheres and engulfing the entire brain. These split-brain findings cast considerable confusion into debates about localization of brain function as they seem to demonstrate separate consciousnesses in the opposing hemispheres of the brain. These patients demonstrate an acute inability to monitor inter-hemispheric behavior, manifesting in a condition called alien hand syndrome (AHS) (Gazzaniga, 2005; Joseph, 2011a, 2011b; Sperry, 1968). Patients with AHS, quite literally, have to physically fight for control over the behavior of their alien hand (Joseph, 2011a, 2011b) because its actions fall exclusively under the control of the non-linguistic right hemisphere. Interestingly, this hand behaves in ways the linguistically capable left hemisphere cannot explain, and this behavior seems to be generated from a conscious locus of control that functions outside of their left hemisphere's perception (Joseph, 2011a, 2011b; Sperry, 1968).

Sperry received a Nobel prize in 1981 for his discoveries into the fundamental processing differences between the two hemispheres, using split-brain patients. However, his suggestion (Sperry, 1968) that there are non-linguistic, yet conscious, mechanisms of behavioral control located in the right hemisphere has inspired considerable research into split-brain phenomenon and a lively debate into the differing functions of the two brain hemispheres (Gazzaniga, 2005). For example, while it has been found that linguistic processing is a weakness of the right hemisphere, which extends even to visual tasks like reading (Zaidel & Peters, 1981), the right hemisphere can be thought of as the brain's creative interpreter of fundamentally ambiguous information (Corballis, 2003; Ramachandran et al., 1998). This is because the right hemisphere engages in problem-solving novel solutions, while the left hemisphere puts those solutions into words. It is believed that what is occurring in hemispheric neglect patients is that stroke damage to the right hemisphere has impaired the patient's ability to interpret novel situations, so they can no longer adequately process the reality of their own paralysis. Instead, their linguistically intact left hemisphere creates excuses for a situation it cannot comprehend. Interestingly, it has been demonstrated by Ramachandran et al. (1998) that these excuses follow the familiar Freudian patterns of the psychological defense mechanisms (1992).

Interestingly, this lack of perceptive self-insight cannot be said to be localized to the right hemisphere. AHS has been found to affect the right hand of individuals with left medial frontal lobe damage also (McNabb et al., 1988). Similarly, the insight issues of Wernicke's patients discussed earlier are the result of left hemispheric damage and belie this hypothesis. However, these regions of the brain do play some role in the perceived ability to choose (Fig. 2.8).

I used the wording, "perceived ability to choose," carefully. There is considerable debate in the neurological community as to the level of freedom available in human choice. Benjamin Libet (2004) performed experiments that showed that the human mind was already contemplating and organizing the muscular response to an, as yet unmade choice, milliseconds before the conscious mind made the choice (for a brief video of the experiment https://www.youtube.com/watch?v=OjCt-L0Ph5o). Dennet (2017) explained that this novel result suggests that rather than consciously experiencing the moment a choice is made, what is consciously experienced is confabulated by a brain that has already made a choice. This suggests that what has been historically considered free choice is constrained by deterministic, non-conscious mechanisms. However, others like Roskies (2011) have argued that the neuroscientific evidence cannot prove, one way or the other, free will's existence.

While split-brain patients further complexify notions of free will, they do seem to confirm that the actions of the brain related to the act of choosing reside in the frontal

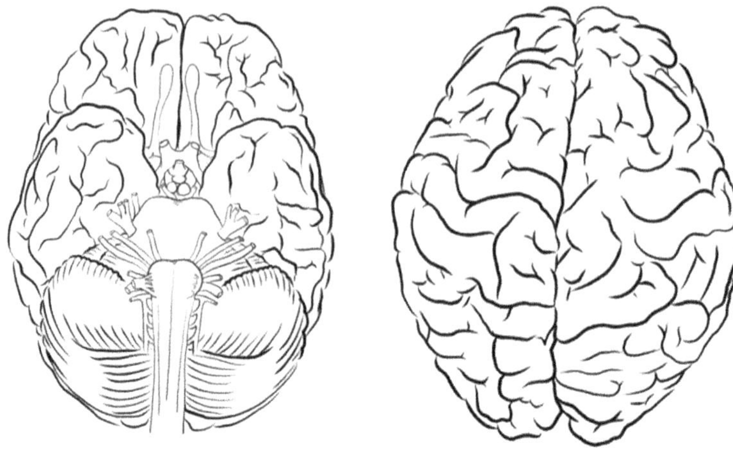

Fig. 2.8 Hemispheres

and parietal lobes (Joseph, 2011a; Roskies, 2010). It is also clear that both hemispheres seem to engage in distinct forms of processing when approaching choice, with the left hemisphere employing language and logical reasoning and the right employing more social and spatial reasoning (Joseph, 2011a, 2011b; Ramachandran et al., 1998; Sperry, 1968). Damage to either the right or left frontal medial motor areas can affect conscious perceptions of choice, and if this damage is accompanied by anterior damage to the corpus callosum, then the condition of AHS will arise (Joseph, 2011a). A clean severing of the neural pathways linking the two hemispheres' supplementary motor areas can lead to two independently focusing attentions (Luck et al., 1989), and two seemingly conscious entities residing inside the same skull, exercising a freedom to choose behaviors outside the other's conscious perception (Joseph, 2011a, 2011b; Sperry, 1968).

From a metacognitive perspective, patients with brain lesions also demonstrate that a powerful level of metacognitive awareness can be brought to bear, even in the face of such debilitating injury. This is the ability to produce adaptive behavior even in the face of an extreme neurological loss. Ultimately, the brain shows a remarkable degree of plasticity and an ability to heal itself (Bethune & Doidge, 2015). Phineas Gage, mentioned earlier, was able to demonstrate a remarkable level of recovery from his injuries through learning and development over his lifespan, going on to become a stagecoach driver in Chile where his livelihood depended on the use of many of the skills initially damaged by his injury (Macmillan & Lena, 2010). It has been shown that anosognosia/neglect patients can regain a level of self-awareness of their deficits over time (Bethune & Doidge, 2015). Even when a condition persists due to a neurological insult, like in the case of HM, a remaining level of metacognitive self-awareness can be used to compensate for the condition (Corkin, 2002).

2.7.3 *Synesthesia and Acquired Savant Syndrome*

In fact, brain injury results not only in the loss or impairment of cognitive ability, but some brain injuries can also cause the appearance of extreme skills in mathematics, geometry, music, and artistic expression. Anecdotal historical evidence of savants is common. Stories of individuals like 'Blind' Tom Wiggens, who despite being blind and possibly autistic, became the first African American to give a command performance at the White House for President James Buchanan. Plus, popular portrayals like Dustin Hoffman's character in the movie "Rainman" have served to romanticize the idea in the mind of the public. Often these savants are born with otherwise debilitating neurological disorders, and yet still possess extreme mental powers. However, growing evidence is beginning to show that such conditions are more than just an accident of birth, they are in fact the result of specific brain injury (Piore, 2013; Snyder et al., 2003). There are presently at least 50 identified cases of individuals developing extreme cognitive abilities after receiving a head injury, resulting in a condition described as acquired savant syndrome (Hughes, 2010).

One of the most surprising cases is the story of Daniel Tammet, who became a synesthete, able to perceive numbers as shapes and colors, following epileptic seizures at age three (Tjentz, 2012). For most synesthetes, their condition causes numbers to slightly glow a distinct color. However, Tammet's condition came with a corresponding vision of a shape. Tammet credits his synaesthesia with his ability to make incredibly complex calculations at lightning speeds (Treskate, 2012). For many with synesthesia, there is an interaction between abstract cognitive symbols and perceived sensory experiences, which allows for deeper processing of certain kinds of information, like the extreme mathematical skills demonstrated by Tammet. Interestingly, most people who have the condition do not realize they have it, and finding out if one has the condition requires a degree of metacognitive realization. In fact, diagnosing synesthesia was not possible until fairly recently. There are several synesthesia tests that, while not standardized, identify the condition by how quickly test subjects identify the frequency of the number two in a field of fives (Eagleman et al., 2007). Because synesthetes perceive a uniform color corresponding to a given digit, they can identify numbers from a field of differing numbers quicker and with fewer mistakes than non-synesthetes.

In a sense, unlike the earlier discussed Wernicke's or neglect patients who have lost the ability to consciously perceive a dimension of the cognitive world that undamaged individuals take for granted, these individuals suddenly become aware of perceptual dimensions that were previously repressed in their undamaged brain. This perhaps suggests that there are, potentially, neurological governors that restrict our conscious access to certain categories of perception (Snyder et al., 2003) and thereby restrict our ability to metacognitively process information. This line of research also invites the question of whether metacognition or other processes could unlock these perceptual restrictions. For example, Snyder et al. (2003); also see Snyder et al. (2006) demonstrated that transcranial magnetic pulses can be applied to the left frontal temporal

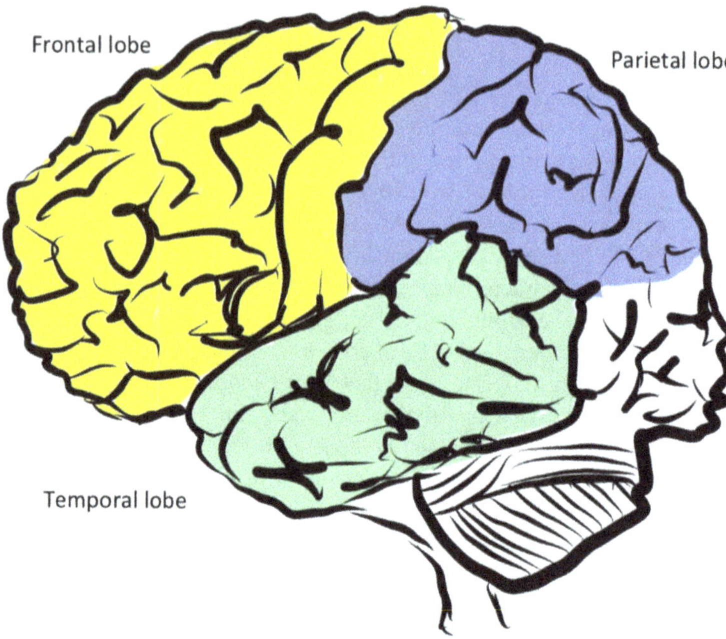

Fig. 2.9 Temporal lobe. *Note* Temporal, Frontal and Parietal lobes

lobes of functionally normal individuals to produce states of improved mathematical and creative performance seen in savants (Fig. 2.9).

2.7.4 Neuroplasticity

Neuroplasticity is the brain's ability to reshape and even heal itself. Neuroplastic phenomena were at one time considered rare, and even negligible phenomena. Directed animal studies into memory and learning, like those carried out on sea slugs by Kandel (2001), have demonstrated that learning produces neurostructural changes. However, the field has been most impacted by the pioneering work of researchers like Doidge (2007, 2016), and the introduction of neuroimaging techniques, which has made neuroplasticity the area of intense study it has become. The most compelling aspects of this research show there are direct morphological effects on brain regions associated with use (Gaser & Schlaug, 2003; Levitin, 2006; Maguire et al., 2000; Sluming et al., 2002) that are powerfully related to metacognition.

When it comes to learning, humans are doing more than simple operant conditioning (Skinner, 2011). We demonstrate the ability to regulate our behavior toward learning (Dewey, 2007; Flavell, 1979). This feature of regulation is conscious, effortful, and metacognitive in nature. It allows for goal-directed executive control and can also produce identifiable morphological changes in the brain. For example, a study of London cabbies by Maguire et al. (2000) demonstrated that as cabbies come to memorize all of the streets and roads in London as required for their job, measurable anatomical changes in the size of their hippocampus occur. While this study is generally cited as evidence for a hippocampal role in memory formation, it is also evidence of metacognitive self-regulation affecting brain plasticity.

This effect is not limited to memory. There have been demonstrated impacts on the brain's linguistic areas in the middle frontal gyrus as well as the hippocampus during language acquisition (Sluming et al., 2002). The most widespread neuroplastic effects were found in studies of students learning to play musical instruments (Gaser & Schlaug, 2003; Levitin, 2006). The development of this skill not only demonstrated volumetric increases in the size of the hippocampus, but also increased synaptic density in motor areas, and improved organization of white matter (Gaser & Schlaug, 2003; Levitin, 2006; Sluming et al., 2002).

While the neurological relationship between metacognitive regulation, practice, learning, and the brain are recent discoveries, a similar kind of metacognitive regulation also can be applied to the physical body. There are presently 131,700,000 (Statistic Brain Research Institute, 2018) people with gym or health club memberships. We can assume that by virtue of their gym membership, they intended to directly regulate their behavior to produce changes to their physical being in one way or another, be it to look more fit, lose weight, improve their cardiovascular health, or any of a myriad of reasons. It is clear there is a form of metacognitive self-regulation involved in the act of physical fitness. Efforts may wax and wane, just as in studying, but through a conscious process of metacognitive self-regulation what is practiced becomes habituated, and physically affects all areas of the body involved in the process, producing morphological changes to the targeted areas. By virtue of this interaction, humans can develop their physical brain in much the same way they can develop their physical body or any practicable skill.

Neuroplasticity research also suggests that humans can counteract and even stave off the effects of disabilities if they are able to harness their self-regulatory behavior through metacognition. There are many examples of individuals using their personal powers of metacognitive regulation to identify ways to rise above a disability or adversity, but perhaps none is more incredible than the story of John Pepper (Doidge, 2016). In 1968, John Pepper was diagnosed with Parkinson's disease. His response was to learn as much as he could about the illness. Then, from this knowledge, he went on to develop a personalized exercise routine that involved daily focused walking to combat the disease's progression. By the time he reached his 60 s, when most Parkinson's patients lose the ability to walk and begin to succumb to their disease, Pepper was coming off his medication, walking five miles per day, and by most evaluative standards moving quite normally (Doidge, 2007, 2016). His story, and others, point to the ability of exercise routines, like Pepper's, to trigger the production of brain-derived neurotrophic factor (BDNF) and other growth factors that stimulate neurogenesis (Cotman & Berchtold, 2002). These neurological compounds have been shown to increase resistance to brain insult, improve learning, boost mental performance, and affect conditions that can lead to both muscle and brain impairment (Adami et al., 2018).

The knowledge of BDNF and the beneficial effects of physical fitness on the musculoskeletal nervous system have changed the way surgeons and physical therapists interact with patients. After most modern procedures, surgeons rarely require more than 48-h bed rest, and most are requiring immediate physical therapy. Along with targeted therapeutic exercise, physical therapists are told "effective exercise instruction is based on knowing a patient's learning style" (Kisner et al., 2017; p. 27). Their goal is to expand their patient's metacognitive knowledge about the brain to positively impact self-regulatory adherence to restorative therapeutic routines. Metacognitive regulation plays an important role in the physical and neurological healing made possible by learning and exercise (Cotman & Berchtold, 2002).

2.7.5 Personal Resilience

In my youth, I was hurt by the experience of failures that aroused disapproval and feelings of incompetence. I was often wrong, and I could not understand why. Often the explanations given made no sense to me either. I can now look back and see how my dyslexia affected both my receptive and expressive language even before I started writing, something I did not realize until I had a child of my own.

My son demonstrated a linguistic quality that I had up to that point only noticed in certain students I had taught, and never related to myself. However, now my son was demonstrating the behavior in a way that was startlingly familiar. This was the tendency to talk only in terms of actions, frequently dropping the subjects of sentences altogether. It was an impediment to clear articulation. When my son would do this, I would gently remind him to include a subject so that I would know what he was talking about. I believe my insight into my son's communication issues kept him off an Individualized Educational Plan (IEP), but for me, things were different. I can remember the frustration I caused. I was frustrated, too. What I did not understand at the time was that the frustration was coming from my own failure to communicate, and my teachers' failure to identify my communication failure for me in a way that would have helped me overcome it. Over time, when a teacher became frustrated with me, I would become frustrated right back. It was cathartic, but also impaired my ability to learn.

My arguing was a learned skill, supported by a broader American entertainment culture of stereotypical conflicts between young and old, students and teachers, parents and children. My mindset was that of a disturbed postmodernist, in that I saw all ideals as constructs of their holders' self-interest. In high school, before I met my tutor, no one could really win an argument with me, as my idea of winning an argument was a complete emotional evisceration of an opponent. Facts were simply one in the arsenal of verbal weapons used to break down an opponent. In this style of arguing, the only goal was to make the other person feel stupid, and my experience with that feeling made me good at it. However, I was not the best. I had friends, of course, who were superior. Sadly, I learned from them because when we were not dissembling a teacher or parent, we were disassembling each other's self-esteem. At that time, I was embedded in a culture of deception and self-defense.

What I developed as a teenager was a mindset with debilitating consequences for learning. Emotion, rather than being a guide through obscurity, became a weapon. At least part of this attitude came from the majority of adults I was exposed to who were under the impression that if discipline was done right, then the child should "show remorse," usually in the form of crying. After enduring many moments of tear-filled humiliation, I learned how to choke back the tears. I adapted this into my argumentative beliefs and style, and I became primarily focused on hurting my opponents on as deep an emotional level as I could muster. Due to my familiarity with failure, I knew what kinds of arguments would hurt the most: the ones that hurt me the most. These were arguments that attacked and trivialized the things you most cared about, and I had an uncanny knack for identifying those things in others. I think the reason the concept of metacognition affected me so powerfully was that it revealed this quality about myself to me, a quality I despised in others that I was also guilty of.

I also feel this change for me was dramatic. One moment I was locked into thinking about exchanges in purely emotional terms, where things like having the last word and trying to make the other person cry were as important as maintaining my own fragile composure, and the next moment I realized how pointless and insipid this behavior was. A large part of this change I owe to my other PAL professor.

When I entered the PAL Program at Curry during the summer of 1989, Joe became my PAL professor. He was a Catholic deacon who also worked in the prison system and literally wore his religious beliefs out there for everyone to see. His standard dress was a black short-sleeved shirt and clerical collar. Joe approached every subject in a way that would lead you back to examine your own beliefs and prejudices. Where my tutor Ned was able to tap into the personal and emotional aspects of learning and self-discovery, Joe was able to tap into the dynamic, intellectual, and scientific aspects of metacognitive thinking. He nurtured and fed a developing obsession for brain science, which enabled me to actually understand, from a scientific and biological sense, the work that Ned had done with me earlier.

Joe had a gift for breaking very difficult concepts into easy to understand and relatable parts. Many times I remember walking out of his office on the second floor of the PAL library absolutely energized by our conversation. Through his work with me, I came to realize that not only could I understand advanced college-level material, despite my obvious functional weaknesses, but that my ideas were important to the discussion. I became a voracious reader of anything on the subject of neurology, learning, or learning disabilities because of his tutelage. Thanks to him, I attempted to read texts that were well beyond my ascribed reading level and came to realize that not only could I read such texts, but I could also express ideas on those subjects. Joe fed my sparks of insight until they became a smoldering academic interest that would become the foundation of a future career, and what has brought me to the point of writing this.

By examining my macabre enjoyment of arguing I have learned that I have a real skill at spotting weaknesses in certain types of arguments, a skill that has served me well in my present career. But in my youth, most adults hated to argue with me. This was because my natural skills, in conjunction with my mindset that the only way to win an argument was to punch people in the emotional and metaphorical breadbasket, made me toxic to anyone who thought they were presenting some kind of truth. I know I was exhausting for most educators, asking questions, changing the subject, and endlessly reframing the debate so that the idea presented seemed trivial. I would push back on sensible arguments with the intention of getting them to no longer make any sense. However, rather than getting offended by my behavior, Joe seemed to enjoy my argumentative quality.

In fact, Joe would use it, spin it, turn it on its head and direct it right back at me, in the most pleasant and jovial of ways. With him, we were playing with ideas to figure out where they were stupid, and not labeling the other person as stupid for having that idea, which would have been my usual course of action. With Joe, my nit-picky arguments became an expression of my intellectual curiosity. He taught me how to transform my curiosity into inquiry, as valid as any other person's intellectual inquiry. The argument became a tool he would use in a very reasoned and systematic way to work with me to break down ideas. Soon, his mental tools of inquiry became my mental tools, and a source of one of my greatest intellectual strengths.

I believe what metacognition creates is the ability to perceive dichotomies as merely manifestations of the same thing. These are the kinds of phenomena that are encapsulated in the Dauist taijitu symbol, commonly called the Yin Yang. Metacognition promotes the ability to see these dichotomous yet unitary phenomena because they are representative of many aspects of the human condition. For me, my greatest intellectual strength was actually what stood in the way of me receiving the information I needed to learn. Joe never told me that. However, I believe I learned it from him. It was my internalization of this process-driven approach to thinking, which he had brought me to, that led me to my own startling self-realizations. I discovered my own mental trap, a trap I created and reinforced repeatedly through my interactions with others.

Back-and-forth exchanges with another person help parcel out, intellectually, differences between what is said and what is meant by what is said. As a person with a language-based learning disability, I have to gauge whether I'm saying what I truly mean, and judge my understanding of what is being expressed to me. From this vantage point, communication is a desperate, emotional, back-and-forth exchange that amazingly allows us to understand the mind of another person. Of course, this is only if we want to understand. To the unhealthy mind, this back-and-forth exchange is a mechanism of obfuscation. Rather than expanding understanding, communication can be used to protect the ego and prevent understanding by degrading our sense of self and compassion for others.

In my youth, I wanted to show "them" they were wrong about me. I hated those people that labeled me disabled, those teachers and others that predicted and encouraged my failure. I needed an enemy to hate, an enemy to battle. However, through the metacognitive teachings of Ned, Joe, and Dr. Webb, my hate was processed into achievement. My achievement created more things in the world that I came to care about and love. I still find it ironic that my hate drove my expanding achievement, and expanded my capacity for love, but I now see they are aspects of a similar phenomenon. My capacity for hate moved from being directed at an actual person, to an abstract "them," and then an abstract system that produces the conditions, social and environmental, that block development.

2.8 Resting State and the Default Mode

It may also be that the human brain is particularly attuned toward self-reflection during times of quiet contemplation. Several studies have found (Buckner & Carroll, 2007; Moran, Kelley, & Heatherton, 2013; Spreng et al., 2009) that people engage in self-referential processing when they are not attending to the outside world. This is because the brain engages in a specific neuronal activation, which occurs when the brain is at rest, called the default network (Damoiseaux et al., 2006). The brain's resting state can be thought of as what the brain is doing when it is not doing anything, and this is why the brain's resting state is sometimes called the default mode.

What is interesting about the default mode is that the region of peak activation during rest is in an area of the medial prefrontal cortex (MPFC) called Brodmann's area 10 (BA 10), which has been found to be engaged in self-referential processing (Denny et al., 2012). The MPFC is the largest of prefrontal regions in the brain (Öngür et al., 2003), and has been found to activate when people reflect on their emotions (Ochsner et al., 2004), think about their personality (Kelley et al., 2002), or their past and future (Spreng & Grady, 2010; Spreng et al., 2009). For this reason, the MPFC/BA 10 has important connections to metacognition and self-reflection.

However, along with demonstrating strong reactions during self-reflective tasks, the MPFC region, ironically, has also shown activation while processing social information (Moran et al., 2013). These regions are considered by some researchers to be part of the "social brain" (Heatherton, 2011; Lewis et al., 2011). Research by Meyer and Lieberman (2018) and Spunt et al. (2015) have further localized these to more specific regions, with MPFC/BA 10 being involved with self-reference, and dorsal medial prefrontal cortex/Brodmann's area 9 (DMPFC/BA 9) being more involved with social referencing. This seems to suggest strong neuro-physical relationships between introspective self-reflective thought and a natural tendency to connect introspections to social relationships (Meyer & Lieberman, 2018). It may be that during quiet times, when we disengage from our subjective thinking, the natural tendency of our default mode is to self-reflect on ourselves and our social relationships.

2.9 The Neuron

The neuron is the most fundamental part of our brain's architecture. The complexity of the brain is derived from its physical system of fractally branching neurons, spread like a web throughout the body. The brain is made of roughly 100,000,000,000,000 neurons (Swanson, 2003, p. 11). Neurons are made up of three basic parts. First, is the main cell body, which contains the nucleus, then the axon, which transmits messages, and finally, the dendrites that receive chemical messages. These chemical messengers, called neurotransmitters, diffuse across a tiny gap between the cells called a synapse. These neurotransmitters connect to receptor sites on the synapse of the receiving dendrite through a lock and key method where the shape of the neurotransmitter fits into a suitably shaped receptor site (Calvin & Ojemann, 2010; Lefkowitz, 2004) (Fig. 2.10).

Individual neurons are among the most diverse cell types in the body. They fall into three distinct categories. Sensory neurons are responsible for carrying information from the sense organs. Motor neurons carry information from the muscles and glands of the body, and often have long axons. The third class of neuron is the interneuron, which lie between connections of sensory and motor neurons and play a role in regulating excitatory and inhibitory patterns in neural networks (Swanson, 2003, pp. 37–38) All neurons are thought to work by transmitting information using electrical impulses that travel through the axons and plasma membrane to the synapse, where the impulse is converted into a chemical signal (Barnett & Larkman, 2007). When this chemical signal crosses to the other side of the synaptic cleft, it is converted into electrical impulses that are sent down the axon to the synapse between the next neuron. The alternating of electrical and chemical signals between neurons are thought to produce the vast and rich neurological behavior associated with the brain and nervous system (Medina, 2011; Swanson, 2003). This neuronal system of electrical and chemical transmissions of information is common to the nervous systems of all organisms, except single-celled protozoa such as paramecium and euglena.

It is believed that individual neurons function in the brain much like the individual switches in computer processors. Each neuron is specialized and becomes electrically excited or inhibited in response to specific information (Calvin & Ojemann, 2010). For example, in the case of sight, specialized sensory neurons called rods and cones detect photons entering the eye. These neurons respond only to specific wavelengths of light: red, green, or blue. The differing intensities with which these neurons respond

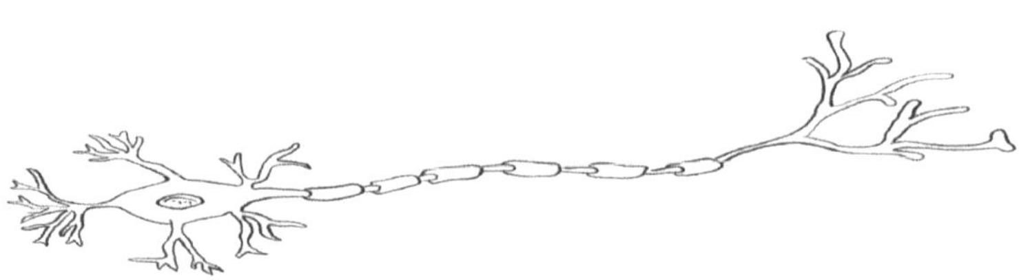

Fig. 2.10 The neuron

to each color lead to a gradual building of the perception of the other colors we perceive. This information is sent to interneurons that may, in turn, become excited by qualities of shape, or movement. Chains of interconnected neurons respond in a binary, excitatory, or inhibitory fashion as the information moves through a vast neural network to the occipital lobe at the back of the brain. From the occipital lobe, a complete visual picture is sent toward the more frontal regions of the brain (Medina, 2011; Swanson, 2003).

As this picture is moved forward through the brain, other neurons are excited or inhibited in more complex and highly specialized ways, adding information to the perception. Much like a computer builds its interface through a computational system of binary bits of information, represented as ones and zeros, the brain builds its perceptual reality through a computational process of excited or inhibited neuron behavior (Medina, 2011). The first computational model of neuron function was a model proposed by Hodgkin and Huxley in 1952.

This model assumes that brains are analogous to the hardware of a computer. It has not been until fairly recently that neurologists have begun to understand enough about computer science, and visa-versa, to develop theories about the software that runs on this neuronal hardware that produces cognition. The chief thrust of this research has been driven by computer programmers trying to program a computer with more human-like cognitive capacities. Presently, computers have been programmed to carry out many human activities, from chess to telemarketing phone calls. Self-referencing programs, trained on large language models like Open AI's Chatbot GPT, have demonstrated a tremendous ability to produce useful media and information using natural language prompting in narrowly defined task-focused domains. However, iterations of these large language model AI's are beginning to demonstrate strikingly human levels of performance and even the beginnings of a general intelligence that can marshal resources across domains to solve tasks in fields as diverse mathematics, coding, vision, medicine, law, and psychology (Bubeck et al., 2023).

While the AI of computers is often magnitudes more efficient than human intelligence at specific programmable tasks, with skills of generation in those domains approaching, and in some cases surpassing, our own. However, computer scientists have not been able to program a machine with what is known as General Artificial Intelligence (GAI). A machine with GAI would possess the cognitive flexibility and a capacity for problem-solving that is natural for most animals and humans. While many computer scientists would love to produce a working GAI, there are presently no clear computational solutions to the problem because there does not seem to be a good computational analog to metacognition or understanding (Penrose, 1989; Pinker, 2018). However, this does not rule out that GAI will not emerge as the processing power of these systems increases. Recent investigations by Bubeck et al. (2023) have demonstrated that the pre-release version of Chatbot GPT-4 successfully passed a version of the classic false-belief test task designed by Josef Perner and Heinz Wimmer in 1983 to test the development of Theory of Mind in children. To be sure the program did not simply parrot back an answer found in a search an updated version of the test was used. In this version a character named Alice saved a photo in a specific file on her computer. Another character, named Bob, moves the file to a different file without notifying Alice. Chatbot GPT-4 was able to correctly deduce that when Alice returned to work she would not find the picture where she expected because she did not have knowledge that the file had been moved (Bubeck et al., 2023). This level of insight into the workings of a human mind has not been achievable before this point with artificial systems.

Up until this point, computational theories have focused less on developing a working GAI and more on computationally modeling specific kinds of brain activity. One computational model of what could be taking place in the frontal lobes is called adaptive resonance theory (Grossberg, 1999). It explains that the brain achieves selective and inhibitory control through a top-down filtering mechanism that enhances task-relevant information and inhibits similar, but irrelevant information. Along with being among the first neuro-computational cognitive approaches to brain function, the model addressed a problem known as the stability-plasticity dilemma, which is a memory storage dilemma of how one can learn about new objects and events quickly, without being forced to forget previously learned information. By this neural processing model, center-on, or relevant information, is upregulated, and irrelevant, surround-off activity is inhibited. Through this organizing operation, many aspects of neuronal processing are controlled by the prefrontal executive cortex, which uses this dynamic filtering mechanism to globally control task-relevant processing (Shimamura, 2000).

Another computational model is Metcalfe's Composite Holographic Associative Recall Model (Metcalfe, 1993). This model is one of the few computational models that specifically addresses metacognition and frontal lobe function. This model proposes that metacognitive evaluations are based on familiarity checks, computed between new and already stored information in memory, described as novelty monitoring. This monitoring-control operation determines the degree to which new information is bound into episodic memory. Computational models of this conceptualization have done a notable job of simulating aspects of the monitoring and control functions of the frontal lobe. Computational models have also shown that damage to this executive function program produces behaviors similar to those seen in Korsakoff patients who suffer from frontal lobe dysfunction (Metcalfe, 1993; Shimamura, 2000).

Another proposed model, which seeks to computationally explain how executive control is imposed, uses links that associate information with working memory (Kimberg & Farah, 1993). These links allow for the selection of appropriate items based on contextual factors. Surprisingly, these Connectionist Models do not use an inhibitory control mechanism (Cohen & Servan-Schreiber, 1992). Inhibition turns out to be extremely difficult to program. There are, presently, no computationally easy or reliably accurate variables that can be used to help a machine differentiate between an appropriate response from an inappropriate response. This approach (Cohen & Servan-Schreiber, 1992; Kimberg & Farah, 1993) has tried to show that, perhaps, a common contextual factor could be used to produce similar behavioral outcomes to those produced through inhibition.

2.9.1 Neurotransmitters

While fMRI imaging technologies and localized brain injury identify areas of high specialization that correlate to specific areas of the brain, this cannot be the entire story. There is a neurochemical level of interaction in the brain that also exerts a powerful effect on thought and the ability to be self-reflective. This area of neurochemical interaction exists in the tiny spaces between neurons, the synapse, where information is transferred. We know that there are certain compounds and drugs that can seriously impair judgment and other metacognitive behaviors, and anesthesia can remove consciousness altogether. We also know that a proper balance of neurochemicals in the synapses is necessary for effective functioning, and that certain compounds can even enhance function (Sapolsky, 2017).

One neurochemical that exerts a considerable effect on our metacognitive abilities is dopamine. Dopamine is central to the brain's reward pathway. It is part of that wonderful feeling of accomplishment that our brain naturally rewards us with when we achieve a goal. Nerve cells in the midbrain and frontal lobe form the core of a dopaminergic system, which increases activation while learning and receiving an award. However, closer investigation seems to indicate that dopamine is more about the anticipation of receiving a reward, rather than the actual award. Spikes in dopamine are recorded most prominently when working toward, rather than after receiving, a reward (Sapolsky, 2017). By this mechanism, dopamine fuels goal-directed behavior by calibrating the value of a reward with the work it takes to achieve it.

Dopamine release also decreases over time, relative to a given reward. A reward that was at one time very motivating and enjoyable will gradually fail to produce the same spike in dopamine, making it feel less enjoyable and fulfilling. This property of diminishing dopaminergic returns drives human behavior toward ever-expanding goals, but also underlies the human propensity toward addictive behavior (Pessiglione et al., 2008).

How dopamine does what it does remains somewhat mysterious. Dopamine is known to produce affective states that can help improve focus, which is why ADHD medications like Adderall and Ritalin are prescribed (Cook et al., 1995), and why many people drink coffee. Paradoxically, dopamine can also impair focus, which is why drugs that work strongly on the dopamine system like marijuana and painkillers are prescribed, and also abused. Interestingly, dopamine plays an important role in increasing our control over motor activities, as patients with decreased dopamine production also present with motoric disorders like Parkinson's (Sapolsky, 2017).

Testosterone is another neurotransmitter that can affect metacognitive thinking. In popular culture, testosterone is linked to aggressive behavior, but closer investigation reveals this link is weak (Archer, 2006). Testosterone more likely enhances an individual's tendency to fall back on established behavior, making a person who is already prone to aggression more aggressive (Sapolsky, 2017). Testosterone makes individuals more egocentric (Wright et al., 2012), impulsive, and willing to take risks

(Bos et al., 2012), but also increases pro social behavior (Sapolsky, 2017). Testosterone may impact metacognition by decreasing activity in the prefrontal cortex, interfering with the brain's ability to plan and execute. However, testosterone is also a driver of the "'winner' effect in lab animals, where winning a fight increased an animal's willingness to participate in, and its success in, another such interaction" (Sapolsky, 2017, p. 102).

A relatively small number of neurotransmitters have been well-studied. The effects of these compounds on human behavior, and the mechanisms of their function, require more consideration. Scientific understanding is rapidly developing in this domain of investigation, which holds the hope of new treatments and drug options for various conditions. While perhaps not directly involved in the brain's generation of the metacognitive ability, it is clear that these chemicals play a powerful role in determining how metacognitive abilities are deployed by the brain.

2.9.2 Single Neurons and Electrical Brain Stimulation

Another tool of neurological investigation that was briefly touched on earlier and enables the close investigation of the behavior of neurons is called electrical brain stimulation (EBS). EBS has been used since the mid 1800s. The basic procedure of EBS involves applying direct electrical current to specific areas of the brain, producing a corresponding neurological experience or behavior. When electrical current is applied to specific areas, a patient may demonstrate unique responses, ranging from changes in blood pressure and breathing to sensory/motor, emotional, and cognitive experiences (Calvin & Ojemann, 2010).

Research by Lettvin (Gross, 2002) suggested that people have neurons that respond specifically to photos of their grandmother. These subject-specific neurons have come to be called "grandmother cells." Later research done by Quiroga (2013) identified neurons that fired steadily each time images of specific celebrities, like Jennifer Aniston, appeared on a screen, but did not fire at all for other photos. The observed effect remained steady for line drawings, profiles, or even if the celebrity was wearing a mask. Interestingly, these activations seemed to be categorical rather than specific, for example a firing "neuron that responded to Luke Skywalker also fired to Yoda, another Jedi from Star Wars" (Quiroga, 2013, p. 31).

What can be inferred from these studies is the subject of much debate. Equivocally, these findings cannot be evidence of extreme localization, as it would mean that the death of a single neuron would result in the loss of a wide and important concept or memory, such as the memory of one's grandmother (Quiroga, 2013). Another big problem with these studies was first illustrated by Lashley (1923). After repeated motoric EBS experiments on monkeys, he found that correlative results changed over time. It seemed, "One day's mapping would no longer be valid on the morrow." (Quotation Edward G. Boring in Doidge, 2016, p. 106).

These findings do suggest two things. First, that brain structure is more likely composed of networks of neurons that respond to related information rather than interlocking areas of localization. This interrelated neuroanatomy may make the brain far more flexible than previously believed (Doige, 2016). Second, it shows that single neurons can process information that is far more sophisticated and associative than expected from a binary computational system. How the brain makes these sophisticated associations on the neuronal level could have a tremendous impact on our metacognitive understanding and lead to new approaches to learning and self-regulation. This perhaps indicates that there are primitive, or perhaps precursive, metacognitive actions being performed by the brain at a neuronal level.

2.9.3 Electroencephalography

Electroencephalography (EEG) records electrical activity in the brain using electrodes on the scalp. These electrodes can be used to measure and investigate the brain's response to specific cognitive, sensory, or motor events by recording the corresponding electrical frequency spectrum generated by the brain. EEG can identify subtle anomalies in brain wave oscillations that can be used to diagnose epilepsy, tumors, and stroke (Egner & Sterman, 2006). It is also used to help anesthesiologists determine the consciousness level of their patients (Hameroff & Penrose, 2014) and diagnose sleep disorders (Buettner et al., 2019; Islam et al. 2018), as well as degenerative conditions, brain death, or coma. EEG is also a widely used research and treatment for attention deficit hyperactivity disorder (Arns et al., 2013) and auditory processing disorder (Perl & Perl, 2019).

While EEG provides much lower spatial resolution than fMRI and requires sophisticated approaches to data analysis because of its high signal-to-noise ratio, EEG's low cost and high temporal resolution make it better for studying subtle differences in cognitive responses through altered brain wave presentation. EEG can also be used with other neuroimaging techniques to visualize how signals are associated with the actions of certain drugs (Schreckenberger et al., 2004). EEG has also been used in association with machine-learning programs that have been trained to recognize brain wave patterns of epileptics (Buettner et al., 2019), schizophrenics (Shim et al., 2016), and dementia patients (Ieracitano et al., 2020) The combination of EEG with other investigative techniques is revealing information that would have previously been hidden in the EEG data (Burns & Rajan, 2015).

EEG is commonly used in neurofeedback therapy, which uses real-time data of activity in the brain to teach individuals about their brain's function and how self-regulation of this information can be used in the treatment of neurological disorders (Perl & Perl, 2019). These techniques generally use a sound or video to provide an individual with immediate feedback about their brain's activity. This interaction with normally hidden patterns of activation encourages the development of improvements in cognitive capabilities like relaxation, focus, creativity (Omejc et al., 2019), and cognitive flexibility (López et al., 2019). However, there is a dispute about alpha wave neurofeedback's ability to enhance creativity and attention (Beyerstein, 1990). Though there have been considerable methodological advances in neurofeedback studies (Arnold et al., 2013; Knowles et al., 2018), this author is only aware of two double-blind, controlled randomized studies that have undergone peer-reviewed publication (Lansbergen et al., 2011; Perreau-Linck et al., 2010) and neither was able to demonstrate an effect over controlled samples. However, there is good reason to believe that the inability to demonstrate an effect may be a methodological artifact as more recent randomized control studies have identified correlations of considerable significance related to newer attention training techniques (Knowles & Wells, 2018) and neuroplastic effects on cortical function (Ninaus et al., 2015; Ros et al., 2010). Presently, these technologies are developing rapidly and may unlock new approaches to metacognitive monitoring and control.

One of the most valuable aspects of EEG technology is its ability to transmit data that is diagnostically relevant (Iranmanesh & Rodriguez-Villegas, 2017) Diagnostically, EEG can provide data on electrical patterns in the brain that have been related to several difficult-to-diagnose neurological conditions like post-traumatic stress disorder and depersonalization disorder (Salami et al., 2020). An analogous procedure enables the remote control of mechanisms using only brain wave data (Weiss, 2004). This is because EEG produces a comprehensible and relatively stable representation of subtle brain activations through a computer interface. This allows an individual to learn mental control of a computer program or robot through training with an EEG interface (McWhinney et al. 2018; Wan, 2016).

These brain-to-computer interfaces face several hurdles. One is that roughly 15–30% of those who try ultimately fail to gain control over their brain signals (Kober et al., 2013). Possibly the most notable problem with EEG is its considerable sensitivity to interference. Noise produced by body movements or events in the environment can significantly interfere with the technology. However, the technology is developing rapidly and has potentially important applications in prosthetics, rehabilitation, and education as well as commercial products (Padfield et al., 2019).

Neurofeedback has also demonstrated morphological impact (Ninaus et al., 2015). Just as training to remember the streets of London led to changes in the morphological structure in the hippocampus, neurofeedback training has been shown to lead to changes in the anterior insula, left thalamus, right frontal operculum, right putamen, right middle frontal gyrus, and right lingual gyrus (Ninaus et al., 2015). These morphological differences, such as gray matter volumes in these experiments, were able to predict if rhythm training was done using EEG (Ninaus et al., 2015). By presenting a sensory representation of brain activity in real time to assist the self-regulation of brain activity, individuals can learn to monitor brain activity and stimulate specific brain states (Enriquez-Geppert et al., 2017; Sauseng et al., 2007). Neurofeedback has been used in the treatment of motor learning in post-stroke recovery (Pfurtscheller & Neuper, 2006), ADHD (Arns et al., 2013), and epilepsy (Egner & Sterman, 2006). These techniques have also been applied to healthy individuals who want to enhance their peak performance through training cognitive performance (Gruzelier, 2014).

While not every individual responds to neurofeedback in the same way, these interventions hold tremendous promise. They demonstrate a power to bring awareness and control to neurological processes of the mind that are generally so subtle we normally have little practical awareness of them. Because these interventions work to direct the mind's attention to its own internal states and bring a level of self-awareness to these moment-to-moment processes, EEG supported neurofeedback may work through a similar process of introspection seen in meditation (Kober et al., 2017), which has also demonstrated morphological changes in the brain when practiced. Moreover, these studies support findings that a neural network related to self-awareness is active in frontal brain regions, including the insula, anterior cingulate, supplemental motor, dorsomedial, and lateral prefrontal areas (Emmert et al., 2016).

2.9.4 Mirror Neurons

One particular class of neurons that is especially relevant to the study of metacognition is called mirror neurons. Mirror neurons are neurons that activate when one observes directed action. Interestingly, the neuronal activation mirrors the neuronal activation that would occur if a person was actually engaging in the observed behavior (Keysers, 2009; Keysers & Gazzola, 2006; Rizzolatti & Craighero, 2004). Mirror neurons are in many of the same areas that have been correlated with metacognitive activity in the prefrontal parietal lobe, such as the premotor areas, and the inferior parietal cortex (Molenberghs et al., 2009).

Not all researchers are in agreement as to whether mirror neurons are truly a unique class of neuron (Hickok, 2009). Some researchers, like Lingnau, Gesierich, and Caramazza (2009) dispute their existence altogether. This speculation comes from the fact that much of what has been surmised as the function of mirror neurons is based on speculative and highly theoretic extrapolation of neuroimaging data (Hickok, 2009).

Chief among the most controversial findings is that mirror neurons seem to only selectively fire when confronted with goal-directed behavior, like those done during a teacher's demonstration in a classroom, as opposed to just the observation of a movement (Fogassi et al., 2005). The role of the mirror neuron in learning and education has been widely speculated upon since Rizzolatti and Craighero presented their initial findings in 2004. Since this time, there have been continued discoveries of a relationship between these neuron firings in the brains of both teacher and learner in synchrony (Schippers et al., 2010).

Oberman and Ramachandran (2008) have boldly proposed that mirror neurons are the source of human self-awareness. Ramachandran (2000) has further proposed that it was the evolution of mirror neurons in humans that triggered the noted archeological explosion in human capacity called the "Great Leap Forward" (Diamond, 2006; Diamond & Shermer, 1993, Vyshedsky 2014). Anthropologists call this epoch the "Great Leap Forward" because, for much of early hominid history, there was very little innovation in tools and culture. However, suddenly around 60,000 years ago, artifact development advanced rapidly, as evidenced by improvements in tools, art, and culture. It may be that the biological evolution of mirror neurons ushered in an age of new cognitive capacities in Homosapiens, explaining this rapid development.

Other researchers, like Vyshedskiy (2014), have found evidence in the art, technology, and cultural artifacts of this period that demonstrates advances in thinking, imagination, and abstract reasoning which go beyond the learning and imitation paradigm proposed by Ramachandran (2000). I also believe it is justifiable to suggest metacognition as an evolutionary candidate for the "Great Leap Forward" in Homosapiens' cognitive development. It may be that mirror neurons are responsible for the ability to shift between the subjective and objective perspectives described by Nelson's (1996) Metacognitive Model of Consciousness.

Ramachandran's (2000) theory of mirror neurons has elicited a strong response from some critics. This is because it insinuates that a single neuron is capable of far more complex processing than expected from a single neuron. First, because mirror neurons only activate during goal-directed behavior, the question of how a single neuron would know that an action is goal-directed becomes problematic. Kosonogov (2012) has suggested that the mirror neuron cannot possibly be carrying out this function independently and must be activated only after other brain structures have identified goal-directed behavior. To comprehend the intentions of others is highly complex. It generally requires the integration of various kinds of perceptual, historical, and inferential information. A single neuron would not have the power to process even simple social behavior (Churchland, 2012). Based on our present understanding, even the complexity of simple, educationally focused interactions requires the input of large networks of neurons.

References

Abbot, A. (2020). Inside the mind of an animal. *Nature, 584*, 182–185. https://doi.org/10.1038/d41586-020-02337-x

Adami, R., Pagano, J., Colombo, M., Platonova, N., Recchia, D., Chiaramonte, R., Bottinelli, R., Canepari, R., & Bottai, D. (2018). Reduction of movement in neurological diseases: Effects on neural stem cells characteristics. *Frontiers in Neuroscience, 12*, 336. https://doi.org/10.3389/fnins.2018.00336

Aldao, A., Nolen-Hoeksema, S., & Schweizer, S. (2010). Emotion-regulation strategies across psychopathology: A meta-analytic review. *Clinical Psychology Review, 30*(2), 217–237. https://doi.org/10.1016/j.cpr.2009.11.004

Allen, M., Glen, J. C., Müllensiefen, D., Schwarzkopf, D. S., Fardo, F., Frank, D., Callaghan, M. F., & Rees, G. (2017). Metacognitive ability correlates with hippocampal and prefrontal microstructure. *NeuroImage, 149*, 415–423. https://doi.org/10.1016/j.neuroimage.2017.01.060

Amen, D. G., & Carmichael, B. D. (1997). High-resolution brain SPECT imaging in ADHD. *Annals of Clinical Psychiatry, 9*(2), 81–86.

Archer, J. (2006). Cross-cultural differences in physical aggression between partners: A social-role analysis. *Personality and Social Psychology Review*, 10(2), 133–153. https://pubmed.ncbi.nlm.nih.gov/16768651/

Arnold, L. E., Lofthouse, N., Hersch, S., Pan, X., Hurt, E., Bates, B., ... & Grantier, C. (2013). EEG neurofeedback for ADHD: Double-blind sham-controlled randomized pilot feasibility trial. *Journal of Attention Disorders, 17*(5), 410–419.

Arns, M., Conners, C. K., & Kraemer, H. C. (2013). A decade of EEG theta/beta ratio research in ADHD: A meta-analysis. *Journal of Attention Disorders, 17*, 374–383. https://doi.org/10.1177/1087054712460087

Aron, A. R., Robbins, T. W., & Poldrack, R. A. (2014). Inhibition and the right inferior frontal cortex: One decade on. *Trends in Cognitive Sciences, 18*(4), 177–185. https://doi.org/10.1016/j.tics.2013.12.003

Association, A. (2016). 2016 Alzheimer's disease facts and figures. *Alzheimer's & Dementia, 12*(4), 459–509. https://doi.org/10.1016/j.jalz.2016.03.001

Astle, D. E., & Scerif, G. (2011). Interactions between attention and visual short-term memory (VSTM): What can be learnt from individual and developmental differences? *Neuropsychologia, 49*(6), 1435–1445.

Baddeley, A., & Wilson, B. (1988). Frontal amnesia and the dysexecutive syndrome. *Brain and Cognition, 7*(2), 212–230.

Baddeley, A. D., Hitch, G. J., & Allen, R. J. (2009). Working memory and binding in sentence recall. *Journal of Memory and Language, 61*(3), 438–456.

Badre, D., Kayser, A. S., & D'Esposito, M. (2010). Frontal cortex and the discovery of abstract action rules. *Neuron, 66*(2), 315–326.

Barnett, M. W., & Larkman, P. M. (2007). The action potential. *Practical Neurology, 7*(3), 192–197.

Basile, B. M., Hampton, R. R., Suomi, S. J., & Murray, E. A. (2009). An assessment of memory awareness in tufted capuchin monkeys (Cebus apella). *Animal Cognition, 12*(1), 169–180.

Beran, M. J., Perdue, B. M., Futch, S. E., Smith, J. D., Evans, T. A., & Parrish, A. E. (2015). Go when you know: Chimpanzees' confidence movements reflect their responses in a computerized memory task. *Cognition, 142*, 236–246.

Bethune, B., & Doidge, N. (2015). How your brain heals itself. *Maclean's, 128*(4), 40. https://www.macleans.ca/society/health/how-your-brain-heals-itself/

Beyerstein, B. L. (1990). Brainscams: Neuromythologies of the new age. *International Journal of Mental Health, 19*(3), 27–36.

Bonifacci, P., Storti, M., Tobia, V., & Suardi, A. (2016). Specific learning disorders: A look inside children's and parents' psychological well-being and relationships. *Journal of Learning Disabilities, 49*(5), 532–545.

Bos, P. A., Hermans, E. J., Ramsey, N. F., & Van Honk, J. (2012). The neural mechanisms by which testosterone acts on interpersonal trust. *Neuroimage, 61*(3), 730–737. https://doi.org/10.1016/j.neuroimage.2012.04.002

Brookshire, R. H. (2007). *An introduction to neurogenic communitcation disorders.* St. Louis: Mosby-Year Book.

Brown, A. L. (1980). Metacognitive development and reading. In Theoretical issues in reading comprehension: Perspectives from cognitive psychology, linguistics, artificial intelligence, and education (pp 453–481). https://doi.org/10.4324/9781315107493

Brown, A. L., & Smiley, S. S. (1978). The development of strategies for studying texts. *Child Development*, 1076–1088.

Bubeck, S., Chandrasekaran, V., Eldan, R., Gehrke, J., Horvitz, E., Kamar, E., ... & Zhang, Y. (2023). Sparks of artificial general intelligence: Early experiments with GPT-4. arXiv preprint arXiv:2303.12712

Buettner, R. Frick, J., & Rieg, T. (2019). High-performance detection of epilepsy in seizure-free EEG recordings: A novel machine learning approach using very specific epileptic EEG sub-bands. *ICIS 2019 Proceedings: 40th International Conference on Information Systems*, 15–18 Dec 2019.

Buckner, R. L., & Carroll, D. C. (2007). Self-projection and the brain. *Trends in Cognitive Sciences, 11*, 49–57. https://doi.org/10.1016/j.tics.2006.11.004

Burns, T., & Rajan, R. (2015). Combining complexity measures of EEG data: Multiplying measures reveal previously hidden information. *F1000Research, 4*, 137. https://doi.org/10.12688/f1000research.6590.1

Busch, F. N., & Sandberg, L. S. (2012). Combined treatment of depression. *Psychiatric Clinics, 35*(1), 165–179.
Cabeza, R., & Nyberg, L. (2000). Imaging cognition II: An empirical review of 275 PET and fMRI studies. *Journal of Cognitive Neuroscience, 12*(1), 1–47. https://doi.org/10.1162/08989290051137585
Calvin, W. H., & Ojemann, G. A. (2010). *Conversations with Neil's brain: The neural nature of thought and language*. Oxford University Press.
Cantlon, J. F., Brannon, E. M., Carter, E. J., & Pelphrey, K. A. (2006). Functional imaging of numerical processing in adults and 4-y-old children. *PLoS Biology, 4*(5), e125. https://doi.org/10.1371/journal.pbio.0040125
Carter, C. S., Braver, T. S., Barch, D. M., Botvinick, M. M., Noll, D., & Cohen, J. D. (1998). Anterior cingulate cortex, error detection, and the online monitoring of performance. *Science, 280*(5364), 747–749.
Catani, M., & Jones, D. K. (2005). Perisylvian language networks of the human brain. *Annals of Neurology, 57*(1), 8–16. https://doi.org/10.1002/ana.20319
Chan, T. C., Vilke, G. M., Neuman, T., & Clausen, J. L. (1997). Restraint position and positional asphyxia. *Annals of Emergency Medicine, 30*(5), 578–586.
Chomsky, N. (1959). A review of BF Skinner's Verbal Behavior. *Language, 35*(1), 26–58.
Cohen, J. D., & Servan-Schreiber, D. (1992). Context, cortex, and dopamine: A connectionist approach to behavior and biology in schizophrenia. *Psychological Review, 99*(1), 4577. https://doi.org/10.1037/0033-295X.99.1.45
Cook, E. H., Jr., Stein, M. A., Krasowski, M. D., Cox, N. J., Olkon, D. M., Kieffer, J. E., & Leventhal, B. L. (1995). Association of attention-deficit disorder and the dopamine transporter gene. *American Journal of Human Genetics, 56*(4), 993.
Corballis, P. M. (2003). Visuospatial processing and the right-hemisphere interpreter. *Brain and Cognition, 53*(2), 171–176.
Corkin, S. (2002). What's new with the amnesic patient HM? *Nature Reviews Neuroscience, 3*(2), 153. https://doi.org/10.1038/nrn726
Cotman, C. W., & Berchtold, N. C. (2002). Exercise: A behavioral intervention to enhance brain health and plasticity. *Trends in Neurosciences, 25*(6), 295–301.
Craig, A. D. (2009). How do you feel—now? The anterior insula and human awareness. *Nature Reviews Neuroscience, 10*(1).
Damoiseaux, J. S., Rombouts, S. A. R. B., Barkhof, F., Scheltens, P., Stam, C. J., Smith, S. M., & Beckmann, C. F. (2006). Consistent resting-state networks across healthy subjects. *Proceedings of the National Academy of Sciences, 103*(37), 13848–13853. https://doi.org/10.1073/pnas.0601417103
De Nicolás, A. T. (2003). *Meditations through the Rig Veda: Four-dimensional man*. iUniverse.
Deakin, J. F. W. (1991). Serotonin in panic, anxiety and depression. *European Neuropsychopharmacology, 1*(3), 358–360. https://doi.org/10.1016/0924-977X(91)90566-D
Deary, I. J., Penke, L., & Johnson, W. (2010). The neuroscience of human intelligence differences. *Nature Reviews Neuroscience, 11*(3), 201. https://doi.org/10.1038/nrn2793
Dennett, D. C. (1992). The self as a center of narrative gravity. *Self and Consciousness: Multiple Perspectives, 15*, 275–288.
Dennett, D. C. (2017). *Consciousness explained*. Little.
Denny, B. T., Kober, H., Wager, T. D., & Ochsner, K. N. (2012). A meta-analysis of functional neuroimaging studies of self-and other judgments reveals a spatial gradient for mentalizing in medial prefrontal cortex. *Journal of Cognitive Neuroscience, 24*(8), 1742–1752. https://doi.org/10.1162/jocn_a_00233
D'esposito, M., Detre, J. A., Alsop, D. C., Shin, R. K., Atlas, S., & Grossman, M. (1995). The neural basis of the central executive system of working memory. *Nature, 378*(6554), 279. https://doi.org/10.1016/j.neuron.2010.03.025
Dewey, J. (1997). *How we think*. Dover Publications.
Dewey, J. (2007). *Experience and education*. Simon and Schuster.

Dobyns, W. B. (1996). Absence makes the search grow longer. *American Journal of Human Genetics, 58*(1), 7.
Doidge, N. (2007). *The brain that changes itself: Stories of personal triumph from the frontiers of brain science*. Penguin.
Doidge, N. (2016). *The brain's way of healing: Remarkable discoveries and recoveries from the frontiers of neuroplasticity*. Penguin Books.
Domingos, P. (2015). *The master algorithm: How the quest for the ultimate learning machine Will remake our world*. Basic Books.
Dunlosky, J., & Metcalfe, J. (2009). *Metacognition*. SAGE.
Dweck, C. S. (2008). Brainology transforming students' motivation to learn. *Independent School, 67*(2), 110–119.
Dweck, C. (2013, March 1). *2013 Ridley lecture: Carol Dweck on student mindsets*. Retrieved from https://youtu.be/eGnqgXmlTk4
Dweck, C. (2017). *Mindset-updated edition: Changing the way you think to fulfil your potential*. Hachette UK.
Eagleman, D. M., Kagan, A. D., Nelson, S. S., Sagaram, D., & Sarma, A. K. (2007). A standardized test battery for the study of synesthesia. *Journal of Neuroscience Methods, 159*(1), 139–145.
Eckert, M. (2004). Neuroanatomical markers for dyslexia: A review of dyslexia structural imaging studies. *The Neuroscientist, 10*(4), 362–371. https://doi.org/10.1177/1073858404263596
Egner, T., & Sterman, M. B. (2006). Neurofeedback treatment of epilepsy: From basic rationale to practical application. *Expert Review of Neurotherapeutics, 6*, 247–257. https://doi.org/10.1586/14737175.6.2.247
Ellis, N. (2009). *Awakening Osiris: A new translation of the Egyptian book of the dead*. Red Wheel/Weiser.
Emmert, K., Kopel, R., Sulzer, J., Brühl, A. B., Berman, B. D., Linden, D. E., et al. (2016). Meta-analysis of real-time fMRI neurofeedback studies using individual participant data: How is brain regulation mediated? *Neuroimage, 124*, 806–812. https://doi.org/10.1016/j.neuroimage.2015.09.042
Enriquez-Geppert, S., Huster, R. J., & Herrmann, C. S. (2017). EEG-neurofeedback as a tool to modulate cognition and behavior: A review tutorial. *Frontiers in Human Neuroscience, 11*, 51. https://doi.org/10.3389/fnhum.2017.00051
Erikson, E. H., & Erikson, J. M. (1997). *The life cycle completed* (Extended/ed.). W.W. Norton.
Falk, D. (2012). Hominin paleoneurology: Where are we now?. *Progress in brain research, 195*, 255–272. https://doi.org/10.1016/B978-0-444-53860-4.00012-X
Fernandez-Duque, D., Baird, J. A., & Posner, M. I. (2000). Executive attention and metacognitive regulation. *Consciousness and Cognition, 9*(2), 288–307.
Flavell, J. H. (1979). Metacognition and cognitive monitoring: A new area of cognitive development. *American Psychologist, 34*(10), 906–911. https://doi.org/10.1037/0003-066X.34.10.906
Flavell, J. H., & Wellman, H. M. (1975). *Metamemory* [PDF]. ERIC https://files.eric.ed.gov/fulltext/ED115405.pdf
Fleming, S. M., Huijgen, J., & Dolan, R. J. (2012). Prefrontal contributions to metacognition in perceptual decision making. *Journal of Neuroscience, 32*(18), 6117–6125.
Fleming, S. M., Ryu, J., Golfinos, J. G., & Blackmon, K. E. (2014). Domain-specific Impairment in metacognitive accuracy following anterior prefrontal lesions. *Brain, 137*(10), 2811–2822.
Foa, E. B., & Kozak, M. J. (1986). Emotional processing of fear: Exposure to corrective information. *Psychological Bulletin, 99*(1), 20. https://psycnet.apa.org/; https://doi.org/10.1037/0033-2909.99.1.20
Foer, J. (2012). *Moonwalking with Einstein: The art and science of remembering everything*. Penguin.
Fogassi, L., Ferrari, P. F., Gesierich, B., Rozzi, S., Chersi, F., & Rizzolatti, G. (2005). Parietal lobe: From action organization to intention understanding. *Science, 308*(5722), 662–667. https://doi.org/10.1126/science.1106138
Foote, A. L., & Crystal, J. D. (2007). Metacognition in the rat. *Current Biology, 17*(6), 551–555.

Freire, P. (2018). *Pedagogy of the oppressed*. Bloomsbury Publishing USA (Original work published in 1968).
Friedman, H. R., & Goldman-Rakic, P. S. (1994). Coactivation of prefrontal cortex and inferior parietal cortex in working memory tasks revealed by 2DG functional mapping in the rhesus monkey. *Journal of Neuroscience, 14*(5), 2775–2788. https://doi.org/10.1523/JNEUROSCI.14-05-02775.1994
Gabel, M. S., & McAuley, T. (2018). Does mood help or hinder executive functions? Reactivity may be the key. *Personality and Individual Differences, 128*, 94–99.
Gaser, C., & Schlaug, G. (2003). Brain structures differ between musicians and non-musicians. *Journal of Neuroscience, 23*(27), 9240–9245.
Gazzaniga, M. S. (2005). Forty-five years of split-brain research and still going strong. *Nature Reviews Neuroscience, 6*(8), 653. https://doi.org/10.1038/nrn1723
Gerhard, S., Daducci, A., Lemkaddem, A., Meuli, R., Thiran, J. P., & Hagmann, P. (2011). The connectome viewer toolkit: An open source framework to manage, analyze, and visualize connectomes. *Frontiers in Neuroinformatics, 5*, 3.
Gilboa, A., Shalev, A. Y., Laor, L., Lester, H., Louzoun, Y., Chisin, R., & Bonne, O. (2004). Functional connectivity of the prefrontal cortex and the amygdala in posttraumatic stress disorder. *Biological Psychiatry, 55*(3), 263–272.
Goleman, D. (2006). *Emotional intelligence*. Bantam.
Grafton, H. (2006). Dartmouth study finds how the brain interprets the intent of others. *Science Daily*. www.sciencedaily.com/releases/2006/02/060216191651.ht
Gross, C. G. (2002). Genealogy of the "grandmother cell". *The Neuroscientist, 8*(5), 512–518. https://doi.org/10.1177/107385802237175
Grossberg, S. (1999). The link between brain learning, attention, and consciousness. *Consciousness and Cognition, 8*(1), 1–44. https://doi.org/10.1006/ccog.1998.0372
Gruzelier, J. H. (2014). EEG-neurofeedback for optimising performance. I: A review of cognitive and affective outcome in healthy participants. *Neuroscience and Biobehavioral Reviews, 44*, 124–141. https://doi.org/10.1016/j.neubiorev.2013.09.015
Haier, R. J., Colom, R., Schroeder, D. H., Condon, C. A., Tang, C., Eaves, E., & Head, K. (2009). Gray matter and intelligence factors: Is there a neuro-g? *Intelligence, 37*(2), 136–144. https://doi.org/10.1016/j.intell.2008.10.011
Hallowell, E. M. M., & Ratey, J. J. (2011). *Driven to distraction: Recognizing and coping with attention deficit disorder from childhood through adulthood*. Anchor.
Hameroff, S., & Penrose, R. (2014). Reply to seven commentaries on "Consciousness in the universe: Review of the 'Orch OR' theory." *Physics of Life Reviews, 11*(1), 39–78.
Hamilton, E. (1961). *The collected dialogues of Plato, including the letters*. Pantheon Books.
Hampton, R. R. (2009). Multiple demonstrations of metacognition in nonhumans: Converging evidence or multiple mechanisms? *Comparative Cognition & Behavior Reviews, 4*, 17.
Hart, J. (1965). Memory and the feeling-of-knowing experience. *Journal of Educational Psychology, 56*(4), 208–216. Retrieved from https://doi.org/10.1037/h0022263
Harten, M. D. (2014). *An evaluation of the effectiveness of written reflection to improve high school students' writing and metacognitive knowledge and strategies* (Dissertation). Boston University School of Education.
Harzem, P. (2004). Behaviorism for new psychology: What was wrong with behaviorism and what is wrong with it now. *Behavior and Philosophy*, 5–12.
Hattie, J. (2012). *Visible learning for teachers: Maximizing impact on learning*. Routledge.
Heatherton, T. F. (2011). Building a social brain. In A. Todorov, S. T. Fiske, & D. Prentice (Eds.), *Social neuroscience: Toward understanding the underpinnings of the social mind* (pp. 274–283). Oxford University Press. https://doi.org/10.1093/acprof:oso/9780195316872.003.0017
Hickok, G. (2009). Eight problems for the mirror neuron theory of action understanding in monkeys and humans. *Journal of Cognitive Neuroscience, 21*(7), 1229–1243. https://doi.org/10.1162/jocn.2009.21189

Hier, D. B., Mondlock, J., & Caplan, L. R. (1983). Behavioral abnormalities after right hemisphere stroke. *Neurology, 33*(3), 337–337. https://doi.org/10.1212/WNL.33.3.337

Hofstadter, R. (1992). *Social darwinism in American thought (Vol. 16).* Beacon Press.

Hughes, J. R. (2010). A review of savant syndrome and its possible relationship to epilepsy. *Epilepsy & Behavior, 17*(2), 147–152. https://doi.org/10.1016/j.yebeh.2009.12.014

Hulbig, P. R. (2021). Fundamental principles of metacognition: A qualitative study of metacognition, pedagogy and transformation. Lesley University. https://www.proquest.com/openview/31dce8c293a0439393ad856023e3dac0/1?pq-origsite=gscholar&cbl=18750&diss=y

Ieracitano, C., Mammone, N., Hussain, A., & Morabito, F. C. (2020). A novel multi-modal learning based approach for automatic classification of EEG recording in dementia. *Neural Networks, 123*, 176–190. https://doi.org/10.1016/j.neunet.2019.12.006

Iordanou, K. (2016). Developing epistemological understanding in scientific and social domains through argumentation. *Zeitschrift Für Pädagogische Psychologie, 30*(2–3), 109–119. https://doi.org/10.1024/1010-0652/a000172

Iqbal, A., Khan, R., & Karayannis, T. (2018). Developing brain atlas through deep learning. arXiv preprint arXiv:1807.03440. https://arxiv.org/abs/1807.03440

Iranmanesh, S., & Rodriguez-Villegas, E. (2017). A 950 nW analog-based data reduction chip for wearable EEG systems in epilepsy. *IEEE Journal of Solid-State Circuits, 52*(9), 2362–2373. https://doi.org/10.1109/JSSC.2017.2701939

Islam, M., Rahim, M., Akter, H., Kabir, R., & Shin, J. (2018). Optimal IMF selection of EMD for sleep disorder diagnosis using EEG signals. In *Proceedings of the 3rd International Conference on Applications in Information Technology*, no. 3, pp. 96–101.

James, W. (1890). *The principles of psychology* (Vol. 1, p. 188). Dover.

Jarvis, P. (2004). *Adult education and lifelong learning: Theory and practice.* Routledge.

Jefferies, L. N., Smilek, D., Eich, E., & Enns, J. T. (2008). Emotional valence and arousal interact in attentional control. *Psychological Science, 19*(3), 290–295.

Jonides, J., Smith, E. E., Koeppe, R. A., Awh, E., Minoshima, S., & Mintun, M. A. (1993). Spatial working memory in humans as revealed by PET. *Nature, 363*(6430), 623–625.

Joseph, R. (2011a). The neuroanatomy of free will: Loss of will, against the will" alien hand. *Journal of Cosmology, 14*, 6000–6045.

Joseph, R. (2011b). The split brain: Two brains-two minds. *Journal of Cosmology, 14*, 108–154. http://cosmology.com/Cosmology11.html

Kandel, E. R. (2001). The molecular biology of memory storage: A dialogue between genes and synapses. *Science, 294*(5544), 1030–1038. https://doi.org/10.1126/science.1067020

Kegan, R. (1982). *The evolving self: Problem and process in human development.* Harvard University Press.

Kegan, R. (1996). *In over our heads: The mental demands of modern life.* Harvard University Press.

Kelley, W. M., Macrae, C. N., Wyland, C. L., Caglar, S., Inati, S., & Heatherton, T. F. (2002). Finding the self? An event-related fMRI study. *Journal of Cognitive Neuroscience, 14*(5), 785–794. https://psycnet.apa.org/https://doi.org/10.1093/clipsy.bpg016

Kertesz, A., & Dobrowolski, S. (1981). Right-hemisphere deficits, lesion size and location. *Journal of Clinical and Experimental Neuropsychology, 3*(4), 283–299. https://doi.org/10.1080/01688638108403133

Keysers, C., & Gazzola, V. (2006). Towards a unifying neural theory of social cognition. *Progress in Brain Research, 156*, 379–401. https://doi.org/10.1016/S0079-6123(06)56021-2

Keysers, C. (2009). Mirror neurons [PDF]. *Current Biology, 19*(21), R971–R973. https://web.archive.org/web/20130119224448/http://www.bcn-nic.nl/txt/people/publications/2009_Keysers_CurrentBiology.pdf

Kikyo, H., Ohki, K., & Miyashita, Y. (2002). Neural correlates for feeling-of-knowing: An fMRI parametric analysis. *Neuron, 36*(1), 177–186. https://doi.org/10.1016/S0896-6273(02)00939-X

Kimberg, D. Y., & Farah, M. J. (1993). A unified account of cognitive impairments following frontal lobe damage: The role of working memory in complex, organized behavior. *Journal of Experimental Psychology: General, 122*(4), 411. https://psycnet.apa.org; https://doi.org/10.1037/0096-3445.122.4.411

Kisner, C., Colby, L. A., & Borstad, J. (2017). *Therapeutic exercise: Foundations and techniques*. Fa Davis.

Kleinginna, P. R., & Kleinginna, A. M. (1981). A categorized list of emotion definitions, with suggestions for a consensual definition. *Motivation and Emotion, 5*(4), 345–379. https://doi.org/10.1007/BF00992553

Knight, R. T. (1984). Decreased response to novel stimuli after prefrontal lesions in man. *Electroencephalography and Clinical Neurophysiology/evoked Potentials Section, 59*(1), 9–20. https://doi.org/10.1016/0168-5597(84)90016-9

Knight, R. T. (1997). Distributed cortical network for visual attention. *Journal of Cognitive Neuroscience, 9*(1), 75–91. https://doi.org/10.1162/jocn.1997.9.1.75

Knight, R. T., Scabini, D., Woods, D. L., & Clayworth, C. C. (1989). Contributions of temporal-parietal junction to the human auditory P3. *Brain Research, 502*(1), 109–116. https://doi.org/10.1016/0006-8993(89)90466-6.

Knight, R. T., Staines, W. R., Swick, D., & Chao, L. L. (1999). Prefrontal cortex regulates inhibition and excitation in distributed neural networks. *Acta Psychologica, 101*(2–3), 159–178. https://doi.org/10.1016/S0001-6918(99)00004-9

Knowles, M. M., & Wells, A. (2018). Single dose of the Attention Training Technique increases resting alpha and beta-oscillations in frontoparietal brain networks: A randomized controlled comparison. *Frontiers in Psychology, 9*, 1768.

Kober, S. E., et al. (2017). Ability to gain control over one's own brain activity and its relation to spiritual practice: A multimodal imaging study. *Frontiers in Human Neuroscience, 11*, 271. https://doi.org/10.3389/fnhum.2017.00271

Kober, S. E., Witte, M., Ninaus, M., Neuper, C., & Wood, G. (2013). Learning to modulate one's own brain activity: The effect of spontaneous mental strategies. *Frontiers in Human Neuroscience, 7*, 695. https://doi.org/10.3389/fnhum.2013.00695.

Kornell, N. (2014). Where is the "meta" in animal metacognition? *Journal of Comparative Psychology, 128*(2), 143.

Kosonogov, V. (2012). Why the mirror neurons cannot support action understanding. *Neurophysiology, 44*(6), 499–502. https://doi.org/10.1007/s11062-012-9327-4

Kozlovskiy, S. A., Vartanov, A. V., Pyasik, M. M., & Nikonova, E. Y. (2012). Functional role of Corpus callosum regions in human memory functioning. *International Journal of Psychophysiology, 3*(85), 396–397. https://doi.org/10.1016/j.ijpsycho.2012.07.092

Kuhn, D., Cheney, R., & Weinstock, M. (2000). The development of epistemological understanding. *Cognitive Development, 15*(3), 309–328.

Lachman, J. L., & Lachman, R. (1980). Age and the actualization of world knowledge. In L. W. Poon, J. L. Fozard, L. S. Cermak, D. Arenberg, & L. W. Thompson (Eds.), *New directions in memory and aging* (pp. 285–311). Eribaum.

Lacey, S., Stilla, R., & Sathian, K. (2012). Metaphorically feeling: Comprehending textural metaphors activates somatosensory cortex. *Brain and language, 120*(3), 416–421.

Lansbergen, M. M., et al. (2011). ADHD and EEG-neurofeedback: A double-blind randomized placebo-controlled feasibility study. *Journal of Neural Transmission, 118*, 275–284. https://doi.org/10.1007/s00702-010-0524-2

Lashley, K. S. (1923). Temporal variation in the function of the gyrus precentralis in primates. *American Journal of Physiology-Legacy Content, 65*(3), 585–602. https://doi.org/10.1152/ajplegacy.1923.65.3.585

Lashley, K. S. (1950). In search of the engram. In *Society for Experimental Biology, Physiological mechanisms in animal behavior. (Society's Symposium IV)* (pp. 454–482). Academic Press. https://doi.org/10.1007/978-1-4612-6063-9_5

Lefkowitz, R. J. (2004). Historical review: A brief history and personal retrospective of seven-transmembrane receptors. *Trends in Pharmacological Sciences, 25*(8), 413–422. https://doi.org/10.1016/j.tips.2004.06.006

Levitin, D. J. (2006). *This is your brain on music: The science of a human obsession.* Penguin.

Lewis, J., & Litchfield, B. (2011). Effects of self-regulated learning strategies on preservice teachers in an educational technology. *Education,* 455–464.

Libet, B. (2004). Mind time. In *The temporal factor in consciousness* (p. 248). Harvard University Press.

Lingnau, A., Gesierich, B., & Caramazza, A. (2009). Asymmetric fMRI adaptation reveals no evidence for mirror neurons in humans. *Proceedings of the National Academy of Sciences, 106*(24), 9925–9930. https://doi.org/10.1073/pnas.0902262106

Lipot, S. (1956) *Ego analysis* Ch. XIX (Arthur C. Johnston, Trans.), p. 268.

Linton, D. (1999, Nov., 18). Authorities: Mother may have watched as son starved. *The Sun Chronicle.* https://www.thesunchronicle.com/authorities-mothermay-have-watched-as-son-starved-to-death/article_a88b0515-99cd-5b51-a4a4-b9e0592f3309.html

Macmillan, M., & Lena, M. L. (2010). Rehabilitating Phineas Gage. *Neuropsychological Rehabilitation, 20*(5), 641–658. https://doi.org/10.1080/09602011003760527

Maguire, E. A., Gadian, D. G., Johnsrude, I. S., Good, C. D., Ashburner, J., Frackowiak, R. S., & Frith, C. D. (2000). Navigation-related structural change in the hippocampi of taxi drivers. *Proceedings of the National Academy of Sciences, 97*(8), 4398–4403.

Mancini, G., Short, R., Mulcahy, R., & Andrews, J. (1991). Social cognition and social competence: Instructional issues. In R. Mulcahy, R. Short, & J. Andrews (Eds.), *Enhancing learning and thinking* (pp. 193–206). Preager.

Marques, J. C., Li, M., Schaak, D., Robson, D. N., & Li, J. M. (2020). Internal state dynamics shape brainwide activity and foraging behaviour. *Nature, 577*(7789), 239–243.

Maxwell, N. (2020). When disabilities aren't welcome at church. *Focus on the Family.* https://www.focusonthefamily.com/pro-life/special-needs/whendisabilities-arent-welcome-at-church/

Mazzoni, G., & Nelson, T. (Eds.). (1999). *Metacognition and cognitive neuropsychology.* Psychology Press.

McCurdy, L. Y., Maniscalco, B., Metcalfe, J., Liu, K. Y., de Lange, F. P., & Lau, H. (2013). Anatomical coupling between distinct metacognitive systems for memory and visual perception. *Journal of Neuroscience, 33*(5), 1897–1906.

McNabb, A. W., Carroll, W. M., & Mastaglia, F. L. (1988). Alien hand" and loss of bimanual coordination after dominant anterior cerebral artery territory infarction. *Journal of Neurology, Neurosurgery & Psychiatry, 51*(2), 218–222.

Medina, J. (2011). *Brain rules: 12 principles for surviving and thriving at work, home, and School.* ReadHowYouWant.com.

Merriam, S. B., & Caffarella, R. S. (2007). *Learning in adulthood: A comprehensive guide* (2nd ed.). Jossey-Bass Publishers.

Mesulam, M. (1981). A cortical network for directed attention and unilateral neglect. *Annals of Neurology, 10*(4), 309–325. https://doi.org/10.1002/ana.410100402

Metcalfe, J. (1993). Novelty monitoring, metacognition, and control in a composite holographic associative recall model: Implications for Korsakoff amnesia. *Psychological Review, 100*(1), 3. https://doi.org/10.1037/0033-295X.100.1.3

Metcalfe, J., & Shimamura, A. P. (1994). *Metacognition: Knowing about knowing.* MIT Press. https://doi.org/10.7551/mitpress/4561.001.0001

Meyer, M. L., & Lieberman, M. D. (2018). Why people are always thinking about themselves: Medial prefrontal cortex activity during rest primes self-referential processing. *Journal of Cognitive Neuroscience* (Early Access), 1–9.

Milberg, W., & Blumstein, S. E. (1981). Lexical decision and aphasia: Evidence for semantic processing. *Brain and Language, 14*(2), 371–385. https://doi.org/10.1162/jocn_a_01232

Mitchell, S. (1988). trans. Tao te Ching. AuthorHouse.

Molenberghs, P., Cunnington, R., & Mattingley, J. B. (2009). Is the mirror neuron system involved in imitation? A short review and meta-analysis. *Neuroscience & Biobehavioral Reviews, 33*(7), 975–980. https://doi.org/10.1016/j.neubiorev.2009.03.010

Moran, J. M., Kelley, W. M., & Heatherton, T. F. (2013). What can the organization of the brain's default mode network tell us about self-knowledge? *Frontiers in Human Neuroscience, 7*, 391. https://doi.org/10.3389/fnhum.2013.00391

Mountcastle, V. B. (1984). Central nervous mechanisms in mechanoreceptive sensibility. *Handbook of Physiology, 3*, 789–878. https://doi.org/10.1002/cphy.cp010318

Nelson, T. O. (1996). Consciousness and metacognition. *American Psychologist, 51*(2), 102–116. https://doi.org/10.1037/0003-066X.51.2.102

Nelson, T. O., & Narens, L. (1990). Metamemory: A theoretical framework and some new findings. In G. H. Bower (Ed.), *The psychology of learning and motivation* (pp. 125–173). Academic.

Nelson, T. O., Metcalfe, J., & Shimamura, A. P. (1994). *Metacognition: Knowing about Knowing*. MIT Press.

Nielsen, M., Langley, M. C., Shipton, C., & Kapitány, R. (2020). Homo neanderthalensis and the evolutionary origins of ritual in homo sapiens. *Philosophical Transactions of the Royal Society B, 375*(1805), 20190424. https://doi.org/10.1098/rstb.2019.0424

Ninaus, M., et al. (2015). Brain volumetry and self-regulation of brain activity relevant for neurofeedback. *Biological Psychology, 110*, 126–133. https://doi.org/10.1016/j.biopsycho.2015.07.009

Oakley, B., Knafo, A., Madhavan, G., & Wilson, D. S. (Eds.). (2011). *Pathological altruism*. Oxford University Press.

Oberman, L. M., & Ramachandran, V. S. (2008). Reflections on the mirror neuron system: Their evolutionary functions beyond motor representation. In *Mirror neuron systems* (pp. 39–59). Humana Press. https://doi.org/10.1007/978-1-59745-479-7_2

Ochsner, K. N., et al. (2004). Reflecting upon feelings: An fMRI study of neural systems supporting the attribution of emotion to self and other. *Journal of Cognitive Neuroscience, 16*(10), 1746–1772. https://doi.org/10.1162/0898929042947829

Omejc, N., Rojc, B., Battaglini, P. P., & Marusic, U. (2019). Review of the therapeutic neurofeedback method using electroencephalography: EEG Neurofeedback. *Bosnian Journal of Basic Medical Sciences, 19*(3), 213. https://doi.org/10.17305/bjbms.2018.3785

Öngür, D., Ferry, A. T., & Price, J. L. (2003). Architectonic subdivision of the human orbital and medial prefrontal cortex. *Journal of Comparative Neurology, 460*(3), 425–449. https://doi.org/10.1002/cne.10609

Owen, A. M., Roberts, A. C., Hodges, J. R., & Robbins, T. W. (1993). Contrasting mechanisms of impaired attentional set-shifting in patients with frontal lobe damage or Parkinson's disease. *Brain, 116*(5), 1159–1175. https://doi.org/10.1093/brain/116.5.1159

Pace, S. F. (1991). Government processes for including thinking skills in the curriculum. In R. Mulcahy, R. Short, & J. Andrews (Eds.), *Enhancing learning and thinking* (pp. 21–34). Preager.

Padfield, N., Zabalza, J., Zhao, H., Masero, V., & Ren, J. (2019). EEG-based brain-computer interfaces using motor-imagery: Techniques and challenges. *Sensors, 19*(6), 1423. https://doi.org/10.3390/s19061423

Palmer, J. (2013) Quantum smell idea gains ground. *BBC*. http://www.bbc.com/news/science-environment-21150046

Pandya, D. N., & Barnes, C. L. (1987). Architecture and connections of the frontal lobe. In E. Perecman (Ed.), *The frontal lobes revisited* (pp. 41–72). The IRBN Press.

Pannu, J. K., & Kaszniak, A. W. (2005). Metamemory experiments in neurological populations: A review. *Neuropsychology Review, 15*(3), 105–130.

Penfield, W., & Boldrey, E. (1937). Somatic motor and sensory representation in the cerebral cortex of man as studied by electrical stimulation. *Brain, 60*(4), 389–443. https://doi.org/10.1093/brain/60.4.389

Penrose, R. (1989). *The emperor's new mind: Concerning computers, minds, and the laws of physics*. Oxford U. Press.

Penrose, R. (1994). *Shadows of the mind* (Vol. 4). Oxford University Press.

Perl, M., & Perl, D. (2019). EEG amplitude neurofeedback: A review of the research. *APJNT Journal*, 44. https://apjnt.org/wp-content/uploads/2019/04/Moshe_Perl_APJNT_Journal_No1_Vol1_2019.pdf

Perreau-Linck, E., Lessard, N., Levesque, J., & Beauregard, M. (2010). Effects of neurofeedback training on inhibitory capacities in ADHD children: A single-blind, randomized, placebo-controlled study. *Journal of Neuropathy, 14*, 229–242. https://doi.org/10.1080/10874208.2010.501514

Pessiglione, M., Petrovic, P., Daunizeau, J., Palminteri, S., Dolan, R. J., & Frith, C. D. (2008). Subliminal instrumental conditioning demonstrated in the human brain. *Neuron, 59*(4), 561–567. https://doi.org/10.1016/j.neuron.2008.07.005

Pesaran, B., Nelson, M. J., & Andersen, R. A. (2008). Free choice activates a decision circuit between frontal and parietal cortex. *Nature, 453*(7193), 406. https://doi.org/10.1038/nature06849

Peterson, B. S., Skudlarski, P., Gatenby, J. C., Zhang, H., Anderson, A. W., & Gore, J. C. (1999). An fMRI study of Stroop word-color interference: Evidence for cingulate subregions subserving multiple distributed attentional systems. *Biological Psychiatry, 45*(10), 1237–1258.

Petrides, M., Alivisatos, B., Meyer, E., & Evans, A. C. (1993). Functional activation of the human frontal cortex during the performance of verbal working memory tasks. *Proceedings of the National Academy of Sciences, 90*(3), 878–882. https://doi.org/10.1073/pnas.90.3.878

Pfurtscheller, G., & Neuper, C. (2006). Future prospects of ERD/ERS in the context of brain computer interface (BCI) developments. *Progress in Brain Research, 159*, 433–437. https://doi.org/10.1016/S0079-6123(06)59028-4

Phelps, E. A. (2004). Human emotion and memory: Interactions of the amygdala and hippocampal complex. *Current Opinion in Neurobiology, 14*(2), 198–202.

Picardi, A., & Gaetano, P. (2014). Psychotherapy of mood disorders. *Clinical Practice and Epidemiology in Mental Health: CP & EMH, 10*, 140.

Pinker, S. (2018). *Enlightenment now: The case for reason, science, humanism, and progress.* Penguin Random House.

Piore, A. (2013). When brain damage unlocks genius. *Popular Science*. https://www.popsci.com/science/article/2013-02/when-brain-damage-unlocks-geniuswithin/

Pintrich, P. R. (2002). The role of metacognitive knowledge in learning, teaching, and assessing. *Theory into Practice, 41*(4). 219–225.

Price, M. A. (1991). Teaching thinking to preschoolers. In R. Mulcahy, R. Short, & J. Andrews (Eds.), *Enhancing learning and thinking* (pp. 53–66). Preager.

Quiroga, R. Q., Fried, I., & Koch, C. (2013). Brain cells for grandmother. *Scientific American, 308*(2), 30–35.

Radua, J., Phillips, M. L., Russell, T., Lawrence, N., Marshall, N., et al. (2010). Neural response to specific components of fearful faces in healthy and schizophrenic adults. *NeuroImage, 4*(1), 939–946. https://doi.org/10.1016/j.neuroimage.2009.08.030

Ramachandran, V. S., & Hubbard, E. M. (2003). The phenomenology of synaesthesia (PDF). *Journal of Consciousness Studies, 10*(8), 49–57.

Ramachandran, V. S., Altschuler, E. L., & Hillyer, S. (1997). Mirror agnosia. *Proceedings of the Royal Society of London B: Biological Sciences, 264*(1382), 645–647. https://doi.org/10.1098/rspb.1997.0091

Ramachandran, V. S., Blakeslee, S., & Shah, N. (1998). *Phantoms in the brain: Probing the mysteries of the human mind* (p. 224). William Morrow.

Ramachandran, V. S. (2000). *Mirror neurons and imitation learning as the driving force behind "the great leap forward" in human evolution.* http://williamlspencer.com/mirrorneurons.pdf

Ramachandran, V. S. (2004). *A brief tour of human consciousness: From impostor poodles to purple numbers.* Pi Press, an imprint of Pearson Technology Group.

Ricoeur, P. (1984). *Time and Narrative, Vol. 1.* Chicago: University of Chicago Press. https://doi.org/10.7208/9780226713519.

Rizzolatti, G., & Craighero, L. (2004). The mirror-neuron system. *Annual Review of Neuroscience, 27*, 169–192. https://doi.org/10.1146/annurev.neuro.27.070203.144230

Roediger, H. L., & Finn, B. (2009). Getting it wrong: Surprising tips on how to learn. *Scientific American*, 499–504.

Roper, M. K. (1969). A survey of the evidence for intrahuman killing in the pleistocene. *Current Anthropology, 10*(4), 427–459. http://www.jstor.org/stable/2740555.

Ros, T., Munneke, M. A., Ruge, D., Gruzelier, J. H., & Rothwell, J. C. (2010). Endogenous control of waking brain rhythms induces neuroplasticity in humans. *European Journal of Neuroscience, 31*(4), 770–778. https://doi.org/10.1111/j.1460-9568.2010.07100.x

Roskies, A. L. (2010). How does neuroscience affect our conception of volition? *Annual Review of Neuroscience, 33*, 109–130. https://doi.org/10.1146/annurev-neuro-060909-153151

Roskies, A. L. (2011). Why Libet's studies don't pose a threat to free will. *Conscious Will and Responsibility*, 11–22.

Salami, A., Andreu-Perez, J., & Gillmeister, H. (2020). Symptoms of depersonalisation/derealisation disorder as measured by brain electrical activity: A systematic review. Neuroscience & Biobehavioral Reviews. https://doi.org/10.1016/j.neubiorev.2020.08.011

Sapolsky, R. M. (2017). *Behave: The biology of humans at our best and worst*. Penguin.

Sauseng, P., Hoppe, J., Klimesch, W., Gerloff, C., & Hummel, F. C. (2007). Dissociation of sustained attention from central executive functions: Local activity and interregional connectivity in the theta range. *European Journal of Neuroscience, 25*, 587–593. https://doi.org/10.1111/j.1460-9568.2006.05286.x

Schippers, M. B., Roebroeck, A., Renken, R., Nanetti, L., & Keysers, C. (2010). Mapping the information flow from one brain to another during gestural communication. *Proceeding of the National Academy of Sciences*, 201001791. https://doi.org/10.1073/pnas.1001791107

Schnyer, D. M., Verfaellie, M., Alexander, M. P., LaFleche, G., Nicholls, L., & Kaszniak, A. W. (2004). A role for right medial prefrontal cortex in accurate feeling-of-knowing judgments: Evidence from patients with lesions to frontal cortex. *Neuropsychologia, 42*(7), 957–966. https://doi.org/10.1016/j.neuropsychologia.2003.11.020

Schreckenberger, M., Lange-Asschenfeld, C., Lochmann, M., Mann, K., Siessmeier, T., Buchholz, H. G., ... & Gründer, G. (2004). The thalamus as the generator and modulator of EEG alpha rhythm: A combined PET/EEG study with lorazepam challenge in humans. *Neuroimage, 22*(2), 637–644.

Scientific Racism (2023, January 21). *Harvard Library*. https://library.harvard.edu/confronting-anti-black-racism/scientific-racism

Seghier, M. L. (2012). The angular gyrus: Multiple function ad multiple subdivisions. *The Neuroscientist, 19*, 43–61. https://doi.org/10.1177/1073858412440596

Seth, A. (2021). *Being you: A new science of consciousness*. Penguin.

Shibolet, Y. (2019). Towards a Framework for Embodied Narrativity: An enactive study of narrative phenomenology, through the lens of interactive digital media (Master's thesis).

Shimamura, A. P. (2000). *Toward a Cognitive Neuroscience of Metacognition*. https://doi.org/10.1006/ccog.2000.0450

Shim, M., Hwang, H. J., Kim, D. W., Lee, S. H., & Im, C. H. (2016). Machine-learning-based diagnosis of schizophrenia using combined sensor-level and source-level EEG features. *Schizophrenia Research, 176*(2–3), 314–319.

Skinner, B. F. (2011). *About behaviorism*. Vintage.

Sluming, V., Barrick, T., Howard, M., Cezayirli, E., Mayes, A., & Roberts, N. (2002). Voxel-based morphometry reveals increased gray matter density in Broca's area in male symphony orchestra musicians. *NeuroImage, 17*(3), 1613–1622.

Smith, J. D., Shields, W. E., Allendoerfer, K. R., & Washburn, D. A. (1998). Memory monitoring by animals and humans. *Journal of Experimental Psychology: General, 127*(3), 227.

Snyder, A. W., Mulcahy, E., Taylor, J. L., Mitchell, D. J., Sachdev, P., & Gandevia, S. C. (2003). Savant-like skills exposed in normal people by suppressing the left fronto-temporal lobe. *Journal of Integrative Neuroscience, 2*(02), 149–158. https://doi.org/10.1142/S0219635203000287

Snyder, A., Bahramali, H., Hawker, T., & Mitchell, D. J. (2006). Savant-like numerosity skills revealed in normal people by magnetic pulses. *Perception, 35*(6), 837–845. https://doi.org/10.1068/p5539

Sperry, R. W. (1968). Hemisphere deconnection and unity in conscious awareness. *American Psychologist, 23*(10), 723. https://doi.org/10.1037/h0026839

Spreng, R. N., & Grady, C. L. (2010). Patterns of brain activity supporting autobiographical memory, prospection, and theory of mind, and their relationship to the default mode network. *Journal of Cognitive Neuroscience, 22*(6), 1112–1123. https://doi.org/10.1162/jocn.2009.21282

Spreng, R. N., Mar, R. A., & Kim, A. S. N. (2009). The common neural basis of autobiographical memory, prospection, navigation, theory of mind and the default mode: A quantitative meta-analysis. *Journal of Cognitive Neuroscience, 21*, 489–510. https://doi.org/10.1162/jocn.2008.21029

Stajkovic, A. D., Locke, E. A., & Blair, E. S. (2006). A first examination of the relationships between primed subconscious goals, assigned conscious goals, and task performance. *Journal of Applied Psychology, 91*(5), 1172. https://doi.org/10.1037/0021-9010.91.5.1172

Statistic Brain Research Institute (2018, July 23). https://www.statisticbrain.com/gym-membership-statistics/

Stein, S., & Volpe, B. T. (1983). Classical "parietal" neglect syndrome after subcortical right frontal lobe infarction. *Neurology, 33*(6), 797–797. https://doi.org/10.1212/WNL.33.6.797

Stratton, S. J., Rogers, C., Brickett, K., & Gruzinski, G. (2001). Factors associated with sudden death of individuals requiring restraint for excited delirium. *The American Journal of Emergency Medicine, 19*(3), 187–191. https://doi.org/10.1053/ajem.2001.22665

Sutton, J. E., & Shettleworth, S. J. (2008). Memory without awareness: Pigeons do not show metamemory in delayed matching to sample. *Journal of Experimental Psychology: Animal Behavior Processes, 34*(2), 266–282. https://doi.org/10.1037/0097-7403.34.2.266

Swanson, L. (2003). *Brain architecture: Understanding the basic plan* (pp. 263). 198 Madison Avenue, Oxford University Press.

Tanner, K. D. (2012). Promoting student metacognition. *CBE—Life Sciences Education, 11*(2), 113–120.

Templer, V. L. (2019). Slow progress with the most widely used animal model: Ten years of metacognition research in rats, 2009–2019. *Animal behavior and cognition, 6*(4), 273.

Teuber, H. L. (1955). Physiological psychology. *Annual Review of Psychology, 6*(1), 267–296. https://doi.org/10.1146/annurev.ps.06.020155.001411

Thakkar, A. N., Karande, S., Bala, N., Sant, H., Gogtay, N. J., & Sholapurwala, R. (2016). Is anxiety more common in school students with newly diagnosed specific learning disabilities? A cross-sectional questionnaire-based study in Mumbai, Maharashtra, India. *Journal of Postgraduate Medicine, 62*(1), 12.

Tjentz (2012, August 17). 10 people who gained extraordinary abilities from brain damage. https://www.bestpsychologydegrees.org/10-people-who-gainedextraordinary-abilities-from-brain-damage/

Todd, J. J., & Marois, R. (2004). Capacity limit of visual short-term memory in human posterior Parietal cortex. *Nature, 428*(6984), 751–754. https://doi.org/10.1038/nature02466

Treskate (2012, October 19). Brainman. [Video]. YouTube. https://www.youtube.com/watch?v=Kf3-el-dJAw

Tyng, C. M., Amin, H. U., Saad, M. N., & Malik, A. S. (2017). The influences of emotion on learning and memory. *Frontiers in Psychology, 8*, 1454.

Vaillant, G. E. (1993). *The wisdom of the ego.* Harvard University Press.

Virués-Ortega, J. (2006). The case against BF Skinner 45 years later: An encounter with N. Chomsky. *The Behavior Analyst, 29*(2), 243–251.

Vitiello, B. (2009). Combined cognitive-behavioural therapy and pharmacotherapy for adolescent depression. *CNS Drugs, 23*(4), 271–280.

Von Aster, M. G., & Shalev, R. S. (2007). Number development and developmental dyscalculia. *Developmental Medicine & Child Neurology, 49*(11), 868–873. https://doi.org/10.1111/j.1469-8749.2007.00868.x

von Plessen, K., Lundervold, A., Duta, N., Heiervang, E., Klauschen, F., Smievoll, A. I., et al. (2002). Less developed corpus callosum in dyslexic subjects—a structural MRI study. *Neuropsychologia, 40*(7), 1035–1044. https://doi.org/10.1016/S00283932(01)00143-9

Vyshedskiy, A. (2014). *On the origin of the human mind* (2nd ed.). [S.l.]: Createspace Indep Pub. ISBN 978-1492963615

Wagner, A. D., Shannon, B. J., Kahn, I., & Buckner, R. L. (2005). Parietal lobe contributions to episodic memory retrieval. *Trends in Cognitive Sciences, 9*(9), 445–453.

Wan, F., Da Cruz, J. N., Nan, W., Wong, C. M., Vai, M. I., & Rosa, A. (2016). Alpha neurofeedback training improves SSVEP-based BCI performance. *Journal of Neural Engineering, 13*(3), 036019.

Weinert, F. E. (1987). Introduction and overview: Metacognition and motivation as determinants of effective learning and understanding. In F. Weinert & R. Kluwe (Eds.), *Metacognition, motivation, and understanding* (pp. 1–16). Erlbaum.

Weiss, R. (2004, Dec., 13). Mind over matter: Brainwaves guide a cursors path. *Washington Post.* https://motorlab.pitt.edu/press/mind_over_matter2.pdf

Witelson, S. F. (1985). The brain connection: The corpus callosum is larger in left-handers. *Science, 229*(4714), 665–668. https://doi.org/10.1126/science.4023705

Witelson, S. F., Kigar, D. L., & Harvey, T. (1999). The exceptional brain of Albert Einstein. *The Lancet, 353*(9170), 2149–2153. https://doi.org/10.1016/S0140-6736(98)10327-6

Woods, D. L., & Knight, R. T. (1986). Electrophysiologic evidence of increased distractibility after dorsolateral prefrontal lesions. *Neurology, 36*(2), 212–212. https://doi.org/10.1212/WNL.36.2.212

Woolsey, C. N., Erickson, T. C., & Gilson, W. E. (1979). Localization in somatic sensory and motor areas of human cerebral cortex as determined by direct recording of evoked potentials and electrical stimulation. *Journal of Neurosurgery, 51*(4), 476–506. https://doi.org/10.3171/jns.1979.51.4.0476

Wright, N. D., Bahrami, B., Johnson, E., Di Malta, G., Rees, G., Frith, C. D., & Dolan, R. J. (2012). Testosterone disrupts human collaboration by increasing egocentric choices. *Proceedings of the Royal Society B: Biological Sciences, 279*(1736), 2275–2280. https://doi.org/10.1098/rspb.2011.2523

Yamaguchi, S., & Knight, R. T. (1991). Anterior and posterior association cortex contributions to the somatosensory P300. *Journal of Neuroscience, 11*(7), 2039–2054.

Yazar, Y., Bergstrom, Z. M., & Simons, J. S. (2012). What is the parietal lobe contribution to long-term memory? *Cortex, 48*, 1381–1382.

Young, A. W., Ellis, H. D., Szulecka, T. K., & De Pauw, K. W. (1990). Face processing impairments and delusional misidentification. *Behavioural Neurology, 3*(3), 153–168. https://doi.org/10.3233/BEN-1990-3303

Yussen, S. R., & Levy, V. M., Jr. (1975). Developmental changes in predicting one's own span of short-term memory. *Journal of Experimental Child Psychology, 19*(3), 502–508.

Zaidel, E., & Peters, A. M. (1981). Phonological encoding and ideographic reading by the disconnected right hemisphere: Two case studies. *Brain and Language, 14*(2), 205–234.

Zeng, J., Tan, S., Li, B., & Huang, J. (2016). Large-scale JPEG steganalysis using hybrid deep-learning framework. arXiv preprint arXiv:1611.03233.

Zurif, E. B., Caramazza, A., Myerson, R., & Galvin, J. (1974). Semantic feature representations for normal and aphasic language. *Brain and Language, 1*(2), 167–187.

Chapter 3
Information Processing

How information is processed to produce meaning is, perhaps, even more relevant to the study of metacognition than understanding the underlying biological connections that make metacognition possible for the human mind. The information-processing perspective attempts to explain how the physical organ of the brain takes in information and turns it into comprehensible knowledge. What are the features of understanding and thought in their most abstract, conceptual form?

One aspect of metacognition that is of particular interest when considering how information is processed has to do with the level of conscious awareness that a person approaches their understanding of their learning or behavior. For some researchers (Veenman et al., 2002), the concept of metacognition must include both conscious and subconscious processes. Metacognition in this case would include less than conscious constructs, such as one's neurological makeup or environmental factors (Bandura, 1989), that regulate behavior. Other researchers like Nelson (1996) have maintained the narrow view that metacognition represents a uniquely conscious activity and that it is the conscious nature of metacognition that leads to higher-order processing. This lack of clarity around the essential nature of consciousness affects the ability to clearly define what constitutes a metacognitive skill, strategy, or behavior (Veenman et al., 2006), and how one would use metacognition in a pedagogical sense.

The practice of metacognition uses a process of bringing otherwise unconscious elements of an individual's learning into a state of conscious awareness for active conscious investigation. It has been suggested that it is the simple process of self-reflection itself that produces more effective modes of processing through recursion (Hofstadter, 1979). Such an insight runs parallel with educational pedagogy in very practical ways. It has been found that educational routines that promote self-reflection are highly functional (Dunlosky, 2013; Hattie, 2012). A potential reason for this could be because they are modeled around an underlying, fundamental quality of information processing. If true, then educational programs that can better support this style of information processing will be most successful as they would be most in line with the brain's natural process.

P. R. Hulbig, *The Pedagogy of Self-Authorship*,
https://doi.org/10.1007/978-3-031-41436-7_3

There is reason to believe that there could be what has been described as a master algorithm (Domingos, 2015) at work behind human cognition. The best evidence for this theory has been the tremendous developments made in the field of computation and specifically artificial intelligence (AI). These computational models are supported by neuroimaging studies that seem to indicate an emergent consciousness, ending in the neurons of the frontal lobe. Of particular interest, AI researchers have found that self-referential programs based on simple heuristics, rather than complex linear programs, produce more stable and flexibly functioning computer interfaces and robotics (Domingos, 2015; Hofstadter, 1979; Kelly, 1995). This emergent, computational view would impact the concept of metacognition and learning because it would suggest that human-level conscious behavior results from a coalescence of vast stores of information being integrated from moment to moment by the brain. By this line of thinking, higher levels of conscious behavior result from larger stores of knowledge and experience.

However, programming a computer that can execute metacognition, even in a rudimentary way, has proven to be exceedingly difficult. The chief problem is the ability of the mind to formulate a new, and conceptually more abstract, representation of phenomena that appear unrelated at a low level of understanding (Hulbig, 2018a, 2018b). This is an expansion of a perceptual problem known as the binding problem (Revonsuo & Newman, 1999), and it poses a considerable problem to the computational study of metacognition as it is through this abstract process that new understandings are generated. Computers are very good at putting things in categories, but they are not very good at developing the categories themselves. The ability to make new categories is more abstract than the constituent parts of the categories. This ability enables more advanced behavior over time rather than simply repeating actions.

Moreover, our chief way of conceptualizing information processing is through computation, which is a linear process. While computational processes can connect or categorize information, the capacity and flexibility of computation is limited by the computer's linear, "word at a time," (Backus 1978, p. 613) processing architecture. This limits its ability to access stored processing instructions and the stored data needed for processing simultaneously, a problem called Von Neumann's bottleneck (Backus 1978). It may be that this bottleneck is a functional and fundamental limitation of computation.

This has led to the claim that computation, as presently constituted, will never be able to abstract or forge new novel connections, categorizations, and symbolic representations necessary to produce novel understandings (Penrose, 1989, 1994). Computers presently lack an algorithm capable of making metacognitive, inquisitive, creative, and spontaneous understandings. Similarly, seemingly automatic functions of human cognition, such as the ability to make analogies and metaphors, are far from automatic in computation systems. They seem to require humans to interpret the data and apply human understanding to the production of new algorithms to support the computational process (Domingos, 2015).

The difference between human and AI information processing is akin to the difference between being able to follow a list of instructions and being able to generate a list of instructions. Though there have been several examples of modern convolutional neural-networking-style computation systems that have been capable of producing computer programs (Basin et al., 2004; Domingos, 2015) and even articles for major publications (Keohane, 2017), these programs are all based on relationships discovered by humans and added into the system as a list of instructions for organizing the data they have access to, and not the result of any genuine understanding.

3.1 Neural Networks and Computation

Interestingly, this problem is analogous to an age-old debate in education between teaching discipline and the skills that follow from direction, versus fostering critical thinking and the skills that follow from creativity. While human beings can do both reasonably well, computers are only able to follow directions, albeit in an exceptionally fast and accurate way when compared to humans. Presently, there is wide agreement that it is the integration of neural networks dedicated to specific types of processing that produce the advanced cognitive capabilities of humans (Churchland 2011; Medina, 2011; Swanson, 2003; Gerhard et al., 2011). This concept best fits with what has been discovered through the various lines of investigation we have covered so far in this discussion. This approach is further supported by advances in the field of machine learning. The advent of artificial neural networks has led to the solutions to several computational problems that were once considered intractable, like image identification, speech recognition, and other general inflexibilities demonstrated by numerical computation (Domingos, 2015; Zhang et al., 1998). Historically, computational learning models have been limited by the linear nature of computational coding, a technological lack of storage, and limited networking capability.

The idea of programming software that uses networks of distributed information to solve problems actually can be traced back to the earliest investigations of machine learning (Domingos, 2015). However, this line of inquiry came to be seen as an investigational dead end due to the limits of computation. To make even simple judgments computationally can require access to massive networks of disparate information that seemed to border on the infinite. However, the last 20 years have seen exponential improvements in computational processing hardware and storage capacity. As computer hardware has improved, so has the possibility of programming large expansive neural networks capable of accurate problem-solving. Krizhevsky et al. (2012) were among the first researchers to demonstrate the power of computational neural networks by using a graphics processing unit to train a computational neural network with five convolutional layers and 60 million parameters on a set of 1.3 million images. Since this time, the use of convolutional neural networks (CNN) has become standard in most search operations, particularly in deep learning and data mining programs that can detect subtle patterns in large data sets (McCann et al. 2017), because of their many convolutional layers of processing.

The power of the CNN model is that it requires relatively minimal processing to produce results (Domingos, 2015). Historically, it was believed that for computers to solve even rudimentary problems all aspects of that problem would need to be hand-engineered, meaning that the programmer would need to consider every possible input into a system, and pre-program each of these possibilities into a coded solution. The problem of this computational approach is on display in early, adventure-style computer games like Colossal Cave Adventure (https://rickadams.org/adventure/) where the player can interact with an expansive textual environment. However, gameplay was confounded by the non-exact nature of human communication. Humans can express ideas using a seemingly infinite possible collection of word configurations, whereas computers are limited to only pre-programmed considerations. Due to this computational limitation, much of the play in these kinds of early computer games revolved around the player trying to decipher which words or phrases the program could actually understand. This was because each entered response needed to exactly match the program's pre-programmed list of expected responses. If you are unsure of what I am explaining here, please go to the above website and spend five to ten minutes playing Colossal Cave Adventure. I am sure you will quickly realize the limitations of this style of programming for yourself, as you will find yourself spending an inordinate amount of time trying to figure out which text commands the game will actually accept.

Rather than having to program for every possible permutation of an input, CNN allows programs to filter and categorize large sets of data based on similar attributes. It does this in a neurologically analogous way by passing information through the convolutional layers that, like neurons, process data relevant only to its receptive field. This information is then pooled into related categories and given different weighted values. This process, in conjunction with the ability to self-reflect on the accuracy of earlier responses, has allowed algorithmic programs to make increasingly more accurate responses, so much so that this computational style is called deep learning. The power of computational neural networks is evidenced by the fact that today the best checkers, chess, go, Atari 2600 video game, and even Jeopardy players are all computers running variations of these self-referencing CNN algorithms (Domingos, 2015; Mnih et al., 2015).

The success of machine learning has also highlighted potential shortcomings in trying to understand what the human brain does through the surrogacy of computers. The first, and most pronounced shortcoming, is the amount of data these systems require to make reasonable answers to the problems they are confronted with. In the case of IBM's Watson system (Ferrucci et al., 2010) that defeated the world's reigning human Jeopardy champ Ken Jennings, a vast database of 15 terabytes of general human knowledge was required. This is 16,492,674,416,640 bytes of information! In general, humans do not approach problems with such a store of information on hand.

This point is particularly significant when considering the learning and problem-solving abilities of children, who could not possibly have access to the stores of knowledge that computers do to make similar judgments. Essentially, this is a variation of Noam Chomsky's (2006) poverty of stimulus argument that was used to disprove early behaviorist conceptions of language development. Behaviorists could never achieve a compelling explanation for how a child could learn the complexities of a native language as quickly as they did, considering the dearth of proper linguistic examples provided in their environment. Similarly, computational approaches to learning fail to approximate human learning and understanding (Berwick et al., 2011; Penrose, 1989) by this same poverty of stimulus reasoning.

The problem is more than simple exposure. Even successful algorithms, like the ones that learned how to play Atari video games on their own (Mnih et al., 2015), are clearly not performing a learning function that is akin to what humans do. First, the program itself uses raw pixels as its input data and derives its output from a value function estimate of future rewards. Humans, inversely, perceive the input of the video game holistically. Clusters and configurations of pixels are viewed as whole objects, like tanks or walls (Goldstein, 2009). These approaches produce very different learning behaviors. Whereas humans will make large movements that become, through repetition, more inhibited and exact, the computer program initially makes small moves. Even after 100 trials, it still appears that the computer has little real understanding of what it is doing. Humans generally understand the main objective of a game like Breakout after only a few trials.

The reason for the program's different learning behavior is that it is processing, systematically, through all possible single-pixel states. Machine learning, in this sense, is an extreme extension of the old "not seeing the forest for the trees" metaphor. Except what these algorithms are doing is literally building a map of the forest tree by tree and storing it in memory to get through the forest later. Because machines do not get bored, they can play the game until they can narrow down their movements to a point where it looks like actual gameplay. After hundreds of hours of more game play, computers begin to identify the most optimal way of playing a video game, which they then replicate flawlessly ever after (Mnih et al., 2015). Again, this is very different from even highly skilled human players, who always must remain vigilant not to make a mistake and can rarely replicate gameplay exactly. It is also important to note that the computer could become extremely good at some games like Video Pinball and Breakout, while it was unable to figure out other games like Asteroids and Ms. Pac-Man (Mnih et al., 2015).

Even deep-learning programs, like the one described above, require tremendous amounts of continued "hand programming" to help the fledgling algorithm along. Hand programming is not analogous to the help human students receive from teachers, who may help their students by identifying salient features or maybe even modeling the proper learning behavior. When programmers have to hand program a deep-learning algorithm, it means they are going directly into the code of the program and changing the way it processes and perceives the information. So, while these programs can, in some sense, learn from their past experience, this learning is limited in scope, and they cannot be taught, or learn, in a traditional human sense.

In fact, these programs require humans to watch their development, as they lack the metacognitive ability to self-monitor, and will continue to develop unproductive responses that fall outside of their algorithmic purview. In other words, if a computer algorithm can detect a certain class of errors, it must be programmed to do so. Perhaps the most famous and humorous example of this difficulty occurred when Eric Brown tried to prepare IBM's computer Watson for its television performance on Jeopardy by letting it learn natural human language through studying the language on the internet. Ultimately, he had to go back and hand program the algorithm because the process resulted in Watson peppering its general communications with swear words and slang taken from a site called The Urban Dictionary (Ferrucci et al., 2010).

So, while computational neural networks are based on a theory that is analogous to present theories of neuron function, they do not appear to be actually functioning in an analogous way. It is also telling to point out that, despite the complexity and power of the present generation of computational programs and hardware, it appears to be impossible to program the human capacity for understanding (Penrose, 1989, 1994). Despite the tremendous advances in the field of machine learning, it is unclear if what is being demonstrated can't even be designated as a precursor or a kind of proto-metacognition. Unlike humans that possess an ever-expanding understanding of the world punctuated by pronounced developmental leaps in their ability to abstract information from what is known, computers doggedly follow a step-by-step process. They cannot expand out of their pre-programmed parameters without direct human intervention. Even their capacity for self-reference is algorithmic and restricted to parameters already present in their programming. This is very different from the kind of cognitive flexibility in the face of ambiguity that is seen in the cognitive processes of humans and some animals.

3.2 The Problem of Understanding

It has been suggested that at present we do not really understand how the brain works because of the difficulties computers have with subjective qualia, suggesting that these experiences are non-computational (Penrose, 1989). This would explain why we have been able to produce advanced computational devices, but not a generalized artificial intelligence capable of thinking and problem-solving in a manner that is seen in humans (Penrose, 1994). The process of metacognition and understanding do not appear to have computational solutions (Penrose, 1989, 1994).

Gödal's (1992) succinct Incompleteness Theorem, which derailed Alfred North Whitehead and Bertrand Russell's work to solidify the logical foundation of mathematics and determinism in 1931, also seems to indicate that computation will never be capable of the kind of self-regulation and self-understanding that forms the core of human metacognitive capacity. The ability to mathematically represent qualia, such as the experience of the redness of a rose, a feeling of love, or even the basic physical sensation of touching an object, all seem to be features of cognition that cannot be represented computationally. This indicates that there are whole classes of cognitive ability that are not well-explained by our present theories. This class consists of experiential states, of which understanding (Penrose, 1989, 1994) and metacognition are advanced iterations.

One of the potential solutions to this algorithmic problem could be found in quantum computation. Deutsch (2011), one of the founding fathers of quantum computing and famous for formulating a description of the universal quantum computer, has presented a theory that human intelligence represents a special kind of computer, a universal problem solving system. His descriptions of an advanced type of computer capable of flexibly identifying and solving problems would also certainly possess a level of metacognitive insight. It may be that as quantum technology is developed, new insights into how our brains process information will be gained. Presently, this technology is at the beginning stages of development, but that development is increasing at a breakneck pace. In 2018, the United States passed the National Quantum Initiative Act, establishing priorities for a 10-year plan to accelerate the development of quantum computer systems (Giles, 2018). This research holds great potential and could reveal new ways that computation could inform our understanding of human cognition.

However, computation may not lead to greater discoveries if there truly is an underlying dualism, sometimes called the mind–body problem, where there are divisions between the physical and psychic world that cannot be breached. If this philosophical view turns out to be true, then looking for a computational answer to what consciousness is will always remain a scientific dead end. However, there are philosophies that conjecture that there is no mind-matter duality. Many Eastern cultures approach the idea of consciousness this way. Mathematician Alfred North Whitehead (1957) proposed in Process and Reality that consciousness is an abstraction produced by what he called an occasion of experience. These occasions of experience have both mental and material aspects, making conscious abstractions drawn from experience.

Whitehead's (1957) concepts support an alternative view that consciousness represents a multifaceted and unique type of neural processing that promotes problem-solving (Block, 1994), which is, in fact, fundamental to matter in the universe. Rather than using the classical computing approaches of binary bits of information regulated in the synapse, it has been proposed by philosophers and cognitive scientists like Chalmers (1996) that consciousness is the result of biological systems arising out of quantum processes in the brain. Physicist and cosmologist Tegmark (2014), for example, has proposed that there is a fundamental mathematical quality to the universe that produces consciousness. Much like matter states, such as solid, liquid and gas, that can be described by their mathematical structure, consciousness can likewise be described mathematically and comes into existence as the result of this structure. This purely mathematical approach to the problem of consciousness has grown out of earlier theoretical work by Julian Tioni, who proposed the integrated information theory of consciousness that argues that consciousness is a fundamental property of the universe that can be quantified by a quantity called "phi". This theory predicts that the more phi a system has, the more conscious it is, and that phi can be used to distinguish conscious from unconscious systems.

Roger Penrose has proposed a more mechanical exploitation of quantum-level properties through the use of exceedingly small subcellular structures called microtubules, which may be involved in how sensory neurons use quantum mechanical properties to produce conscious perception. Along with being ubiquitous in neurons, microtubules form the cilia structures at the base of all classes of sensory receptors (Swanson, 2003) and orchestrate the division of genetic material during mitosis (Hameroff & Penrose, 2014). There is building evidence that quantum mechanical properties may be more involved in biological processes than previously appreciated (Gleiser, 2014; Verny, 2020).

Though much of the evidence for biological exploitation of quantum physics comes from the study of plants (Olaya-Castro & Fassioli, 2011; Romero et al., 2014; Yarris, 2010) and animals (Mouritsen, 2018; Pinzon-Rodriguez et al., 2018), there is some evidence of probable quantum processes being involved in the sensory processing of humans (Verny, 2020). Palmer (2013) found that, along with the classically understood lock and key molecular mechanisms, the human sense of smell also uses quantum properties to produce our experience of smell. Palmer (2013) found that humans could smell the difference between hydrogen with one neutron and hydrogen with two neutrons, also called deuterium. These two compounds fit into the same lock and key receptors of the nose, but because of the quantum vibrational differences between the two substances caused by a difference of only one neutron, the sensation is perceived as two distinguishably different smells. Previously intractable problems in cellular biology, like photosynthesis (Olaya-Castro & Fassioli, 2011; Yarris, 2010) and the migratory ability of geese (Pinzon-Rodriguez et al., 2018), indicate that macro-scale biological organisms can actually use physical properties that only exist at exceedingly small, quantum-level physical scales (Verny, 2020).

Penrose's (1989) solution to this problem suggests that subcellular neuronal structures regulate experiential states and produce understanding by exploiting subatomic properties, such as quantum entanglement. Quantum entanglement (QE) is an extremely well-verified property of subatomic matter (Horodecki et al., 2009; Kaiser, 2014). It is particularly relevant because QE has been shown to be related to information transfer between particles (Bennett et al., 1993; Horodecki et al., 2009). It is also behind a not well-understood property of binding discrete parts together to form physically larger single entities. For example, when quarks are subsumed into protons or protons and electrons from atoms, or atoms form molecules. The implications of quantum phenomena such as entanglement and the collapse of the wave function are potentially profound as it would suggest higher levels of conscious behavior result from potentially higher levels of conscious organization and awareness within the environment.

Practically speaking, this would suggest learners and teachers must work to forge a deep relationship between each other, the environment, and their understanding to bolster their ability to identify and connect perceptions to learning (Hulbig, 2018a, 2018b). The impact of this conflict on educational pedagogy is subtle, but real. If metacognition is a wholly conscious phenomenon, then educational practices like gaining attention, making connections, and individual motivation become critical to practice. Inversely, if metacognition is an emergent phenomenon, one which brings together conscious, subconscious, and environmental components, then educational practices like routine, exposure, and the manner of presentation become most important.

The extent to which quantum mechanical properties may be involved in cognition may be underappreciated. It has been assumed that quantum mechanical properties of matter are so remotely removed that their effect on everyday physical properties, at our size and scale, is negligible. Tegmark (2000) proposed that the mathematics of quantum mechanics seemed to indicate that the insides of living cells are too wet, warm, and noisy (Tegmark, 2000) to produce useful quantum collapses like those proposed by Penrose (1989). However, there is building evidence that quantum mechanical properties do indeed exercise important physical effects at everyday scales (Mouritsen, 2018; Olaya-Castro & Fassioli, 2011; Palmer, 2013; Pinzon-Rodriguez et al., 2018; Romero et al., 2014; Verny, 2020; Yarris, 2010).

For example, our sun's most important quality, which nurtures all life on this earth, is its ability to radiate heat and light and is the result of a macro expression of quantum tunneling phenomena (Siegel, 2015). Discoveries of physical and biological systems using quantum properties, such as recent discoveries in plants during photosynthesis (Romero et al., 2017) and geese during migration (Hiscock et al., 2016) and even investigations into human smell and the processing of olfactory stimuli (Turin, 1996; Palmer, 2013), make it clear that large biological systems can harness quantum phenomena. While no theory about the nature of consciousness has wide acceptance or support, Penrose and Hameroff's Orch OR theory of consciousness (Hameroff & Penrose, 2014) has withstood initial attempts to falsify it using mathematics (Tegmark, 2000). Recent investigation has shown quantum excitation in microtubules, and that anaesthetic drugs dampened this excitation (Lewton, 2022). Microtubials have demonstrated an ability to harvest light particles (Kalra et al., 2022), also lending support to the theory. Discovering the influence of a quantum phenomena like entanglement on a physical system like microtubials could be the first step towards explaining important elements of how our conscious processing works and the role of relationship on thinking, learning and teaching.

3.3 Metaing

There is a need to describe the most abstract features of metacognition and ground its educational practice in not just neuropsychological but also physical, biological, and conceptual phenomena. When one realizes that the reason metacognition works so well as an educational routine is because it reflects, in practice, fundamental qualities of human learning, rationales for denying any person such an important developmental form of education fails to stand up to scrutiny. The depth to which metacognition can be grounded in a multidisciplinary scientific approach should be seen as a call to action to more purposefully integrate these developmental practices of education more deeply into societies, communities, and the educational lives of individuals. It also opens pathways that integrate fields like education, psychology, and health care with the needs of the individuals they serve.

The explanation for the uncommon effectiveness of metacognitive educational routines stems from an alignment with underlying neurobiological and developmental processes of learning. The fact that metacognition can be grounded in scientific data so far afield from its origins in educational psychology only further lends support to the broader thesis of this book, which is that metacognitive education is critical to the development of all learners. More than this, it suggests that presently distant lines of research are converging on fundamental qualities of learning that extend beyond the field of education, allowing for deeper understanding and control of the regulatory abilities that produce self-transformation.

The subjective first-person experience of metacognition is a neurocognitive experience whose core features can be extrapolated to form the basis of an educational routine. This is why metacognitive educational elements have been shown to achieve high levels of success in supporting student learning (Dunlosky & Metcalfe, 2009; Hattie, 2012). This is particularly true for students with learning differences who do not perform well using more traditional educational models and must find the ways of doing things that are most effective for them. This is because the metacognitive experience bears a fundamental relationship to core elements of physical, biological, and information-processing systems of thought.

The human capacity for understanding and self-control can be identified, ordered, and directed back upon itself by the individual in a way that produces new knowledge and behavior. This process refines learning behaviors and develops an individual's capacity for understanding by providing for an ever-evolving expansion of their ability to develop complex behaviors and self-control. Metacognition can be thought to exploit foundational elements of the learning process to produce higher-order thinking. It is a tool of learning that can be used by all kinds of learners, at many different ages and developmental levels of appreciation, making it better suited to address the diverse needs of individuals.

Education, by this formula, is cyclical and expansive. Unlike more linear approaches to education that place arbitrary limits on both the individual and on what can be taught, metacognitive procedures are cyclical, expansive, and eventually become self-reinforcing and self-directing. This is because metacognitive learning expresses a quality that is manifested across abstract fields of thought and has at its base an integrative, synthetic phenomenon called **metaing** (Hulbig, 2018a, 2018b), which integrates quantitative and qualitative dimensions of experience to produce new understanding.

3.4 Problem Solving and Metaing

It has been observed by Deutsch (2011) in his book, *The Beginning of Infinity*, that humans are an organism that have evolved a capacity for universal problem-solving. Much like a Turing machine, which uses patterns of ones and zeros as its mechanism of universal computation, the human brain uses a mechanism of explanation that imbues an infinite capacity for problem-solving. Deutsch (2011) identified explanation and error correction as fundamental qualities of a universal problem-solving mechanism. Processes of explanation and error correction have historically been considered primary components of learning. This suggests the existence of a generalized educational routine capable of imparting a practice of personal problem-solving.

Historically, institutions have struggled to produce standardized, non-biased curriculums because they have not focused on providing support to individuals in solving the problems of their life, society, and culture independently. The need for a new teaching pedagogy capable of enabling students to form a problem-solving that seeks to enlist what is known about the neuropsychological processes of learning to develop the student's individual capacity for skill development and personal achievement, which are indicative of human learning, is more critical than ever before.

One finding of this study was that metacognition demonstrates both conscious and unconscious qualities. Conscious qualities of learning are those the learner is aware of. Subconscious qualities of learning are those that the learner is not aware of. However, they can be brought into consciousness through a direction of attention. There are also non-conscious elements, which are more mechanical or abstract elements of brain function, like the transference of protons into bursts of neuroelectric charge in the eye, which are aspects of the process of sight that the learner cannot consciously experience. Interestingly, these processes can be understood through learning and produce useful explanations about vision. While all indications are that the process of metacognition must be conscious, some aspects that fall under metacognitive control like strategies and habits become more subconscious routines through practice. So while the ability to have cognitions about cognitions seems to necessitate a conscious awareness, there appears to be a level of consciousness represented all the way down through the cognitive process. Conscious elements of experience are integrated with non-conscious elements to become tools of thought used and integrated by ever more sophisticated manifestations of behavior. To quote Subject G, "I don't think you can have one without the other."

The brain's ability to synthesize information cannot be simulated by computers, and no approaches to programming seem likely to describe this discrepancy (Penrose, 1994). Not only is it becoming clear that metacognition is a far more intractable computational problem than previously appreciated, but also it has confounded explanations in a classically physical way. In response to the lack of substantive progress toward a model of cognition using the logic of computation and classical physics, it is proposed that phenomena underlying the human ability to understand are the result of the brain's ability to harness quantum physical properties (Penrose, 1989; Hameroff & Penrose, 2014; Kerskens, 2022).

The concept of metaing, at this time, is believed to only be a part of the phenomena of understanding and is intended to be a conceptual place marker for a component of cognition that is not well explained using classical theoretical concepts. However, there is a quality of learning that displays a strongly analogous relationship to certain quantum phenomena, such as entanglement, that allows for a non-physical and non-local transference of information (Einstein et al., 1935; Bell, 1964). A practical implication of this line of thinking may be that to truly understand learning we may first need to better understand quantum-level physical interactions.

3.5 Meta Integration

Metaing is an integrative power in the mind. A metaing process binds identified ideas into larger concepts, enabling our minds to synthesize and produce a single bounded consciousness capable of identifying boundaries within its field of perception and predicting the most effective ways of interpretation. Through this metaing interaction, boundaries are perceived and functional constraints can be synthesized to make further identifications. From these perceived boundaries, holistic entities emerge, made up of parts that themselves can be identified and bound to other identifications in useful ways.

Metaing is a power of the mind that is built off the idea of recursion (Chomsky & Kenstowicz, 1999; Hofstadter, 1979; Pinker, 2003). Recursion is a process where the steps of a procedure involve invoking the procedure itself, producing a similar representation at a different scale. In linguistics, this would be represented by the sentence, "Chompski thinks language is recursive," which can be expanded to include another related perspective, for example, "Pinkard thinks that Chompski thinks that language is recursive," or "I think that Pinkard thinks that Chompski thinks that language is recursive." Such a linguistic cognitive structure can be built to include an infinite number of individuals concluding the same thing. Recursion has also been demonstrated both visually and mathematically (Fig. 3.1).

Mathematical recursion example

$$a(n) = a(a(n-1)) + a(n - a(n-1))$$

Note: Hofstadter-Conway $10,000 Sequence (Weisstein, 2002)

Visual recursion example

Note: Visual example: M C Escher Print, Escher Art, "Smaller and Smaller", Circa 1956,

Fig. 3.1 Examples of recursion

Metaing differs from recursion in that it creates a non-similar bounded whole. While recursion generates multiple iterations of essentially the same thing, metaing produces something new; a cognitive representation that can be understood as separate from its constituent parts. For example, words are made of recurring patterns of just 26 letters, but from these recurring patterns of letters one is able to generate an infinite number of words. In turn, recurring patterns of words can be structured into sentences that express infinite ideas, and from these ideas, patterns can be expressed that produce new ideas feeding the initial process of letter, word, and idea production. So, while recursion speaks to a repeating pattern, metaing speaks to an extrapolation of meaning from these recurring patterns that, in turn, can form new patterns that, in turn, produce new knowledge.

Tools of thought can be constructed from certain constituent parts of perception that allow for a new abstract level of perceptual experience. The perceptual experiences produced by the new understanding become the constituent parts of the new tools of thought that will, in turn, produce new understandings. This process develops over time, from a state of subjective, concrete, sensory experience to one of more objective, abstract understandings that bind details into metarepresentations that produce various kinds of abstract understanding. By this underlying metaing phenomena, qualitative features of cognition are integrated with the quantitative. An integration is apparent in the metaphors used to describe abstractions. For example, highly actionable abstract boundaries are often expressed in visual terms such as "clear", while less actionable abstractions are described as "unclear" or "distorted". Moreover, there is evidence that the phenomena of metaphor exert a strong influence on the human psyche and behavior (Lobel, 2016). An integrative metacognitive property would explain how the brain formulates metaphors and why metaphors would exhort such a powerful force on human understanding and behavior.

A visual metaphor that could be used to describe the process of metaing was first demonstrated in a short film by Szasz (1968) and was most recently recreated by astrophysicist Obreschkow (2018). This visual effect is caused by zooming out from a fixed point, like a picnic in the park to a point where the whole park, whole state, whole country, and whole world constitute the frame of the visual image. This experience can also be generated by *Google Maps,* or experienced while taking off and landing in a plane. The visual transformation that is experienced is an example of the mind's metaing capacity in the visual field, as it is forced to build new representations of information that account for the increase in visual data. I am suggesting that this kind of transformation happens with all information processed by the mind. As the amount of data related to a given concept is widened, our perception produces new patterns and representations as related ideas aggregate to produce meta-constructions akin to the transformations that are seen as the image of the park gets subsumed into the geometric pattern of city blocks and the fractal images of large-scale geographic elements.

3.6 Science and Metacognition

Metacognitive understanding has eluded a full scientific and mathematical explanation and yet is identifiable across the literature. Rather than an explanation, science has done better at identifying the environments and experiences that influence its expression. For example, in educational psychology, scientists have devised tests to identify the kinds of environments that promote metacognitive thinking (Brown, 1978; Dunlosky & Metcalfe, 2009). Likewise, neurobiologists have devised scientific procedures and equipment capable of identifying the general parts of the brain that are activated during certain kinds of metacognitive thinking (Carter et al., 1998; Fernandez-Duque et al., 2000; Peterson et al., 1999). However, a fully descriptive explanation of what is occurring when the human mind shifts during metacognition remains forthcoming.

What is most relevant to this discussion is the simple fact that individuals can subjectively investigate their thinking in ways that are scientific in form, but permanently unscientific because of their subjective nature. However, this is not to say that a person cannot approach their subjective experience scientifically. A person can train themselves to look at subjective experience as data, and even devise tests for these experiences to confirm their accuracy. This is why science is often thought of as one of the core academic subjects, with language, mathematics, and social studies.

However, while it is the conscious training and practice in scientific thought that separates the thinking of scientists from the thinking of non-scientists, these differences appear to be only in their degree. They are like the differences we see displayed by professionals in other fields who derive their expertise, not simply from a God-given talent, but through a process of nurturing their talent by spending 10,000 or more hours engaged in that field of expertise (Gladwell, 2008; Wong, 2015). Other than spending an extreme amount of time on a task, the only real difference between scientific thinking and the problem solving thinking of regular folk is the caliber of evidence. Because a subjective experiment can be wholly contained and evaluated internally, it is not fully considered science because true science requires social consensus. Social consensus is necessary to be sure that mistakes were not made. It is a form of error correction that is built into the scientific system that attempts to prevent mistakes from going unnoticed and protect the truth against charlatans and liars.

The impact of charlatans and liars in the field of science can have broadly negative effects on society. For example, Andrew Wakefield, a British physician researcher, presented fraudulent research linking the measles, mumps, and rubella (MMR) vaccine to autism. Wakefield later was found to have manipulated data and was involved in a money-making scheme to sell vaccine alternatives. Even though the Lancet retracted his paper in 2010, and the United Kingdom revoked his medical license, Wakefield became a prominent and wealthy anti-vaccination advocate, and one of the chief spreaders of vaccine disinformation during the global pandemic (Godlee et al., 2011; Rao & Andrade, 2011). While the detrimental impact of purposeful manipulation by a scientist is terrible, even well-intentioned scientists can simply be wrong too. The problem for a subjective application of the scientific method is its lack of objective raw data that can be shared and checked for error.

Scientists themselves must demonstrate high levels of metacognitive self-regulation if they are going to engage in objective science that makes actionable predictions (Popper, 1982). Science requires high levels of organizing, planning, executing, and evaluating to be effective. Why the scientific method has this unreasonable effectiveness has become a focus of work by physicists like Deutsch (2011), who sees the steps of the scientific method as being deeply embedded in the processes of identification and organization that stimulate understanding, and the only difference between the thinking of scientists and nonscientists is the degree of error correction they have been trained in. Duetsch's (2011) work suggests that there is a very real relationship between the scientific method and the underlying processes of human learning. Relationships between the scientific methods and fundamentals of the learning processes have been an area of intense study by educational psychologists for many years (Cowles, 2017) and demonstrate a common problem solving routine that drives human development (Gopnik & Wellman, 2012; Ratcliffe, 2006).

3.6.1 Human Development

Piaget (1952) was among the first to suggest that children actively construct their own understanding of the world through a process of assimilation and accommodation. He proposed that children go through four distinct stages of cognitive development: sensorimotor, preoperational, concrete operational, and formal operational (Piaget, 1952), and sparked the question of whether these clearly identifiable stages of development were genetically determined or part of a process of refinement in cognitive processing. Vygotsky's (1978) answer to this question was social developmental theory, which emphasized the role of culture and social interactions in cognitive development, where the development of language and communication drove the development of thinking. Vygotsky stressed how important the support of a more skilled individual was on individual learners.

For many years, human developmental theory was dominated by competing genetic, cognitive, and social-environmental theories in what is known as the nature versus nurture argument. For example, Rosch (1978) found that people tend to group objects into categories based on their perceived similarity rather than by their physical properties, as would be expected by more objective environmental interactionist approaches. This provided evidence that humans have innate cognitive representations of objects and categories that are likely genetically inborn. Inversely, other investigations showed that young children have a limited understanding of both the physical world (Carey, 2000), and the beliefs and intentions of others (Gopnik, 1993). This understanding becomes more sophisticated as they grow older through a process of integrating experience over time.

Research into the cognitive abilities of animals complicated this nature versus nurture argument as evidence of animals having cognitive abilities similar to those of humans was demonstrated (Premack's 1971). What has been found is the species with the most human-like cognitive abilities was the chimpanzee, which shares 95% of the same DNA sequence and 99% of coding DNA sequences (Wong, 2014). However, with a genetic difference that was so small, DNA could not account for all the behavioral differences seen between humans and chimpanzees. Moreover, certain analogous behavioral presentations that were historically thought to be unique to humans have been found in species as genetically distant as bees (Avarguès-Weber et al., 2018; Reina et al., 2018; Choi et al., 2020). Premack and Woodruff (1978) proposed a third option to the nature nurture debate called theory of mind.

Theory of mind is more a description than a theory. What theory of mind describes is the capacity to understand or predict what is occurring in the mind of another. Animal intelligence is limited in the sense that animals have narrowly adapted theory of mind capacities, often serving only one goal. For example, predators may evolve a limited theory of mind relative to figuring out how their prey thinks to support their hunting. Social animals evolve an even more sophisticated theory of mind to support the social understanding necessary for communal living. Humans, however, have developed the capacity to apply theory of mind to teach, and teach in a way that transcends all activities (Premack & Woodruff, 1978).

Theory of mind balances and contextualizes the polarities of the nature versus nurture argument, suggesting that it is an integration of understanding the physical environment and the mental environment that produces this third factor called a theory, which affects learning and development. It also provides a stable cognitive-behavioral metric with which to assess intelligence between species and individuals. In humans, the sophistication of an individual's theory of mind can be thought of as a sliding scale relative to the person's ability to conceptualize other beliefs, judgments, desires, intentions, emotions, and behaviors. It has proven indispensable in helping to explain the underlying deficits of autism (Baron-Cohen, 1991), neurodevelopmental disorders (Korkmaz, 2011), and the effects of trauma (Pang et al., 2022). Dorris et al. (2022) have also suggested that it is the development of theory of mind that regulates expressions of empathy across the lifespan.

The realization that the construction of a theory of mind grows out of an individual's biological nature and the level of nurturing support received from their environment led to deeper investigation into exactly what was occurring when individuals develop a theory of mind, resulting in what has been called Theory-theory.[1]

Theory-theory is a science of folk psychology (Ratcliffe, 2006). It posits that there is an underlying system of problem-solving built off the holding of theories that has perhaps evolved to help humans understand the intentions of other humans and predict their behavior. The initial search for a folk psychology grew from the assumption that there may be a common underlying cluster of beliefs, heuristics, or rules of thumb that form the common, unschooled concept of psychology (Gopnik & Wellman, 2012). Theory-theory, in a sense, invalidated this idea by identifying that

[1] I would like to point out how the discussion of theory- theory suffers from the same problem of recursivity as discussions of metacognition, where there is a blending or overlapping of third person and first person expressions.

there was no underlying folk psychological belief. However, there seemed to be a practical heuristic involving the making of theories themselves, and then using those theories to predict and guide behavior (Ratcliffe, 2006).

In the vein of Piaget, psychologists investigated when the earliest presentations of this process of theory development began, revealing that from a very young age children can be observed developing theories to explain and guide behavior (Bonawitz et al., 2012). These observations demonstrated children apply a very clear pattern of behaviors when problem-solving, starting with a theory, followed by an exploration stage that tested the theory, and then an explanation phase that attempted to make sense of what happened during the exploration but also devise a new and better theory (Bonawitz et al., 2012). The relationship between these problem-solving steps taken by children and the scientific method did not go unnoticed, and led to the development of the child scientist theory of human development (Gopnik, 1996; Gopnik & Wellman 2012; School & Leslie, 1999).

The child scientist theory suggested not only that children behaved like little scientists, but that perhaps the best scientists were thinking like children. This idea that there is something important and pure about the thinking of children is not a new one and can be traced back to the enlightenment ideas of Rousseau (1762). The child scientist theory has had a strong influence on modern teaching pedagogy, producing curriculum and encouraging teachers to produce lessons that are more interactive and require students to develop and test theories. Perhaps the most successful and widespread approach is project-based learning (Chen & Yang, 2019).

What is truly fascinating about theory of mind, theory-theory, and the child scientist theory is that they have not only led to inspiring innovation in teaching pedagogy, but also studies into animal intelligence and the neurology of perception. As mentioned, theory of mind itself grew out of animal studies and continues to be an important crossover theory connecting human cognition to its evolutionary roots (Krupenye & Call, 2019). However, investigations of the neurology of human perception connect this heuristic of theory creation to the fine-grain construction of our cognitive perceptual state.

In his book *Visual Intelligence*, Hoffman (2000) presents several of the heuristics that support the brain's construction of its visual experience. These rules that underpin how we build our perceptual experience seem to be analogous to the rules of grammar that guide our construction of meaning from sound. Rather than hard and fast rules, they are more like general hypotheses that are used to predict what is seen and heard. But they are not so rigidly applied that they cannot be affected by the presentation of new or incongruent information. In fact, there is an analogous experience of illusion that occurs across sensory modalities. These are perceptions where the heuristics used to build the perception violate the rules of perception being used by other cognitive systems creating an identifiable paradox, like the picture that can simultaneously be viewed as either a young lady or old woman, and the child's toy that produces a noise that can be interpreted as saying both "Green Lantern" and "Brainstorm."

Cognitive heuristics do not seem to be simply ingrained but rather developed through interaction with the environment. For example, newborn infants require time to develop full visual capability. However, it has been shown that this is not simply a process of biological maturation (Hubel & Wiesel, 1970). If the eyes of a young child are covered for an extended period of time during the maturation process, the child will not develop the ability to see despite having fully biologically developed eyes and nervous systems.

Infants must interact with their environment to develop these underlying heuristics. A similar phenomenon may be an underlying cause in some cases of dyslexia (Hogan et al., 2014). This is because it is common for children who are later diagnosed to have had tubes placed in their ears at a very young age to prevent the ear canal from being blocked with wax and fluid. Much like the developmental impact on sight when the eyes don't receive proper visual stimulation, early blockages can have a similar effect on the capacity to develop proper hearing, despite there being no discernable damage to the ears' physical or neurological capacity for hearing.

The relationship between biologically centered heuristic theories of perception and psychological interactionist theories, like theory-theory, suggests a process that generates and evaluates theories through physical interaction. Spelke's (1994) work on the development of core knowledge, which proposed that infants have innate, domain-specific systems for understanding physical objects, space, number, and biological organisms, provides further evidence for the idea that humans have these ingrained heuristics that are used to make mental simulations to understand the physical world.

3.6.2 Simulation Theory

The simulation theory of human development posits that humans use simulations or "mental models" built on predictive heuristics to understand the world around them. Heidegger's (1927) ontology of human existence, which proposed that humans understand the world through their practical engagement with it rather than through detached observation, was perhaps the earliest modern expression of simulation theory. In *Being and Time*, Heidegger (1927) provided the philosophical foundation for the idea that humans use mental simulations to understand the world. Like other theories that have attempted to conceptualize human thinking, the most powerful support for Heidegger's idea of humans using mental models to simulate and understand has come from the study of children (Bruner, 2017; Spelke, 1994).

One researcher whose work illuminated this connection between the development of mental models and problem-solving was Bruner (2017, 2009). Bruner (2017, 2009) is known for his work on the development of representation, which proposed that children construct mental models or simulations of the world through the process of abstraction. Bruner's (2017, 2009) research provided evidence that humans use mental simulations to understand the world. This work was expanded upon by Leslie (1994), a theory of mind researcher, who proposed that children develop an understanding of other people's minds by simulating their own mental states in response to their behaviors. In other words, humans use their own cognitions to produce mental simulations of other people's mental states and use that knowledge to regulate their behavior.

This relationship between how sensory information is guided by heuristics to create a useful simulation of our environment is strikingly analogous to what is seen in children when they use their prior knowledge about their experiences to create useful simulation that regulates their behavior. Research across fields seems to be converging on a process that uses past experience to actively construct predictive perceptions to guide and support our actions (Seth, 2021). This connection is important because it extends through both the biological and psychological developmental processes, and could indicate there is an interactive problem-solving process that transcends both. Such interdisciplinary correlations lend strong support to the child scientist theory. However, perhaps the most powerful evidence that there is an underlying biological heuristic compelling the problem-solving behavior of children can be found in the roots of our modern development of a scientific method.

3.6.3 Roots of the Scientific Method

While the theory of mind can accommodate both the nature and nurture sides of the human development problem through the extension of theory-theory, the child scientist theory presents a new "chicken and egg" conundrum to human developmental theory. Are children really displaying a natural aptitude for the problem-solving steps of the scientific method? This would suggest that scientific methodology is the natural, inborn method of problem-solving in all humans. Or it could be that the scientific method is simply the most powerful approach to problem-solving we have developed collectively over hundreds of years and we are projecting this understanding onto our understanding of how children think. In a sense it's the old argument: The only tool I have is a hammer so all problems can be solved by treating them like a nail. If this is the case, then as we progress as a society and develop new methods of problem-solving that are more powerful than the present scientific method, the relationship with child development will fall out of conceptual alignment. Another thing that could happen, if this is the case, would be to drive us to discover more subtle differences between the scientific method and what children do to solve problems.

However, the solution to this chicken and egg problem may have already been found in the origins of the scientific method itself. While the historical origins of scientific approaches to thinking can be traced back to the earliest days of Greek philosophy, the modern scientific method traces its roots to a mere century ago. Before the 1900s, scientific practices were more axiomatic and tied to ideas of proof, cause and effect, and reason. Hence why the Enlightenment Era is also sometimes called the Age of Reason.

The steps of the scientific method were not formalized until the beginning of the twentieth century. Rather than a review of the scientific practices of the 1700 and 1800s, the scientific method was born out of the study of children (Cowles, 2017). The researcher who outlined these steps was not a physicist, biologist, or psychologist. It was the American educator and pragmatist philosopher Dewey (1910). In his seminal book *How We Think*, Dewy (1910) outlined discoveries into human learning made at his Laboratory School. Here we find the first steps of the scientific method identified as "five distinct steps in reflection.... (i) a felt difficulty; (ii) its location and definition; (iii) suggestion of possible solution; (iv) development by reasoning of the bearings of the suggestion; (v) further observation and experiment leading to its acceptance or rejection; that is, the conclusion of belief or disbelief" (Dewey, 1910, p. 72). These were the steps of a reflective problem-solving process, identified in children and reiterated through a formalized method that can be practiced and refined into the scientific profession.

John Dewey's Laboratory School, also known as the University of Chicago Laboratory School, was a research-focused school founded by Dewey in 1896. The school was based on Dewey's educational philosophy, which emphasized hands-on, experiential learning and the integration of academics with real-life experiences. Students at the school were encouraged to learn through observation, experimentation, and problem-solving, rather than through rote memorization. The school formally investigated both the development of critical-thinking skills and the pedagogy of different subjects, such as science, mathematics, and the humanities, until it was closed in 1967. Because Dewy approached the subject of education as an integrated study of pedagogical practice and child development, he was able to see this relationship between problem-solving and learning, and describe its basic heuristic elements.

The study of pedagogy reveals that perhaps the secret ingredient of all lessons is the ability to support a student's natural learning process. However, when taken together with building evidence across fields investigating neurobiological and developmental processes of human thinking, what emerges is a step-by-step methodological approach to problem-solving based on our best understanding of how it is done naturally. This would support child scientist theory's key pedagogical insight that at its root, teaching students involves a simple refinement of natural skills already present. The introduction of metacognition into this process would individualize it by supporting a student's ability to see how their own unique cluster of abilities can be marshaled in the service of this natural problem-solving ability.

References

Avarguès-Weber, A., d'Amaro, D., Metzler, M., Finke, V., Baracchi, D., & Dyer, A. G. (2018). Does holistic processing require a large brain? Insights from honeybees and wasps in fine visual recognition tasks. *Frontiers in Psychology, 9*, 1313.

Backus, J. (1978). Can programming be liberated from the von Neumann style? A functional style and its algebra of programs. *Communications of the ACM, 21*(8), 613–641.

Bandura, A. (1989). Human agency in social cognitive theory. *American Psychologist, 44*(9), 1175.

Baron-Cohen, S. (1991). Precursors to a theory of mind: Understanding attention in others. In A. Whiten (Ed.), *Natural theories of mind: Evolution, development, and simulation of everyday mindreading* (pp. 233–251). Basil Blackwell. ISBN 9780631171942.

Basin, D., Deville, Y., Flener, P., Hamfelt, A., & Nilsson, J. F. (2004). Synthesis of programs in computational logic. In *Program Development in Computational Logic* (pp. 30–65). Springer, Berlin, Heidelberg.

Bell, J. S. (1964). On the Einstein Podolsky Rosen paradox. *Physics Physique Fizika, 1*(3), 195.

Berwick, R. C., Pietroski, P., Yankama, B., & Chomsky, N. (2011). Poverty of the stimulus revisited. *Cognitive Science, 35*(7), 1207–1242. https://doi.org/10.1111/j.1551-6709.2011.01189.x

Bennett, C. H., Brassard, G., Crépeau, C., Jozsa, R., Peres, A., & Wootters, W. K. (1993). Teleporting an unknown quantum state via dual classical and Einstein-Podolsky-Rosen channels. *Physical Review Letters, 70*(13), 1895. https://doi.org/10.1103/PhysRevLett.70.1895

Block, N. (1994). On a confusion about a function of consciousness. *Behavioral and Brain Sciences,* 227–227.

Bonawitz, E. B., van Schijndel, T. J., Friel, D., & Schulz, L. (2012). Children balance theories and evidence in exploration, explanation, and learning. *Cognitive Psychology, 64*(4), 215–234.

Brown, A. L. (1978). Knowing when, where, and how to remember; a problem of metacognition. *Advances in Instructional Psychology,* 1.

Bruner, J. (2017). *A study of thinking*. Routledge.

Carey, S. (2000). The origin of concepts. *Journal of Cognition and Development, 1*(1), 37–41.

Carter, C. S., Braver, T. S., Barch, D. M., Botvinick, M. M., Noll, D., & Cohen, J. D. (1998). Anterior cingulate cortex, error detection, and the online monitoring of performance. *Science, 280*(5364), 747–749.

Chalmers, D. J. (1996). *The conscious mind: In search of a fundamental theory.* Oxford University

Chen, C. H., & Yang, Y. C. (2019). Revisiting the effects of project-based learning on students' academic achievement: A meta-analysis investigating moderators. *Educational Research Review, 26*, 71–81.

Chomsky, N. (2006). *Language and mind*. Cambridge University Press.

Choi, S. H., Rao, V. D., Gernat, T., Hamilton, A. R., Robinson, G. E., & Goldenfeld, N. (2020). Individual variations lead to universal and cross-species patterns of social behavior. *Proceedings of the National Academy of Sciences, 117*(50), 31754–31759.

Chomsky, N., & Kenstowicz, M. (1999). *Derivation by phase* (p. 482). MIT Press.

Cowles, H. (2017) Child's play. Aeon.https://aeon.co/essays/how-the-scientific-method-came-from-watching-children-play

Deutsch, D. (2011). *The beginning of infinity: Explanations that transform the world*. Penguin, UK.

Dewey, J. (1910). *How we think*, (pp. 68–78). Lexington, MA, US: D C Heath, vi, 228 pp.

Domingos, P. (2015). *The master algorithm: How the quest for the ultimate learning machine Will remake our world*. Basic Books.

Dorris, L., Young, D., Barlow, J., Byrne, K., & Hoyle, R. (2022). Cognitive empathy across the lifespan. *Developmental Medicine & Child Neurology, 64*(12), 1524–1531.

Dunlosky, J., & Metcalfe, J. (2009). *Metacognition*. SAGE.

Dunlosky, J., Rawson, K. A., Marsh, E. J., Nathan, M. J., & Willingham, D. T. (2013). Improving students' learning with effective learning techniques: Promising directions from cognitive and educational psychology. *Psychological Science in the Public Interest, 14*(1), 4–58.

Einstein, A., Podolsky, B., & Rosen, N. (1935). Can quantum-mechanical description of physical reality be considered complete?. *Physical Review, 47*(10), 777.

Fernandez-Duque, D., Baird, J. A., & Posner, M. I. (2000). Executive attention and metacognitive regulation. *Consciousness and Cognition, 9*(2), 288–307.

Gerhard, S., Daducci, A., Lemkaddem, A., Meuli, R., Thiran, J. P., & Hagmann, P. (2011). The connectome viewer toolkit: An open source framework to manage, analyze, and visualize connectomes. *Frontiers in Neuroinformatics, 5*, 3.

Giles, M. (2018, December 22) President Trump has signed a $1.2 billon law to boost US quantum tech. *MIT Technology Review*, Retrieved 8/2/2018 from: https://www.technologyreview.com/f/612679/president-trump-has-signed-a-12-billon-law-to-boost-us-quantum-tech/

Gladwell, M. (2008). *The 10,000 hour-rule. In Outliers: The story of success* (pp. 35–68). Little, Brown and Company, NY.

Gleiser, M. (2014). Does consciousness compute? *Chronicle of Higher Education, 61*(2), B13 B15.
Gödel, K. (1992). *On formally undecidable propositions of Principia Mathematica and related Systems*. Courier Corporation.
Godlee, F., Smith, J., & Marcovitch, H. (2011). Wakefield's article linking MMR vaccine and autism was fraudulent. Bmj, 342.
Goldstein, E. Bruce (2009). *Sensation and perception*. Cengage Learning.
Gopnik, A. (1993). How we know our minds: The illusion of first-person knowledge of intentionality. *Behavioral and Brain Sciences, 16*(1), 1–14.
Gopnik, A. (1996). The scientist as child. *Philosophy of Science, 63*(4), 485–514
Gopnik, A., & Wellman, H. M. (2012). Reconstructing constructivism: Causal models, Bayesian learning mechanisms, and the theory. *Psychological Bulletin, 138*(6), 1085.
Hameroff, S., & Penrose, R. (2014). Consciousness in the universe: A review of the 'Orch OR' theory. *Physics of Life Reviews, 11*(1), 39–78.
Hattie, J. (2012). *Visible learning for teachers: Maximizing impact on learning*. Routledge.
Heidegger, M. (1927). Heidegger, Martin. Being and Time. https://danassays.wordpress.com/encyclopedia-of-the-essay/heideggermartin/
Hiscock, H. G., Worster, S., Kattnig, D. R., Steers, C., Jin, Y., Manolopoulos, D. E., ... & Hore, P. J. (2016). The quantum needle of the avian magnetic compass. *Proceedings of the National Academy of Sciences, 113*(17), 4634–4639. https://doi.org/10.1073/pnas.1600341113
Hoffman, D. D. (2000). *Visual intelligence: How we create what we see*. WW Norton & Company.
Hofstadter, D. (1979). *Gödel, Escher, Bach: An eternal golden braid*. Basic Books.
Hogan, A., Phillips, R. L., Howard, D., & Yiengprugsawan, V. (2014). Psychosocial outcomes of children with ear infections and hearing problems: A longitudinal study. *BMC Pediatrics, 14*, 1–8.
Horodecki, R., Horodecki, P., Horodecki, M., & Horodecki, K. (2009). Quantum entanglement. *Reviews of Modern Physics, 81*(2), 865. https://doi.org/10.1103/RevModPhys.81.865
Hubel, D. H., & Wiesel, T. N. (1970). The period of susceptibility to the physiological effects of unilateral eye closure in kittens. *The Journal of Physiology, 206*(2), 419–436. https://doi.org/10.1113/jphysiol.1970.sp009022
Hulbig, P. (2018a). Metacognition at the program for the advancement of learning. Lesley Digital Commons. https://digitalcommons.lesley.edu/cgi/viewcontent.cgi?article=1005&context=community_of_scholars
Hulbig, P. (2018b). Toward a metacognitive model of learning and development: A unifying educational paradigm. ResearchGate. https://www.researchgate.net/publication/327118167_Toward_a_Metacognitive_Model_of_Learning_and_Development_a_Unifying_Educational_Paradigm
Kaiser, D. (2014). *Is quantum entanglement real?*. The New York Times, 16.
Kalra, A. P., Benny, A., Travis, S. M., Zizzi, E. A., Morales-Sanchez, A., Oblinsky, D. G., & Scholes, G. D. (2022). Electronic energy migration in microtubules. *ACS Central Science*. Retrieved from https://doi.org/10.1021/acscentsci.2c01114
Kelly, K. (1995). *Out of control: The new biology of machines, social systems, and the economic world*. Addison-Wesley.
Keohane, J. (2017, February 16). What news-writing bots mean for the future of journalism. *Wired*. Retrieved 8/2/2019 from: https://www.wired.com/2017/02/robots-wrote-this-story/
Kerskens, C. M., & Pérez, D. L. (2022). Experimental indications of non-classical brain functions. *Journal of Physics Communications, 6*(10), 105001.
Korkmaz, B. (2011, May). Theory of mind and neurodevelopmental disorders of childhood. *Pediatric Research, 69*(5 Pt 2), 101R–8R.
Krizhevsky, A., Sutskever, I., & Hinton, G. E. (2012). Imagenet classification with deep convolutional neural networks. *Advances in Neural Information Processing Systems, 25*.
Krupenye, C., & Call, J. (2019). Theory of mind in animals: Current and future directions. *Wiley Interdisciplinary Reviews: Cognitive Science, 10*(6), e1503.
Leslie, A. M. (1994). ToMM, ToBy, and Agency: Core architecture and domain specificity. In L. A. Hirschfeld & S. A. Gelman (Eds.), *Mapping the mind: Domain specificity in cognition*

and culture (pp. 119–148). Cambridge University Press. https://doi.org/10.1017/CBO9780511752902.006

Lewton, T. (2022). *A quantum of consciousness*. New Scientist.

Lobel, T. (2016). *Sensation: The new science of physical intelligence*. Simon and Schuster.

McCann, M. T., Jin, K. H., & Unser, M. (2017). Convolutional neural networks for inverse problems in imaging: A review. *IEEE Signal Processing Magazine, 34*(6), 85–95. https://doi.org/10.1109/MSP.2017.2739299

Medina, J. (2011). *Brain rules: 12 principles for surviving and thriving at work, home, and School*. ReadHowYouWant. Com.

Mnih, V., Kavukcuoglu, K., Silver, D., Rusu, A. A., Veness, J., Bellemare, M. G., ... & Hassabis, D. (2015). Human-level control through deep reinforcement learning. *Nature, 518*(7540), 529–533.

Mouritsen, H. (2018). Long-distance navigation and magnetoreception in migratory animals. *Nature, 558*(7708), 50–59.

Nelson, T. O. (1996). Consciousness and metacognition. *American Psychologist, 51*(2), 102–116. https://doi.org/10.1037/0003-066X.51.2.102

Obreschkow, D. (2018). Universe size comparison: Cosmic eye. https://youtu.be/8Are9dDbW24?si=Wf5QiNw8qu8IbbL5

Olaya-Castro, A., & Fassioli, F. (2011). Characterizing quantum-sharing of electronic excitation in molecular aggregates. *Procedia Chemistry, 3*(1), 176–184.

Palmer, J. (2013) Quantum smell idea gains ground. *BBC*. http://www.bbc.com/news/science-environment-21150046

Pang, Y., Zhao, S., Li, Z., Li, N., Yu, J., Zhang, R., Lu, F., Chen, H., Wu, F., Zheng, W., & Gao, J. (2022). Enduring effect of abuse: childhood maltreatment links to altered theory of mind network among adults. *Human brain mapping, 43*(7), 2276–2288.

Penrose, R. (1989). *The emperor's new mind: Concerning computers, minds, and the laws of physics*. Oxford U. Press.

Penrose, R. (1994). *Shadows of the mind* (Vol. 4). Oxford University Press.

Peterson, B. S., Skudlarski, P., Gatenby, J. C., Zhang, H., Anderson, A. W., & Gore, J. C. (1999). An fMRI study of Stroop word-color interference: Evidence for cingulate subregions subserving multiple distributed attentional systems. *Biological Psychiatry, 45*(10), 1237–1258.

Piaget, J. (1952). *The origins of intelligence in children*. International Universities Press.

Pinker, S. (2003). The language instinct: How the mind creates language. Penguin UK.

Pinzon-Rodriguez, A., Bensch, S., & Muheim, R. (2018). Expression patterns of cryptochromegenes in avian retina suggest involvement of Cry4 in light-dependent magnetoreception. *Journal of the Royal Society Interface, 15*(140), 20180058.

Popper, K. (1982). Science: Conjectures and refutations. *Philosophy of Science and the Occult*, 104–111.

Premack, D. (1971). Language in chimpanzee? *Science, 172*(3985), 808–822.

Premack, D., & Woodruff, G. (1978). Does the chimpanzee have a theory of mind? *Behavioral and Brain Sciences, 4*, 515–526.

Rao, T. S., & Andrade, C. (2011). The MMR vaccine and autism: Sensation, refutation, retraction, and fraud. *Indian Journal of Psychiatry, 53*(2), 95.

Ratcliffe, M. (2006). Folk psychology is not folk psychology". *Phenomenology and the Cognitive Sciences, 5*(1), 31–52. https://doi.org/10.1007/s11097-005-9010-y

Reina, A., Bose, T., Trianni, V., & Marshall, J. A. (2018). Psychophysical laws and the superorganism. *Scientific Reports, 8*(1), 4387.

Revonsuo, A., & Newman, J. (1999). Binding and consciousness. *Consciousness and Cognition, 8*(2), 123–127. https://doi.org/10.1006/ccog.1999.0393.PMID10447994

Romero, E., Augulis, R., Novoderezhkin, V. I., Ferretti, M., Thieme, J., Zigmantas, D., & Van Grondelle, R. (2014). Quantum coherence in photosynthesis for efficient solar-energy conversion. *Nature Physics, 10*(9), 676–682.

Romero, E., Novoderezhkin, V. I., & van Grondelle, R. (2017). Quantum design of photosynthesis for bio-inspired solar-energy conversion. *Nature, 543*(7645), 355. https://doi.org/10.1038/nature22012

Rosch, E., & Lloyd, B. B. (1978). Principles of categorization. Fuzzy grammar: A reader. *Oxford University Press on Demand, 7*, 91–106.

Rousseau, J. (1762). Emile, or Education. J. M. Dent. https://oll.libertyfund.org/title/rousseau-emile-or-education

Scholl, B. J., & Leslie, A. M. (1999). Modularity, development and 'theory of mind.' *Mind and Language, 14*(1), 131–153.

Seth, A. (2021). *Being you: A new science of consciousness*. Penguin.

Siegel, E. (2015, June 22). *It's the power of quantum mechanics that allows the sun to shine*. Forbes.

Spelke, E. (1994). Initial knowledge: Six suggestions. *Cognition, 50*(1–3), 431–445.

Swanson, L. (2003). *Brain architecture: Understanding the basic plan* (pp. 263). Oxford University Press.

Szasz, E. (1968). Cosmic Zoom. https://www.youtube.com/watch?v=ZqwcsuZ1-PU

Tegmark, M. (2000). Importance of quantum decoherence in brain processes. *Physical Review E, 61*(4), 4194.

Tegmark, M. (2014). Consciousness as a state of matter. *Chaos, Solitons & Fractals, 76*, 238–270.

Turin, L. (1996). A spectroscopic mechanism for primary olfactory reception. *Chemical Senses, 21*(6), 773–791. https://doi.org/10.1093/chemse/21.6.773

Veenman, M. V. J., Prins, F. J., & Elshout, J. J. (2002). Initial inductive learning in a complex computer simulated environment: The role of metacognitive skills and intellectual ability. *Computers in Human Behavior, 18*(3), 327–341.

Veenman, M. V., Van Hout-Wolters, B. H., & Afflerbach, P. (2006). Metacognition and learning: Conceptual and methodological considerations. *Metacognition and Learning, 1*(1), 3–14. https://doi.org/10.1007/s11409-005-9002-4

Verny, T. R. (2020). The brain-mind conundrum: the rise of quantum biology. *Journal of Prenatal & Perinatal Psychology & Health*, 34(3).

Vygotsky, L. S. (1978). *Mind in society: The development of higher psychological processes*. Harvard University Press.

Weisstein, E. W. (2002). Hofstadter-Conway $10,000 Sequence. https://mathworld.wolfram.com/

Whitehead, A. N., & Sherburne, D. W. (1957). *Process and reality* (pp. 349–350). New York, NY: Macmillan. Retrieved 8/2/2019 from: /http://journalofcosmology.com/JOC20/Whitehead_PR_Part5_Final_Interpratation.pdf

Wong, K. (2014). The 1 percent difference. *Scientific American., 311*(3), 100.

Wong, N. C. (2015). The 10 000-hour rule. *Canadian Urological Association Journal, 9*(9–10), 299.

Yarris, L. (2010). Untangling the quantum entanglement behind photosynthesis: Berkeley scientists shine new light on green plant secrets. Berkeley Lab. http://newscenter.lbl.gov/2010/05/10/untangling-quantumentanglement/

Zhang, G., Patuwo, B. E., & Hu, M. Y. (1998). Forecasting with artificial neural networks: The state of the art. *International Journal of Forecasting, 14*(1), 35–62.

Part II
Regulation

Chapter 4
Pedagogy

This section covers regulation and discusses the pedagogical practices related to the development of metacognition, self-regulation, self-directed learning, self-authorship, and ultimately self-transformation. This chapter will define and describe basic educational practices that support and promote metacognition and self-regulation. This will be done through both research and narrative, as in the earlier chapters, but this section will also include the stories, perceptions, and practices of professors from the Program For the Advancement of Learning (PAL) around the subject of metacognition and how it is taught. The perspectives and experiences of educators like these PAL professors, who have made the development and teaching of metacognition their lives' work, can provide valuable pedagogical insight. The varied perspectives of these interview subjects were analyzed using an inductive/deductive multi-level coding scheme. Coding procedures for data analysis were adapted from Corbin and Strauss' (1990) grounded theory approach and the earlier inductive–deductive analysis approach of Schutz (1972). Data was collected over two interviews, roughly 60 min long and semi-structured around 11 questions regarding pedagogical and neurological perspectives on metacognition, and how they integrate new scientific knowledge into their practice. Coding drawn from these interviews produced a description of a metacognitive teaching strategy that could be applied widely across educational settings.

4.1 Entering the Field

I graduated from Curry with the conviction to be a great teacher. I knew it. Otherwise, I would not have made it this far. How we perceive ourselves is fundamental to our motivation. Our self-perception motivates us toward success or failure. When I perceived success and failure as polarities, I withdrew as far as I could from responsibility, or anything, I felt there was a good chance of failing. When I learned that failure was only made possible by success, I discovered failure could be carefully

P. R. Hulbig, *The Pedagogy of Self-Authorship*,
https://doi.org/10.1007/978-3-031-41436-7_4

avoided or beaten back with effort. After graduating college, I believed in myself, and in my ideas. I wanted to show the world that you could teach in a way that maximized learning through empowering the student. With my experience and enlightened way of looking at thinking, I felt I was going to make a tremendous impact on the way children were taught. But then I got my first teaching job.

My first job was as a public school educational assistant in a third-grade classroom. Before I started, I was briefed on what to expect. This was the beginning of the inclusion movement in public education. I was going to be a one-to-one support person for two students, who in the past would have been excluded from a general education classroom because of their behavioral presentation. One was diagnosed with attention deficit hyperactivity disorder (ADHD) and the other was diagnosed with pervasive developmental delay (PDD). I was honest about my lack of familiarity with PDD, but I was sure about my knowledge and understanding of ADHD. I was told that I would be trained in physical restraint when it came up in the natural course of events, but I was not sure what that meant.

4.2 Pedagogical Perspectives on Metacognition

Metacognitive interventions have been tremendously important to pedagogy, particularly in supporting individuals with neurologically based learning disabilities in academic settings (Brown, 1978; Druckman & Bjork, 1994; Dunlosky & Metcalfe, 2009; Dweck, 2017; Webb, 1989). Moreover, metacognitive self-regulation is considered to be among the most impactful approaches to supporting the academic needs of learners who come from poor and disadvantaged backgrounds (Bransford et al., 2000; Quigley et al., 2019) Many curricular approaches have achieved success integrating research on metacognition into their programs (Dweck, 2008; Medina, 2011; Tanner, 2012; Webb, 1989). Metacognition has been a defining feature of successful education routines (Bransford et al., 2000; Hattie, 2012), and many researchers (Mancini et al., 1991; Pace, 1991; Price, 1991; Weinert, 1987) have identified various ways metacognitive processes affect learning.

Metacognition has also had a strong influence on the development of special education interventions and programs (Dumont et al., 2010; Wong, 1986). Early metacognitive research into specific learning disabilities (SLD) often involved the teaching of phonemic awareness and the development of efficient reading and studying skills (Wong, 1986). Discoveries that regulation skills correlated with low blood flow to regions of the brain's frontal lobes, like what is seen in ADHD (Amen, 1995), led to the identification of a broader category of learning disability termed executive dysfunction (Miller, 2006). Investigation into the nature of executive dysfunction has not only greatly impacted the study of students with learning disabilities like ADHD, but has also led to new diagnostic procedures and treatments for elderly patients with a behavioral-variant form of frontotemporal dementia (Wong et al., 2018).

A common research model in this domain is contrasting high- and low-achieving students in relation to their degree of self-monitoring and evaluation (Andrade, 1999). The highest performing and most independent learners use a number of metacognitive strategies such as: setting goals, planning, monitoring performance, restructuring physical/social conditions to improve learning, managing time efficiently, and self-evaluation (Zimmerman, 2010). Alternatively, those with poor metacognitive skills tend to be identified as a person with SLD and demonstrate a poorer ability to maintain and generalize learned skills (Wong, 1986) or monitor their own comprehension, particularly in reading (Garner, 1981; Garner & Kraus, 1981; Garner & Taylor, 1982). This metacognitive inability to identify inconsistencies in comprehension was earlier described by Markman (1979) as a "comprehension failure" (p. 987). The fact that SLD students demonstrate weaker than average metacognitive skills is perhaps best exemplified by Garner and Kraus (1981) who discovered that most SLD students wrongly assume that the purpose of reading is effective decoding rather than understanding meaning. This assumption was part of a wider mindset that affected the quality of reading comprehension, impacting the SLD student's ability to connect specific tasks to new problems, situations, or interpretational meaning (Dweck, 2017).

Flavell (1979) helped to clarify the nature of these comprehension failures by identifying four interacting processes of metacognition involved with cognitive monitoring. The first process was metacognitive knowledge (MK), which he described as "cognitive creatures" (Flavell, 1979, p. 906). MK is the factual part of knowledge that describes how things are (Anderson, 1981). MK falls into three categories: declarative knowledge (Efklides, 2008), procedural knowledge, and conditional knowledge (Schmitt & Newby, 1986; Schraw & Moshman, 1995). Declarative knowledge is knowledge of personal strengths and weaknesses that work to support an individual's procedural knowledge, which is a general knowledge of the steps involved in how to do a task (Pierce, 2003). Procedural knowledge comes embedded in the context of an event, making it difficult to transfer abstractly (Clark & Voogel, 1985) and producing knowledge that is situationally conditional. For example, an individual who possesses conditional knowledge of an activity would not only be aware of the strategies involved with their thinking when approaching the task, but they would also be aware of the internal and external environmental conditions that would best facilitate their actions and learning.

Flavell's (1979) three other metacognitive processes, metacognitive experience, goal/task, and actions/strategies, have since been consolidated into one category described as metacognitive regulation. Metacognitive regulation includes selecting, predicting, planning, scheduling, goal setting, allocating resources, ordering, coordinating actions and strategies to accomplish a goal. Nelson (1996) described metacognitive control as the real-time conscious and non-conscious decisions made based on the output of a monitoring process. He felt that "Control processes are revealed by the behaviors a person engages in as a function of monitoring," (Nelson, 1996, p. 4) making them accessible for objective scientific study. For example, when a learner notices internal frustration building at a difficult problem, through her use of cognitive monitoring her behavior will change to regulate these feelings. This change in behavior would be considered metacognitive control, which could be identified and potentially measured scientifically. Nelson's framework and research have enabled broader interdisciplinary communication between the fields of neurology, cognitive psychology, and developmental psychology, which have been able to use similar methodologies in their approach to the subject (Schwartz & Perfect, 2002).

Interdisciplinary research into metacognitive monitoring and control increasingly shows its critical role in the maintenance and development of self-regulation (Winne & Azevedo, 2022). Moreover, it was found that pedagogical practices that used metacognitive, learning-to-learn techniques were also most likely to produce more independence and self-directed learning (Winne and Azevedo, 2022) and self-transformation (Hulbig, 2021).

4.3 The World of Work

For my first day of school, I dressed up and wore a goofy tie that I knew any third-grade student would love. First, I was introduced to my PDD student and his father. He was a brilliantly quirky student and seemed to immediately trust me. My ADHD student was the complete opposite. He was guarded and stand-offish with me. When it came time for morning work, I noticed he was not doing it. I asked if he would like a pencil and if he needed any help. He took the pencil and began to write his name in a slow, struggling way. All of a sudden, he yelled, "Fuck this Shit!" as he broke his pencil in half, threw the pieces, and flipped over his desk. At this point, my first formal introduction to physical intervention began.

I had never seen behavior like this, from any person, child or adult. He threw whatever I thought I knew about learning into turmoil and laid bare my inexperience as a teacher. How could I teach someone I could not even get near? His rages were often barely predictable. Everything I thought I knew about education was called into question. The behavior modification techniques I had been taught in college actually had the tendency to provoke his explosive behavior. Plus, you could not ignore the fact that this little boy was deeply hurt by his tantrums and the effect his behavior had on those around him. It was as if he had rage attacks like epileptics have seizures. At times, he was so truly sorry it was heartbreaking. But at other times, he was shockingly condescending, insulting, and manipulative. When I tried to be firm and consistent, he would melt down. When I tried to be accommodating and understanding, he would take advantage of the situation until it provoked a tantrum or other dangerous situation.

The individuals enlisted by administrators to help me with this student were soon out of supportive solutions. No one knew what to do with this child. At this time there was no program to offer, and there were no clear schools of thought that could be used to frame the situation.

There was no history of trauma. He had a wonderfully loving mother and a compassionate and involved stepfather. The classroom teacher I was there to support gave her all to this student, and the staff were consummate professionals in all ways possible. His behavior was so reactive it was dangerous to be any other way. He was obsessed with power and manipulation. Physical interventions were long, threatening struggles. Remorse came with wailing sobs of apology or frightening threats about what would happen next time.

After three months of employment, the school was ready to throw in the towel. I was told if I could not demonstrate some type of improvement, then it was not safe to keep him in school. I would fail my first student. I would fail again.

However, I had become metacognitive, and, rather than seeing the event as a failure, I saw a tremendous opportunity to test my ideas about learning, the ones I had developed in college with the help of Joe, Ned, and others. This was a real-world test, and I had an opportunity to work creatively with him without the fear of being told that I was doing something wrong because, at this stage, my theories on intervention were as good as anyone else's. In the midst of repeated failure, I saw the potential for success, a potential to learn from this student as I helped him.

Through careful observation and reflection, I noticed that there were aspects of his behavior program that were actually setting him off. I also realized that there were patterns of communication that he perceived as condescending that also set him off. I realized I could, in fact, get close enough to communicate, commiserate, and empathize with him. He was actually desperate for control. I came to understand his mind and his disability, and I could predict his unpredictable behavior and use that knowledge to influence his thinking and actually teach him. It turned out that he was extremely smart, yet no one knew how smart he was before this point since his out of control and oppositional behavior made it impossible to assess him in any formal fashion.

By our next progress meeting, the number of physical interventions he required had dropped drastically. By the end of the year, they were even more infrequent. By the end of the next year, this student who was exploding more than three times a week was no longer exploding at all and blended seamlessly into a mainstream class with his peers.

I was clearly doing something right, but what was it? I continued to use metacognition to build theories on teaching, learning, and behavior. When they were shown to be wrong, I would tweak them, change them, or throw them out. In the day-to-day search for real-life solutions, my students were succeeding in measurable ways. Still, I wasn't really sure exactly what I was doing that was producing this success. Grand ideas were put to the side because I needed to learn. How could these kinds of students be successful? No schooling could have provided the kind of education that my daily work was presenting me with, and because I approached the experience metacognitively, I learned more.

As time went by, my ability to work successfully with students with learning and emotional disabilities enabled me to secure a job rebuilding and improving a substantially separate special education classroom in a small public school. My success there led me to be given the responsibility of creating, from the ground up, similar programs for students with learning and emotional needs at both the elementary and middle school level of a much larger school district. The ability to build my own programs from the ground up and run them was an unprecedented opportunity for me, one that complimented my learning style in a way that I do not think I can fully express here. I had finally found a place in the world that respected my talents. I had achieved a place where my insights and achievements were valued, and people genuinely were working to understand and teach all children.

I knew that my knowledge and experience were valuable assets to the school district, but there was so much work to do. There were so many intractable problems related to the day-to-day function of the program that there was little time for anything else. Problems with no clear solutions needed to be solved every day for the success of the program. Plus, I needed to figure out how to teach four content subjects to three or more separate grades, differentiated to account for the diversity of ability and disability. In addition, there was a seemingly endless stream of writing, testing, meetings, and consulting related to the many complicated Individual Educational Programs (IEPs) I was entrusted to implement. Also, I was responsible for the development and implementation of behavior plans, orchestrating crisis interventions, and managing the day-to-day drama that was the lives of my students. How was I managing all this? For me, the answer to this question was best expressed in the lyrics of a song:

> When you love something you develop the mental capacity to reach that thing you love. (Ridenhour, 2007)

4.4 Self-regulated Learning

Self-regulated learning (SRL) refers to the process of actively controlling and managing one's own learning through setting goals, monitoring progress, and making adjustments as needed. As early as 1978 Brown questioned whether the phenomena coming to be described as metacognition resulted from various interactions between conscious and unconscious components of learning. The idea that there are identifiable conscious and unconscious factors that affect a person's ability to regulate their own learning formed the basis of SRL theory. The idea of SRL grew out of work done by Bandura (1997) in social cognitive theory. SRL introduced a broad concept of learning that described how many aspects of behavior are coordinated to contribute to achieving a goal (Lewis & Litchfield, 2011).

SRL suggests that development requires an individual to give simultaneous attention to both the cognitive and metacognitive dimensions of their reasoning (Kuiper & Pesut, 2004), and it has been suggested that metacognition is a substructure of broader self-regulation (Schraw, 2006). However, SRL interventions, to date, have focused on using concrete learning tasks within specific learning contexts (Dignath et al. 2008; Schuster et al., 2020). The task-specific nature of SRL approaches has limited transference between tasks when compared with metacognitive skills that are more developmental and generalizable (Schuster et al., 2020). The ability to take a learning strategy that is effective in one situation and apply it to a different yet analogous situation where it could also be effective is called "far transfer." Metacognitive skills, when paired with SRL strategies in a hybrid manner, have demonstrated both near and far skill transfer (Schuster et al., 2020), and have been shown to enhance performance across learning domains (Cromley & Kunze, 2020; Ohtani & Hisasaka, 2018). This seems to be because of the integrative nature of metacognitive understanding, which abstracts specific strategies of SRL into categorical approaches that increase the flexibility of thinking by providing a menu of response options to problems.

SRL attempts to consider all the processes that stimulate and maintain cognitions, behaviors, and affects, and develop declarative, procedural, and the conditional knowledge of the learning process (Murphy, 2009; Pierce, 2003; Zimmerman, 2010). Early research provided evidence for the idea that SRL is a transactional process (Boekaerts, 1999) that involves the dynamic interaction of multiple factors (Pintrich, 2002). Researchers like Garcia & Pintrich (1993) identified that SRL included critical emotive and motivational links to cognition. Garcia conceptualized SRL as extending beyond the conscious cognitive components of metacognition to include an individual's environmental and social experience. This approach deeply considers the impact of resource-management strategies in the regulation of cognition, motivation, and effort.

Bandura's (1989) initial notions of behavior resulting from the imitation of role models, such as parents and teachers, through exposure and observation, expanded on earlier environmentalist and behaviorist models to include social reinforcement as drivers of behavior. SRL has attempted to bridge aspects of cognitive, environmental, and behavior to identify how individuals can produce adaptive behavior (Zimmerman, 1990). Ideas involved with SRL have become hard to partition from ideas of metacognition. Metacognition's central tenet of self-reflection and learning about learning seems to indicate an active quality of learning and growth, while SRL is an investigation of specific impacts on self-regulation and strategies that are used to address these impacts. Generally speaking, these two approaches are talking about similar features of learning and regulation, though occasionally using different vocabulary or definitions. Future investigations will undoubtedly help to clear up these confusions by illuminating the connections between these fields of research.

The most important aspects of SRL and metacognitive research have been on pedagogy and identifying modes/techniques that enhance the effectiveness of teaching and learning. For example, strong research (Dunlosky et al., 2013) has differentiated between teaching (Hattie, 2012) and learning (Simmons, 2019) techniques that are most effective in supporting learning and development. Much of this research presents a direct challenge to traditional practices and beliefs about teaching and learning, particularly those used most frequently in banking-style schools (Freire, 2018). Often teachers in these institutions are not given the time, or professional development, needed to familiarize and integrate this research into their daily practice (Wong et al., 2018). However, the impact and effectiveness of metacognition and SRL has fundamentally changed the way educators and researchers approach their craft. This is an impact that will no doubt continue to affect the field of education.

4.5 My Pedagogy

When teaching metacognition, I try to keep my own metacognition in sharp focus. It is important for me to remember that I engage in metacognition to forge a level of stability and predictability for myself. This is why I always structure my sessions with students around those things that are producing stress in their lives, and the future demands they must plan for. I tell them that first, we will focus on any immediate crisis of the moment, then we will plan for the future, and then we will talk about metacognition, learning, and the brain. Focusing on the crisis of the moment generally consists of bringing up deadlines that are fast approaching, or passed. It can also be a time when the students can bring up personal problems that are impacting their day-to-day life and weighing heavy on their hearts and minds.

Planning for the future involves a student creating game plans for completing certain tasks, setting goals, and deadlines, plus, studying how similar events occurred in the past. During this stage I directly teach metacognitive regulation. I try to do two things. First, I try to make the program as discussion- based as possible, and target areas where the student has shown either difficulty or interest. Then, I directly teach students about nine cognitive components of problem-solving and how they function, which is modeled on Dr. Webb's (1989) original cognitive ladder model. My hope is to stimulate an enjoyment and habit of thinking about the brain and how thinking works.

If there is a problem affecting students, examining what they think about the problem, what the potential solutions of the problem are, and then attempting to execute a solution, are themselves therapeutic. When success is achieved through this process, students will tend to keep utilizing metacognitive techniques that worked for them. This is because metacognition offers the possibility of a solution to problems, even when there is no clear solution, and compels action even if the action is new and ambiguous. The process itself can come to be seen as a way to keep at bay the crippling anxieties that generally prevent individuals from doing anything about their situation.

Anxiety is an emotional energy that lacks a clear target. It is an energy that is unsure of where it belongs and how it should be expressed. A big piece of the work I do with students is to try and figure out where this emotional energy is coming from so that we can direct that emotional energy at the problem that is producing it. Without support, it is possible for the true source of the student's anxiety to become obscured by psychological defense mechanisms.

When I first start working with a student, my initial metacognitive lesson is to discuss illusions, cognitive biases, and the subconscious factors that affect perception. Often the things that are causing instability are things our defenses are trying to protect us from because they are scary, and we don't even know where to begin to understand them, not to mention how to handle them. We work to keep these things outside of our conscious thought. I try to make it clear to the student, upfront, that we are going to be looking for these hidden and scary impediments to their learning.

4.6 Dr. Webb and the Program for the Advancement of Learning (PAL)

One of the first individuals to champion the educational use of metacognition to help students with learning disabilities better regulate their learning was Webb (1989). Dr. Webb established the PAL Program at Curry College in 1970. Curry is a small four-year liberal arts college in Milton, Massachusetts, with a historic emphasis on developmental education. The college's mission emphasizes, "an inclusive community of diverse learners and educators, committed to continuing our legacy of developing effective communicators with reflective and critical thinking skills" (Curry College Mission Statement, 2020). Today, Curry has a population of 2,800 students, 475 of whom receive services for learning disabilities. PAL was the nation's first college-level program for students with language-based learning difficulties, and it is considered one of the top schools for students with learning disabilities (Sorensen, 2018).

Dr. Webb established PAL to serve students who had the intelligence and drive to succeed in college, but whose history of learning differences posed a major obstacle to their success. Dr. Webb, herself, was no stranger to the obstacles that can obscure one's path to success. Born in 1916 to Lithuanian immigrants who originally named her Goldie, she began using the name Gertrude after a teacher directed her to change it because they considered Goldie too ethnic a name for Roxbury, Massachusetts at that time (McKenna, 2012). She graduated from Teachers' College of Boston in 1937 and achieved a level of education that was uncommon for women at that time. With her husband's support, she became an important leader in the development of Massachusetts Chapter 766 laws that guarantee educational programs for students with special needs (McKenna, 2012).

According to her daughter Heidi, Gertrude's lifelong passion for supporting those with learning differences came from her experience raising her own children and seeing the struggles of students with learning disabilities in her classroom (personal conversation, 2016). When Dr. Webb was director of the PAL program, she would leave a communal jigsaw puzzle on a table for students to work on. Students who lingered to work on the puzzle would be treated to her story of a young boy she once taught who struggled with reading and writing at the school but excelled at such puzzles. Dr. Webb would describe how this experience profoundly affected her thinking about learning because while she excelled at reading and writing, the weaknesses that defined this student's disability, her analogous weakness with jigsaw puzzles was far from being considered a disability. This made her think about individual strengths and weaknesses differently, and question exactly what is meant when a person is described as learning disabled (Webb, personal conversation, 1992).

Dr. Webb's son Marc described her approach to teaching and learning as to first identify what the student can do well and focus on that. While not ignoring weaknesses, she would not make them the focus but allow those things to come along as the student built up the self-confidence needed to best address them properly (McKenna, 2012). Dr. Webb elaborated on this idea in an interview with the Boston Globe in

1992 where she said, "If we can look at all children as potentially successful learners, then we will strengthen their self-image, and they will bring increased energy to the more difficult tasks we would expect of them" (McKenna, 2012). These ideas illuminate a common theme relative to metacognition and the important role of the teacher in developing a student's self-efficacy by developing an understanding of their strengths, weaknesses, and self-confidence.

Webb's approach was to teach self-regulatory behaviors by having students develop a close learning relationship with a PAL professor who would work with the students individually or in small groups. Students would initially meet twice a week for 1 h and 30 min with their PAL professors to help them develop the organizational, regulatory, planning, and social skills needed to succeed in their college course work. Webb felt that group work was a particularly important feature because it allowed students to form learning relationships not only with their professor but also with their peers. Today, the PAL program has expanded on this idea, developing many leadership opportunities for students to mentor and support peers.

Metacognitive knowledge was bolstered through the use of a workbook called *Tuning in to Learning* (Webb, 1989), which introduced students to information about their personal traits and their relationship to the neuro-cognitive functions of the brain. It contained relevant information on learning and sections designed to aid students in their understanding of their learning disability. This workbook was based on an earlier workbook called *Secrets to Successful Learning* (Webb, 1986). Webb strongly believed that understanding the emerging research on the brain was important for learners to come to understand their brain's various functions and bring them under their unitary control (Webb, 1983). She believed that learning disabilities were the result of regions of the brain not working in an integrated fashion and that teachers could, "help our students develop competence through an understanding of the need for the brains to work together" (Webb, 1983, pg. 515).

Dr. Webb felt that by providing a supportive system of self-development, students with learning disabilities could discover their personal and intellectual strengths. For Webb, teachers needed to connect with their students so that discussions about learning and how the brain worked would seem to be natural and not forced. The use of the Wechsler Adult Intelligence Scale (WAIS), which measures cognitive abilities such as memory, attention, and problem-solving, provided a foundation for the idea of metacognition. At PAL, the WAIS was not simply used as a diagnostic tool, but also as a mechanism to direct conversations about learning back to the student (Webb, 1983). In this role, the WAIS became a bridge between highly abstract notions about the brain and learning, and the everyday lived experiences of students. For example, the subtests of the WAIS could be used to both identify a student's specific skills related to hemispheric function and identify how a student could use these strengths to overcome their weaknesses.

In *Tuning in to Learning,* Webb (1989) used many interactive elements and visual models to support understanding of the book's various concepts. Two of her unique constructions were the cognitive ladder and the hierarchical model of active learning. Both were visual models constructed to aid students in their conceptualizations and discussions of how the mind functions. The cognitive ladder, at first glance, appears to be a conceptualization much like Bloom's (1956) taxonomy. Both arrange certain abilities of the mind in a hierarchical format, with the difference that Webb put memory in place of knowledge near the bottom of the hierarchy, and universal truth in place of evaluation at the top. However, Webb's intention was not to use her cognitive ladder to organize educational goals and objectives. The cognitive ladder was intended to represent a cognitive hierarchy of forms of thinking, more in line with Vygotsky's (1934) "tools of thought" (p. 176). The cognitive ladder, like the WAIS, was used to bring abstract components of the mind into an individual's conscious attention to be examined, developing a student's deeper understanding of their mind (Table 4.1).

The hierarchical model of active learning (Webb, 1989) was developed out of another theme that was equally central to Webb's philosophy on metacognitive education. This was the development of the student's sense of self, which for SLD students was frequently damaged by their difficulties learning in school (Webb, 1972). Webb's hierarchical model of active learning was a visual representation of the developmental dynamics underlying motivation, competence, independence and efficacy. For Webb, hope was an important ingredient for success, providing the motivation to work through life's many adversities (Table 4.2).

Without hope, the trauma of failure in school was amplified, even crippling (Webb, 1972). Maintaining hope throughout the developmental process was important since hope was the force drawing the learner forward. Success was a critical element in this process because hope was derived from personal success. Students who achieve enough personal success would develop the hope they need to engage in something new, extending themselves into new areas of learning (Webb, 1989). However, too much failure could cause a student to feel hopeless and retreat from new learning and challenges. With hope, an individual could endure and persevere to find success. Without hope a student would shrink away from challenges, see little chance of

Table 4.1 The cognitive ladder

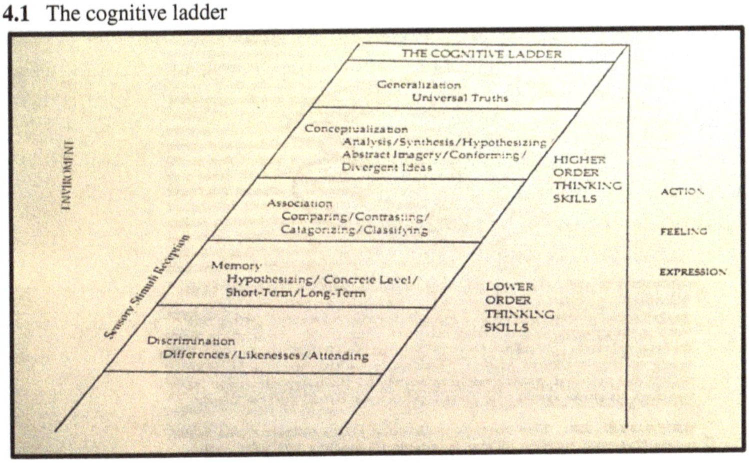

Note Webb's Cognitive Ladder (1989)

Table 4.2 Hierarchical model of active learning

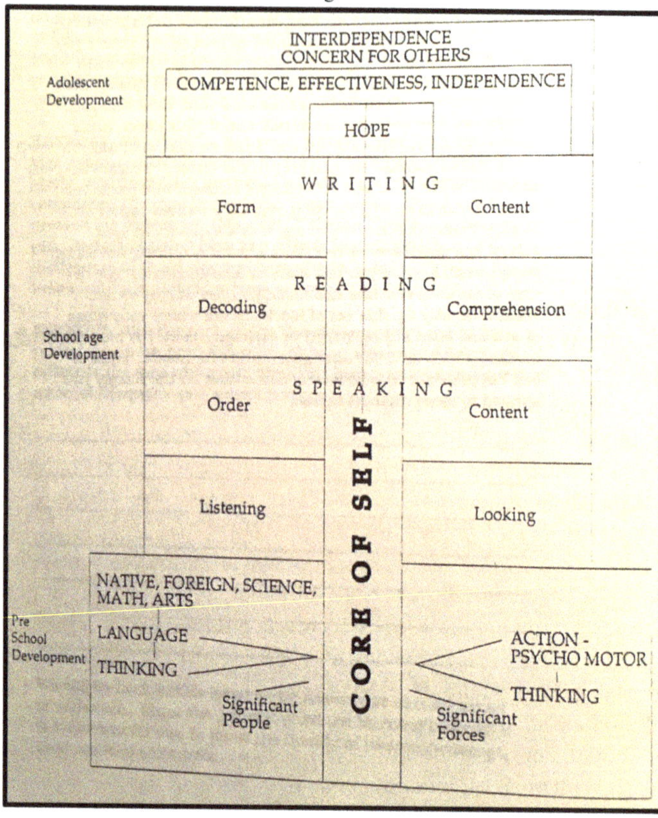

Note The Hierarchical Model of Active Learning (Webb, 1989)

success, and become hopeless. In many ways, Webb's hierarchical model of active learning was an early conceptualization of how the growth-oriented mindset delineated by Carol Dweck (Dweck, 1999, 2017; Dweck & Leggett, 1988) is developed in the individual learner.

Webb's most important insight into metacognitive learning is embodied in the basic structure of the PAL program, using the student–teacher relationship to support metacognitive regulation. Upon entering the program, students are paired with a PAL professor who meets with the student individually or in small groups to discuss their learning, planning, and organization. This metacognitive relationship between student and teacher facilitates personal conversations that evolve over time with the learner's development of self-efficacy and regulation. The goal of these conversations is for the student to develop and apply insights to personal responsibilities and goals. The teacher's responsibility in this process is to guide their student through the personal, interpersonal, and social demands of their lives at school, helping the students to develop strategies to meet these demands. Through an interactive process, the student's powers of reflection, self-assessment, personal improvement, and self-regulation are established, providing a regulatory foundation for the development of new skills.

This interactive process of metacognitive learning was first labeled by PAL professor Dian Goss (Adelizzi & Goss, 1995) as the learning conversation (Pennini, 2006). According to Sue Pennini (2006), the term was first described in the literature by Harris-Augenstein & Thomas (1991) as "a form of dialogue about a learning experience in which the learner reflects on some event or activity in the past. Ultimately, it is intended that people will internalize such conversations so that they are able to review the learning experience systematically for themselves, but at the beginning, the learning conversation is carried out with the assistance of a teacher or tutor" (p. 180, cited in Pennini, 2006). Goss separated her concept, however, by identifying listening as a primary feature of this process (Pennini, 2006). She described these conversations as "about her students *from* them rather than from a report *about* them" (Pennini, 2006, p. 181). This study determined that PAL professors have continued to develop and refine the learning conversation into a highly skilled and specialized approach to learning. Due to the level of complexity and degree of individualization needed to engage in this kind of learning, the program requires senior lecturers to possess a doctorate and extensive educational experience working with neurologically diverse populations.

Curry College has a long and rich history of supporting those with learning disabilities. Alexander Graham Bell, the American inventor who struggled with an SLD, taught and served as chancellor of Curry's School of Oratory in the early 1900s (Abrahams, 2016). Regardless of whether it was always understood, Curry has played a unique role supporting SLD individuals at this level. Since Gertrude Webb's establishment of PAL in the 1970s, Curry and the program have grown both in size and prestige (Sorensen, 2018).

4.6.1 General PAL Practices

PAL professors meet with their students, one on one or in small groups, to have dialectic discussions about learning, organization, planning, studying, and the science of the brain. PAL professors use these discussions to focus their students' attention on potential areas of difficulty to promote problem-solving. These personal conversations between the student and the teacher evolve over time, with the learners developing a level of self-understanding and self-regulation. These are interactions that engage in supporting a student's understanding of the complexity of their own learning and the development of self-sufficiency.

The professor's responsibility in this process is to teach students about their learning and guide them through the demands of their lives in college, supporting the student in their development of the skills and strategies needed to meet these demands. Frequently, living with an SLD leads to a level of cognitive rigidity and pessimism. The PAL approach is to be supportive and help the student develop a personal practice of strategic thinking, planning, and organization that are needed to be successful as college students. Conversations about metacognition encourage, illustrate, and educate students about patterns of thought and behavior that can be used to address their unique learning profiles. These conversations were initially identified by Diane Goss as the Learning Conversation and elaborated by Sue Peninni (2006).

Such a conversational structure has considerable historic roots, as does the practice of identifying the student's strengths and weaknesses for the purpose of using one's strengths to overcome their weaknesses. Nietzsche (1974) believed people should "survey all the strengths and weaknesses of their nature and then fit them into an artistic plan until every one of them appears as art and reason and even weaknesses delight the eye," (Nietzsche, 1974, pp. 232–233). Dr. Gertrude Webb also understood this and made understanding using personal strengths to overcome weaknesses as a foundational PAL technique. With the support of a professor, students learn to examine their strengths and weaknesses to break down the fear and helplessness associated with their neurological conditions.

PAL is very much a college class in the classic sense of the word. However, a PAL class is highly specialized and individualized to study a specific student's learning and development. A learning conversation is used to convey and connect a professor's depth of research and experiential knowledge with the real and everyday learning experiences of their students. Students learn both what the research has to say about learning, as an abstract subject of human inquiry, but also how to connect knowledge to a real-time personal investigation of their own learning as they respond to the demands of their life.

In the preface of the book, *A Closer Look* (Adelizzi & Goss, 1995), Dr. Webb identified the following features of PAL pedagogy:

1. Just about all students start school wanting to learn.
2. Learning is synonymous with growth.
3. Those who do not learn in our schools fail to do so because they have not found their way.
4. Good teachers serve as "coaches" to both those successful at school learning and to those who have not found their way through the conventional system; they understand that the latter think differently.
5. Teacher/coaches are excellent observers; they focus on the uniqueness of their learners.
6. Teacher/coaches are good questioners, encouraging students to "talk," to discuss developing concepts as they clarify their thinking while identifying their preferred learning styles.
7. Teacher/coaches are deep listeners—they search for the meaning behind what they hear, adding that insight to their observations, putting the pieces of the learning puzzle together.
8. Believing that a student's understanding of his/her learning style preferences is foundational to metacognition, teacher/coaches facilitate this understanding in their learners, suggesting how their preferences might be used to bring success.

9. Teacher/coaches do reality checks, encouraging students to evaluate the usefulness of the application of their newly acquired metacognitive knowledge.
10. Teacher/coaches respect their students' potential for success, coaching them as they strive to become independent, competent, and effective learners, able to take charge of their own learning while working collaboratively in a very competitive society (Adelizzi & Goss, 1995, pg. 1–2).

What a PAL professor does is identify their student's strengths and weaknesses, particularly hidden weaknesses and strengths. A secondary goal is to help their students embrace their own individuality and discover how to live a whole and satisfying life. Through dialectic conversations a student's understanding of their disability is made conscious, providing the student with a conceptual framework to overcome and address it. A high level of self-examination is cultivated and practiced through honest self-reflection with an eye for behavioral patterns and habits of mind.

References

Adelizzi, J. U., & Goss, D. B. (Eds.). (1995). *A closer look: Perspectives and reflections on college students with learning disabilities*. Curry College.

Amen, D. (1995). *Images into the mind: A radical new look at understanding and changing behavior*. Mindworks Press.

Anderson, J. R. (1981). *Cognitive skills and their acquisition*. Lawrence Erlbaum.

Andrade, H. G. (1999, April 20). Student self-assessment: At the intersection of metacognition and authentic assessment. Paper presented at the annual meeting of the American Educational Research Association, Montreal, Canada.

Bandura, A. (1997). *Self-efficacy: The exercise of control*. W. H Freeman.

Bandura, A. (1989). Human agency in social cognitive theory. *American Psychologist, 44*(9), 1175.

Boekaerts, M. (1999). Self-regulated learning: Where we are today. *International Journal of Educational Research, 31*(6), 445–457.

Bransford, J. D., Brown, A. L., & Cocking, R. R. (2000). *How people learn* (Vol. 11). National Academy Press.

Brown, A. L. (1978). Knowing when, where, and how to remember; a problem of metacognition. *Advances in Instructional Psychology, 1*.

Cromley, J. G., & Kunze, A. J. (2020). Metacognition in education: Translational research. *Translational Issues in Psychological Science, 6*(1), 15–20. https://doi.org/10.1037/tps0000218

Clark, R. E., & Voogel, A. (1985). Transfer of training principles for instructional design. *Educational Communication and Technology Journal, 33*(2), 113–123. http://www.jstor.org/stable/30220955

Corbin, J. M., & Strauss, A. (1990). Grounded theory research: Procedures, canons, and evaluative criteria. *Qualitative Sociology, 13*(1), 3–21.

Dignath, C., Buettner, G., & Langfeldt, H. P. (2008). How can primary school students learn self-regulated learning strategies most effectively? A meta-analysis on self-regulation training programmes. *Educational Research Review, 3*(2), 101–129.

Druckman, D. E., & Bjork, R. A. (1994). *Learning, remembering, believing: Enhancing human performance*. National Academy Press.

Dumont, H., Istance, D., & Benavides, F. (Eds.). (2010). *The nature of learning, using research to inspire practice*. http://www.educ.ethz.ch/pro/litll/oecdbuch.pdf

Dunlosky, J., & Metcalfe, J. (2009). *Metacognition*. SAGE.

Dunlosky, J., Rawson, K.A.,Marsh, E.J.,Nathan, M. J. & Willingham, D. T. (2013). 'Improving students' learning with effective learning techniques: Promising directions from cognitive and educational psychology', *Psychological Science in the Public Interest, 14*(1), 4–58.

Dweck, C. S. (1999). Caution-praise can be dangerous. *American Educator, 23*, 4–9.

Dweck, C. (2017). *Mindset-updated edition: Changing the way you think to fulfil your potential.* Hachette UK.

Dweck, C. S. (2008). Brainology transforming students' motivation to learn. *Independent School, 67*(2), 110–119.

Dweck, C. S., & Leggett, E. L. (1988). A social-cognitive approach to motivation and personality. *Psychological Review, 95*(2), 256.

Efklides, A. (2008). Metacognition: Defining its facets and levels of functioning in relation to self-regulation and co-regulation. *European Psychologist, 13*(4), 277–287. https://doi.org/10.1027/1016-9040.13.4.277.

Flavell, J. H. (1979). Metacognition and cognitive monitoring: A new area of cognitive development. *American Psychologist, 34*(10), 906–911. https://doi.org/10.1037/0003-066X.34.10.906

Freire, P. (2018). *Pedagogy of the oppressed.* Bloomsbury Publishing USA. (Original work published in 1968).

Garcia, T., & Pintrich, P. R. (1993). *Self-schemas, motivational strategies and self-regulated learning.* https://eric.ed.gov/?id=ED359234

Garner, R. (1981). Monitoring of passage inconsistency among poor comprehenders: A preliminary test of the 'piecemeal processing' explanation. *The Journal of Educational Research, 74*(3), 159–162.

Garner, R., & Kraus, K. (1981). Good and poor comprehender differences in knowing and regulating reading behaviors. *Educational Research Quarterly, 6*(4), 5–12.

Garner, R., & Taylor, N. (1982). Monitoring of understanding: An investigation of attentional assistance needs at different grade and reading proficiency levels. *Reading Psychology, 3*(1), 1–6.

Harri-Augstein, E. S., & Thomas, L. (1991). *Learning conversations: The self organized learning way to personal and organizational growth.* London: Routledge.

Hattie, J. (2012). *Visible learning for teachers: Maximizing impact on learning.* Routledge.

Hulbig, P. R. (2021). *Fundamental principles of metacognition: A qualitative study of metacognition, pedagogy and transformation.* Lesley University.

Kuiper, R. A., & Pesut, D. J. (2004). Promoting cognitive and metacognitive reflective reasoning skills in nursing practice: Self-regulated learning theory. *Journal of Advanced Nursing, 45*(4), 381–391

Lewis, J., & Litchfield, B. (2011). Effects of self-regulated learning strategies on preservice teachers in an educational technology. *Education*, 455–464.

Mancini, G., Short, R., Mulcahy, R., & Andrews, J. (1991). Social cognition and social competence: Instructional issues. In R. Mulcahy, R. Short, & J. Andrews (Eds.), *Enhancing learning and thinking* (pp. 193–206). Preager

Markman, E. M. (1979). Realizing that you don't understand: Elementary school children's awareness of inconsistencies. *Child Development*, 643–655.

McKenna, K. (2012, September) Gertrude Webb; created program for students with learning disabilities. *Boston Globe.* Retrieved February 22, 2019, from https://www.bostonglobe.com/metro/2012/09/16/gertrude-webb-founded-program-for-advancement-learning-curry-college/1XeBht21Z6qV8whrPzwIdJ/story.html

Medina, J. (2011). *Brain rules: 12 principles for surviving and thriving at work, home, and School.* ReadHowYouWant. Com.

Miller, P. H. (2006). A lot of knowledge is a dangerous thing: Learning in children and adults. *Journal of Cognition and Development, 7*(3), 305–308.

Murphy, E. (2009). A framework for identifying and promoting metacognitive knowledge and control in online discussants. *Canadian Journal of Learning and Technology/La revue canadienne de l'apprentissage et de la technologie, 34*(2).

Nelson, T. O. (1996). Consciousness and metacognition. *American Psychologist, 51*(2), 102–116. https://doi.org/10.1037/0003-066X.51.2.102

Nietzsche, F. W. (1974). *The gay science: With a prelude in German rhymes and an appendix of songs* (Vol. 985). Vintage. http://faculty.georgetown.edu/blattnew/intro/gs290.html

Ohtani, K., & Hisasaka, T. (2018). Beyond intelligence: A meta-analytic review of the Relationship among metacognition, intelligence, and academic performance. *Metacognition and Learning, 13*(2), 179–212.

Pace, S. F. (1991). Government processes for including thinking skills in the curriculum. In R. Mulcahy, R. Short, & J. Andrews (Eds.), *Enhancing Learning and Thinking* (pp. 21–34). New York: Preager.

Pennini, S. W. (2006). College students with learning disabilities: A case study (77) [Doctoral dissertation, Lesley]. https://digitalcommons.lesley.edu/education_dissertations/77

Pierce, W. (2003). Metacognition: Study strategies, monitoring, and motivation. Text version of a workshop presented November 17, 2004, at Prince George's Community College. Retrieved from http://academic.pg.cc.md.us/~wpeirce/MCCCTR/metacognition.htm

Pintrich, P. R. (2002). The role of metacognitive knowledge in learning, teaching, and assessing. *Theory into Practice, 41*(4). 219–225.

Price, M. A. (1991). Teaching thinking to preschoolers. In R. Mulcahy, R. Short, & J. Andrews (Eds.), *Enhancing learning and thinking* (pp. 53–66). New York: Preager.

Quigley, A., Mujis, D., & Stinger, E. (2019) Metacognition and self-regulated learning: guidance Report. *Education Endowment Foundation.* Retrieved March 3, 2019 from https://educationendowmentfoundation.org.uk/tools/guidance-reports/metacognition-and-self-regulated-learning/

Ridenhour, C. (2007). How you sell soul (Time is God refrain) [Recorded by Public Enemy]. How You Sell Soul to A Soulless People Who Sold Their Soul? [CD]. NY: Slam Jamz.

Schmitt, M. C., & Newby, T. J. (1986). Metacognition: Relevance to instructional designing. *Journal of Instructional Development, 9*(4), 29–33. https://doi.org/10.1007/BF02908316

Schraw, G., Crippen, K. J., & Hartley (2006). Promoting self-regulation in science education: Metacognition as part of a broader perspective on learning. *Research in Science Education, 36*, 111–139. https://doi.org/10.1007/s11165-005-3917-8

Schraw, G., & Moshman, D. (1995). Metacognitive theories. *Educational Psychology Review, 7*(4), 351–371. https://doi.org/10.1007/BF02212307

Schuster, C., Stebner, F., Leutner, D., & Wirth, J. (2020). Transfer of metacognitive skills inself-regulated learning: An experimental training study. *Metacognition and Learning*, 1–23.

Schutz, A. (1972). *The phenomenology of the social world*. Northwestern University Press. https://openlibrary.org/books/OL5539309M/The_phenomenology_of_the_social_world

Schwartz, B. L., & Perfect, T. J. (2002). Toward an applied metacognition. In T. J. Perfect & B. L. Schwartz (Eds.), *Applied Metacognition* (pp. 1–14). Cambridge University Press.

Simmons, M. (2019, May 8) Memory & learning breakthrough: It turns out that the ancients were right. accelerated intelligence, *Medium.* Retrieved from: https://medium.com/accelerated-intelligence/memory-learning-breakthrough-it-turns-out-that-the-ancients-were-right-7bbd3090d9cc

Sorensen, M. (2018, March 8) Top 10 best colleges for students with learning disabilities. *College Magazine.* Retrieved February 23, 2019, from https://www.collegemagazine.com/top-10-accommodating-schools-students-learning-disabilities/7/

Tanner, K. D. (2012). Promoting student metacognition. *CBE—Life Sciences Education*, 11(2), 113–120.

Vygotsky, L. S. (1934) *Thinking and Speech*, Retrieved September 9, 2019, from: https://www.marxists.org/archive/vygotsky/works/words/Thinking-and-Speech.pdf

Webb, G. (1986). *Secrets to successful learning.* Waltham, Massachusetts.

Webb, G. (1989). *Tuning in to Learning.* Waltham, Massachusetts.

Webb, G. M. (1972). Building a sense of worth. *Academic Therapy, 8*(1), 41–49.

Webb, G. M. (1983). Left/right brains, teammates in learning. *Exceptional Children, 49*(6), 508–515.

Weinert, F. E. (1987). Introduction and overview: Metacognition and motivation as determinants of effective learning and understanding. In F. Weinert & R. Kluwe (Eds.), *Metacognition, Motivation, and Understanding* (pp. 1–16). Erlbaum.

Winne, P., & Azevedo, R. (2022). *Metacognition and self-regulated learning*. The Cambridge Handbook of the Learning Sciences, 93–113.

Wong, B. Y. L. (1986). Metacognition and special education: A review of a view. *Journal of Special Education, 20*(1), 9–29.

Wong, S., Balleine, B. W., & Kumfor, F. (2018). A new framework for conceptualizing symptoms in frontotemporal dementia: From animal models to the clinic. *Brain, 141*(8), 2245–2254. https://doi.org/10.1093/brain/awy123

Zimmerman, B. J. (1990). Self-regulated learning and academic achievement: An overview. *Educational Psychologist, 25*(1), 3–17.

Zimmerman, B. J. (2010). Becoming a self-regulated learner: An overview. *Theory into Practice, 41*(2). https://doi.org/10.1207/s15430421tip4102_2

Chapter 5
Investigation

The discussion of metacognitive pedagogy in this chapter comes largely from the perspective of eight professors who have made the teaching of self-regulation and personal transformation their life's work. It is presented through the interview subject's own words as they were illuminated through the multi-level coding scheme employed for analysis.

These professors were chosen for this interview process because of their senior faculty status at the PAL program, the program whose teachings were responsible for my transformative educational experience. For this reason, a complex multi-level coding scheme was adopted to minimize the impact of personal biases in the analysis and also ground the investigational relationships revealed in the interview subjects' own words. The narrative investigation, which up to this point has been interspersed with the presentation of research from various academic fields, is both data and a research safeguard that demonstrates my subjective and formative experiences to make potential areas of bias apparent to a reader. It is also a demonstration of how first-person, subjective experience can be honestly assessed through objective evaluation.

Initial open coding of the interviews identified statements for relevance regarding the questions asked, or because they seemed interesting, or were identified by the interview subjects as important. This coding was also turned into concise overviews in each subject's own words, expressing their perspectives and what was discussed in the interviews.

5.1 My Role as the Researcher

My role as the researcher in this project has many facets. The nature of the subject of metacognition, its pedagogy, and practices requires a high degree of self-awareness and self-reflection. Because self-reflection is a key component of the subject, I have tried to bring those elements forward for the reader. One way I achieved this was by

P. R. Hulbig, *The Pedagogy of Self-Authorship*,
https://doi.org/10.1007/978-3-031-41436-7_5

choosing research methodologies and procedural approaches to analysis that make reflection on the data visible from many perspectives.

Metacognition also integrates dualistic subjective and objective qualities of mind. For this reason, I have purposefully used first-person narrative to help the reader identify information that is most informatively expressed subjectively. Likewise, I have used third-person narrative when information is most informatively expressed objectively. These shifting narrative styles are analogous to the metacognitive perceptual shifts the mind uses to optimize its cognitive capacity relative to the task at hand. The first-person nature of this section is an example of my aim to bring forward the functional shifts in perceptual understanding metacognition makes possible through both form and format.

As a researcher using a mixed-method approach to investigate metacognition, I committed myself to critically evaluating my thinking by actively identifying my underlying assumptions and actively searching for counterpoints to those assumptions. For example, at the beginning of my doctoral work I was initially fascinated with the self-referencing informational systems being produced by computer programmers working on artificial intelligence (Hofstadter, 1979; Minsky, 1988), and I still believe there is tremendously important work being done in this field that could deeply inform the study of metacognition. However, purposeful research into critics of computational theories led me to critiques (Gödel, 1992; Penrose, 1989) of computational analogs of metacognition and clarified relationships between understanding (Penrose, 1989), metacognitive consciousness (Nelson, 1996), and human development (Keegan, 1982) that became important in my final analysis. This approach has led to a tremendous amount of research, from a wide spectrum of fields and disciplines.

First, and most practically, my role as a researcher was to be an effective interviewer. In this context, my role was to draw out of my interview subjects their insights and the full range of their thoughts on metacognition and its practical practice. To do this, I developed a core structured list of questions. I employed my intuition as a researcher to seize upon opportunities to ask follow-up questions when potential points of interest arose. In my role as an interviewer, I tried to evoke insights through follow-up questions and by inviting interview subjects to share their insights.

The next important facet of my role as a researcher was to detail my embodied, personal experiences with metacognition. This required a deeply personal analysis of how my ideas of metacognition came to be developed through personal experience and reflection. For this, I tried to write a compelling, thoughtful, and exhaustive narrative thick with a description of these experiences and ideas. In this narrative context, I strove to be as honest and detailed as possible to provide the reader with a strong point of reference with which to evaluate the work and its conclusions.

Finally, and most importantly, my role as a researcher was to analyze the data deeply and thoroughly. To identify patterns and common themes in the data, I used a systematic approach of multileveled, organized coding. The multilevel coding scheme included open, axial, and selective coding phases, which were further broken down into a phase of contrasting coding that made subtle patterns in the data visible. Through this analytic procedure, I developed valuable insights into a broad theory of metacognition and its pedagogy that are both insightful and actionable for future research.

In all facets of this research, I tried to remain aware of my standing point, and the lenses through which I viewed and described the data. Careful self-reflection and analysis of my thinking, in conjunction with the support and insight of the professionals on my doctoral committee, provided a crucial perspective. Research into implicit bias (Brownstein, 2019) demonstrates that it is not possible to fully eliminate the shortcomings of my neurological system or the influential lens of my past experience. However, by using the guidance and insight of the professionals on my committee, as well as the tools of reflection built into the study, I have strived to address the existence of biases that may distort perceptions or interpretations of the data.

I do not believe I can be more honest about PAL or the impact the program's approach to metacognitive teaching and learning has had on my individual development. I have had a transformative learning experience. As a result, I have dedicated myself to investigating and identifying metacognition in all of its components. This learning experience has, no doubt, affected my thinking. However, I also believe this experience is the source of valuable points of data. I have tried to present these experiences as plainly and honestly as I can. It is why I have chosen to integrate them into the methodological framework of this study for you to examine and bring into your research.

Mezirow (1975) was the first researcher to identify the central features of transformative learning. Mazirow felt such transformations were most often experienced as the result of a crisis or a major life transition. My experiences with failure in high school fit this formula. However, I also benefited from a third factor that Mezirow came to believe was most important. This third factor is educational experiences induced by a skilled teacher (Mezirow, 1991). His descriptions of the changes in an individual's psychological understanding of the self and how they trigger changes in one's convictions, beliefs, and lifestyle rings very true for me (Mezirow, 1975, 1991).

I have resigned myself to the fact that I am part of this research. My role as a researcher was to collect and present the data related to my personal experiences with metacognition, and how those experiences provoked an educational transformation within me. Care was taken to describe the first-person experiential elements of the educational transformation metacognitive education provokes. This also provided several unique layers of insight to this work: a visceral lived component of the education provided by the PAL program; a historical perspective on the evolution of the program; and the perspective of someone who was both a student and a professor in this program. However, these experiences color my impressions of the data. My hope is that through thick, detailed, careful description and open discussion, any bias that creeps into this study will not go unnoticed and will be addressable in a way that does not detract from the main insights.

My ultimate role as a researcher is to present what I have learned about metacognition and the pedagogical insights of these PAL professors, as well as integrate my years of research into the subject. Through this process, I have been able to penetrate the subject deeply. My personal experiences as a PAL student, a teacher, and a researcher developing and using metacognitive educational techniques have informed my understanding of educational transformation and produced important data to inform the domain of future metacognitive research.

5.2 A Community of Support

Despite all professors in the PAL program ostensibly teaching toward the same goals, approaches were highly individualized. Professors invited the opportunity to express their knowledge about what they did. Some even expressed an interest in hearing how other professors approached the subject of metacognition. Subject A identified wanting to hear specific strategies relative to individual student needs. Subject A:

> …to really hear some of the more interesting things that people have tried and found to be effective in each of the metacognitive areas, executive functioning, all of that. (I'd) be really interested in hearing very specific things, like I had this kid once and …
>
> Just something just to spur the creativity that lets us, I think, create innovative ways of working with students. It kind of sparks things that gets more ideas rolling.

Some even expressed appreciation for the opportunity to share professionally. Subject B noted:

> I think this department used to take time to have collegial conversations of student concerns. There was an effort to kind of put that back together. But we still don't have the time to talk about practice and how we're all using metacognition, or what are we calling metacognition these days.

This idea was corroborated by interview subject G: "I think we don't have enough time to play with ideas like this and then relate them back to our practice."

This need for opportunities for professors to share ideas and experiences pointed to a twofold issue. First, practical research into teaching approaches to metacognitive and self-regulatory skills has been lacking (Tryggvason, 2009), and often focuses on classroom procedures, not the individual interactions between teacher and student seen between PAL professors and their students. There would be educational benefits to identifying specific situational techniques favored by these professors that are aggregated and distributed in a way that makes them more accessible to teachers.

Secondly, the highly interpersonal and individualized nature of the metacognitive education practiced at PAL does not lend itself to easy standardization. Subject C hinted at the difficulty standardizing an approach to what she did:

> It's going to be really hard to translate something like this into a curriculum, it's going to be hard to translate something like this into a program. We have a program here that is staffed by 22 very different, individually different, and high-achieving faculty members, and they're each going to do it in a different way.

5.3 Similarities

Despite the lack of a standardized teaching approach, many broad similarities were identified between the PAL professors and their practice. All agreed with Flavell's (1979) basic definition of metacognition, or expressed it in the more educational terms of Webb (1985), using the phrase learning about learning. However, some identified a feeling that metacognition encompassed more than what is inferred by this definition. For example, Subject D noted: "It's not about just thinking about thinking. It's got to be more than that." Subject G insinuated a desire to expand the definition of metacognition: "I used to define it as thinking about thinking. But now I define it more as being aware of one's thought processes, which includes implicit attitudes, explicit attitudes, emotions ... I really think about thinking as a broader concept than just language."

All identified metacognition as important to their practice. All interview subjects directly identified metacognition as a core educational concept, and expressed feelings similar to Subject C, who said: "I think metacognition as a statement… is what education is all about." Outside of a general agreement of the importance of metacognition and the general definition of thinking about thinking, there were surprising differences.

Some saw the word itself as problematic, "I don't like the word metacognition. I think it sounds like… it's making something sound more intimidating than it is" (Subject E). This was identified as a particular problem with parents by Subject D: "(In) My experience… a lot of parents (do) not get it. And I want them to get it because it's important for them to understand." One way to bridge this gap was offered by Subject E: "I really do see metacognition as self-awareness and in some ways would be more comfortable thinking of it, as aware(ness) of… who you are."

All of the subjects talked about emotion as a confounding factor in the development of metacognitive understanding and thinking. Over half of the subjects specifically identified an underlying emotional component that needed to be addressed before being able to get into the work of self-regulation and self-monitoring. "The problem when you work with adults with learning disabilities and attention deficits is that (they) have had their needs inconsistently addressed" (Subject B). Students with emotional issues were identified by Subject C as having the most difficulty in college: "Students who have some other difficulty with self-regulation… stemming from a psychiatric/psychological challenge with depression, anxiety, obsessive–compulsive. Those students are having a very difficult time."

5.4 Findings

Abstract features were identified during axial coding. Statements were cataloged based on themes—intrapersonal, interpersonal, or societally constructed. Intrapersonal statements were statements pertaining to an individual's subjective practice of metacognition, self-awareness and self-control. Interpersonal codes pertain to dialectic discussions or small group interactions between a teacher, or other individuals, that support metacognition and self-regulation. Societally constructed statements were those that referred to metacognition through the lens of a theorist or institution. These codes represented wider social and institutional perspectives on metacognition.

The coding scheme of intrapersonal, interpersonal, and societally constructed themes were identified during the earlier pilot study (Hulbig, 2016) and from differences in practice identified in the broader literature related to metacognition (Artino, 2008; Darabi et al., 2007; Downing et al., 2009; Dweck, 2013; Pennini, 2006; Schwarz, 2015). The questions developed for this interview were purposefully designed to allow the interview subjects to choose their definitional perspective without being guided by the frame of the question. Analysis showed deep relationships and made visible abstract interconnections that transcended these three dimensions, demonstrated by responses that overlapped or blended perspectives.

Through this coding system, it became possible to analyze a subject's descriptions of metacognition to reveal aspects of their underlying stance toward the subject. For example, individuals with very personal and individual ideas about metacognition were identified by the number of intrapersonal statements they made during the interview. Similarly, many interactions between student and teacher were identified as intrapersonal, revealing further subcategories related to these professors' pedagogical approach to metacognition. The social construction codes helped identify the professors' reliance on research, institutional, or prescribed learning structures, as well as the limitations these structures imposed.

Axial coding revealed a pattern that allowed subjects to be identified by two qualities. First, the unique nature of the metacognitive relationship the interviewees aimed to establish with their students. Second was the transformational quality of their metacognitive educational practices. This practice was perhaps best encapsulated by interview Subject H's description:

> The learning conversation is a deeper conversation about their hopes and dreams, passions, their fears, their frustrations, their successes, their social life, the way they think, what I'm noticing that day, what they're noticing that day. I engage in deep listening, so I can be fully present in their discoveries, their tears, their joy.

These conversations between student and professor evolve over time, supporting the learner's development and self-regulation.

The interpersonal quality of these learning conversations would frequently be paired with the development of intrapersonal insights from the professor's personal practice or social insights from the literature. These conversations highlighted an interactive process of elevating the students' powers of reflection and self-assessment that seemed to transcend the intra-, inter- and social framework of this axial coding scheme. There was a clear connection between these interpersonal learning conversations and increased intrapersonal self-regulation, both for the student and the professors themselves. This support aided in the development of new skills and self-regulatory behaviors.

Metacognitive teaching was described as more than just a step-by-step pedagogical approach, but rather a perceived responsibility to engage in guiding students through the transitional gates and social demands of their lives in college. These professors saw their role as supporting their students in developing strategies to meet the demands of college and life. Sometimes the process was simply letting the student know something they did not know before or, as Subject G put it: "You should model the process of metacognition for your students."

Subjects A, C, G, and H described how they used their personal practice of metacognition to confront their cognitive biases, which enabled them to provide a supportive practice to their students. "I'm constantly using metacognition while I'm teaching, and on myself, thinking about my thinking and my approach and my responses to my students (Subject G)." Metacognition was conceived of as a cognitive tool from this frame of reference, one that guided a professor's modeling behavior and the way they addressed their students' fears and anxieties. By drawing from their own personal metacognitive practice, these professors have become more adept at addressing cognitive rigidity both in themselves and their students. This was most eloquently expressed by Subject G: "It's a tool that I use to become more aware of my ability to be open and accepting and kind and loving to people." Regarding their pedagogical practice, Subject B used the metaphor of metacognition as a vehicle to educate students about patterns of thought and behaviors that can be used to address their unique learning. "It's a vehicle for getting some things done."

Most statements correlated to a direct individualized interaction between the professor and their students. This suggested that these professors employed a kind of embodied educational practice, or praxis, that was highly individualized from moment to moment. The identification of this relationship led to a deeper selective coding to identify practical differences between practices of pedagogy and practices of praxis. Abstracting these categories revealed a strongly interactive teaching style. That style drew upon connections between the professor's personal practices of metacognitive self-discovery, research-based practices from psychology and neurology, and a strong relationship between student and professor. Selective coding consisted of two types of coding: single theme and contrasting. Single-theme codes were targeted because of their significance during open and axial coding. Single-theme codes were related to statements about definition, relationship, modeling, institutional problems, and questions. Contrasting codes were themes that could be broken into contrasting stances, such as pedagogy versus praxis, psychological versus neurological, and conscious versus unconscious. What follows is a breakdown of the themes identified through coding.

5.4.1 Relationship

Relationship was mentioned several times as one of the most important elements of teaching metacognition. Subject F reported it was: "Very important to build a positive relationship with them so they want to grow." Subject D observed: "I often think that some of the magic at PAL is that we take the time and have the relationship to go there." The place where their relationship allowed these professors to go with their students was a zone where emotion, action, and learning was integrated with a student's self concept. These codes often blended or overlapped with other codes, identifying them as statements of unique importance to the practice of metacognition. As Subject A noted:

> I think in order to teach anything, including metacognitive strategies, relationship is key … From the relationship, we relax enough to show what we don't have a real good grasp of. That lets whoever is kind of scaffolding in that interaction, allows them to see enough of what's going on inside of you to create something to help you figure out how you move forward.

This learning relationship was succinctly described by Subject B through a story about a student who was having academic problems and needed to have a difficult conversation with a professor: "It was a very mindful kind of thing that we worked through in that moment using that conversation that he was dreading to have with the professor."

There were many descriptions of professors creating an emotionally safe space for their students, as described by Subject E: "It is my relationship with students that allows metacognition to happen, the non-judgmental, and the acceptance, so that it's okay to be honest, even about things that you don't want to be honest about." Subject E also identified this relationship as being one where power between teacher and student was integrated into the relationship:

> I think it's really important to feel some connection before you progress into conversations with metacognition. I also think there has to be some kind of equality before that can happen.

Subject F described the subtle way she used her relationship with students to influence them to grow:

> I try not to make a lot of negative judgments about it because then he won't want to do anything about it. But if I tease him about it, and cajole him a little bit about it, he's more … because I have an excellent relationship with this kid he's more willing to address that behavior in a different way.

Another reason for this relationship was identified by Subject B: "I have students be in the relationship equal in power because I want them to practice their agency." Statements like these suggest that metacognitive education requires a level of equality between teacher and student that is not only quite different from the traditional teaching model but is done for the practical reason of enhancing a deepening of the learning experience itself.

Metacognition seems to integrate abstract cognitions and visceral concrete cognitions in ways that produce new understandings. Several comments suggested that metacognitive learning leads to a general awareness that is qualitatively different and encompassing of multiple data points:

> … a lot of people are completely blind to (it). They don't even believe that it's happening. Like you could be in a group, and you could know, boy, this is not working. And someone else could think that it's moving along beautifully because the language is the cohesive element

> that they're using, and nothing else. No body language, no eyes, you know what I mean? (Subject A).

While this statement from Subject A seems to identify a perhaps missing intuitive or nonverbal element, others indicated that there was a very temporal and embodied element too: "There's a person in the room and there's the past, and somehow we have to get there. We have to bring those two together (Subject D)."

Subject E also connected curiosity with the need for a safe, secure learning relationship: "I think curiosity adds a little lightness to it also, so it's not so heavy and scary. It's interesting, it's going to be interesting." Through curiosity, she could change the emotional energy of the learning. This ability to change the emotional energy of the learning through language was also described by Subject F:

> If you have a relationship with someone and you can go, "I'm doing it again."
>
> It's so much more effective than if (you) just say it to yourself."

The simple phrase, "I'm doing it again" represents a specific constellation of issues and repeated behavior patterns that affected this student's progress. It is a simple phrase that serves to define, identify, and emotionally frame these issues as a curious problem to solve.

There were also several components that were identified as necessary to build this relationship. One was vulnerability:

> Part of building of the relationship is building a rapport and part of building a rapport is being vulnerable, a little bit vulnerable…You don't want to make it too heavy (Subject F).

Subject E described it as:

> One reason I feel like I get along well with my students is that I acknowledge that we're both… We're all just humans, which means we're all imperfect, and we're all working on doing better. I think that that acknowledgement goes a long way in my connection with students.

Subject A identified what they saw as a common block that impaired a teacher's ability to build this kind of relationship:

> People kind of slip into something, like a role or authoritarian gig or something. I think there's less vulnerability in that, and so less of an authentic relationship.

Subject F indicated that a teacher: "must care and not just teach metacognition."

Another necessary component was a high level of authenticity. "I think you have to be brave, and you have to have some level of confidence, at least with the people you're with, in order to be authentic (Subject A)". Some professors described what seemed to be an almost heroic level of courage in their students:

> They come into the program … managing issues like depression, all kinds of depression, anxiety, certainly attention and focus issues, all kinds of language processing difficulties and yet, courageously, they're still here (Subject, B).

Understanding the impact of their student's personal history was important across interviews. Subject H described the need for this sensitivity as: "Sometimes people struggle so hard that they get disconnected, and not only from themselves but from other people." Subject E described how she would like to deeply understand: "how anxiety impacts (them), I want to learn how to undo it so that students can have some way of dealing with that."

Frequent statements by these professors demonstrated a deep respect and admiration for these students and their understanding capabilities. Subject C described her work with a student as:

> There's like this implicit curriculum that we're making explicit for him before he even gets to his content that he's studying. And that he sees his learning as collaborative ... To me (it) is remarkable that he can imagine that ... his cognitive space is amenable to change and he wants people in it.

However, despite common components of honesty, vulnerability, and authenticity, it was still difficult for professors to describe what was happening.

> I don't know how I do it to be honest with you. It's funny, because part of what happens is that a student will walk into my office and they'll sit down and then it just starts to happen, where there's this sort of give and take (Subject E).

Subject F also acknowledged a difficulty pinpointing the exact components necessary for this learning relationship to develop:

> Sometimes I don't really know why because I don't feel like I'm the most attentive teacher or the best teacher or the perfect teacher. But it is about relationship and there is something that I do, and it has maybe to do with being informal rather than formal.

Subject H used the stronger word "connection" to describe metacognition itself:

> What I see about metacognition is ... It's about connection. Not only just a connection to yourself, but connection between the two of us. Connection to the classes. How it connects deeply to your life.

Statements like this suggest the deep and powerful role of relationship in metacognition education that perhaps transcends the simple roles of teacher and student and encompasses both the student's academic demands and emotional experience. Regardless, the relationship between student and teacher achieved by metacognitive learning seems to powerfully affect both the student and the professors as evidenced by this statement by Subject C: "I'm just so honored to be invited into their thinking process and be able to be with them."

5.4.2 *Modeling*

Modeling was a universal theme across interviews. For most, it was an important part of their approach. "You should model the process of metacognition for your students. And necessarily use language to give voice to your awareness (Subject G)."

Some described their modeling approach as, "I'm honest with them. I'm authentic with them. I share my own personal experiences (Subject F)." Others specifically identified that they: "model ways to remember, retrieve, and apply the information (Subject D)." A common modeling intervention expressed by Subject D was to use metacognitive questions because: "They're easy to remember," and were easy to make, "a normal part of what they do on a daily basis." Many described this kind of metacognitive modeling as: "just how you operate, I just automatically do it in my practice with students and in my own life (Subject G)."

The modeling of metacognition was a formative experience for at least one professor who described:

> I had really good models in my home … I remember … the modeling that my mom had done and how critical that was for me for problem solving. Even her voice would change as she tried the new approach, and I would sit there and do my homework and I could hear her be like, "Well what about if," and she'd re-engage with her thoughts in a totally different voice, and I'd be like, "Oh she's got a new idea. I wonder what that one is," and I'd listen and do my homework … After she had died, 10 years after her death, realizing that she had modeled how to mull over thinking, like how to actively engage in thinking and revise it and flip it on its head and do it again and what a gift that was (Subject C).

This described the metacognitive modeling other professors employed during their interviews. All the professors slipped into moments where they described their practice through a re-enactment of the dialogue, using differing tones of voice to show different individuals speaking or differing lines of thought. Some of the richest and most interesting data came through these presentations of discussions professors had with their students. Closer examination revealed that what these professors portrayed was not simply what was said, but also the thinking involved in the exchanges. This example by Subject B demonstrates:

> Initially, I said, "Well, that seems like you're going to have brain freeze. That's a worry, by the way you're talking, it seems like you're going to have brain freeze." Then ultimately, it really was, "I'm scared, I'm anxious and when that happens, I get angry and it comes out as a bad temper, and I flare." He was thinking through his process. "I'm anxious and worried, I'm embarrassed and where this was all headed, this actually is my ... If I start with this, then this happens and then this happens and then I get mad." Before it was sort of free floating, not nailed down at all and then there was this look of recognition, "It's a problem to solve, so I could compartmentalize those feelings and put them somewhere. It's a problem to solve, something I can repeat to myself so I can keep my emotions in check."

This example by Subject B also demonstrates the previously mentioned learning technique of compacting many of the students' problematic behaviors and feelings into a phrase. Here Subject B's use of the phrase, "its a problem to solve" is similar to Subject F's use of the phrase "you are doing it again" with her student. Both serve to take what would seem a wide field of issues and turn them into a single actionable phrase.

This propensity for modeling behavior was deeply integrated into their practice and came out organically as they described their educational practices. The modeling done by these professors was purposeful and intent on revealing a process to better control self-regulation. Interview Subject A identified that teaching metacognition this way allows you: "to see enough of what's going on inside of you to create something to help you figure out how you move forward." This appears to suggest that these professors are using modeling at PAL in a unique way. They are modeling a cognitive interaction, representing not only thoughts and actions but also bringing understanding to multiple perspectives and modes of action in the service of improving one's own action.

5.4.3 *Institutional and Social Barriers*

Recurring themes of conflict between the way metacognition was practiced at PAL and broader social/institutional concepts of learning was found in the data. Subject H succinctly identified this as: "The biggest problem I have with metacognition is academia and the way they misperceive what we do." Subject C described the problem through a conversation with a non-PAL professor:

> "I just want to give them things to do and tell them to do it, that's what I want to do." And I said, "I don't want to give them things to do and tell them to do it… I want to teach them what they could do, and how they could do it." So that when they come to a new situation they can say to themselves, "What could I do and how would I do it?"

Interview Subject C described the reason for this divide in approaches: "It is so much harder on the teacher, I believe, to do the metacognitive work." The source of this problem for Subject C was the difficulty for teachers: "To take the time to teach the students to understand what metacognition is." Others, like Subject D, identified an over-reliance on reaching curriculum standards: "You know why it's not done all the time? Because we worry so much about covering content." Subject G identified a common implicit bias that she believed greatly impacted a professor's ability to develop metacognitive thinking in their students: "If professors believe motivation is a personality choice or personal choice, then when the students aren't motivated, they get to blame the student."

For Subject H this problem was also exacerbated by a lack of neurodiversity in the teaching profession. "We need a better balance in education. You know, I mean, we need more people to think out of the box because there are more and more students who are outside of the box." This lack of neurodiversity negatively affected students with specific learning disabilities (SLD) because:

> They need to see that there are people who think outside of the box. They need to see that there are people who, who don't think linearly… it is sort of like having a bunch of black students and white teachers. If we do not have mixed teachers, students don't have somebody they can look at and say, ahh, I know this person (Subject H).

A number of statements indicated professors noticed a broad increase in social conditions that negatively impact metacognitive development. "This is a very challenging time, but it will probably become challenging in other ways down the road. I just feel like everybody's being pierced and interrupted. It's very hard to set the sort of boundaries needed for reflection and thought, real thought (Subject A)." Three areas of social disruption were identified by Subject C. The first was, "They can use the computer and they can use the internet to access information faster than I will be able to simply because they're native about the process. But then when I watched them access that information, I realize they're not being critical consumers of the information." The second was, "We're seeing students who have been parented in a different way than they were parented 15 years ago, 20 years ago, 30 years ago, and that type of parenting could be influencing the type of development we see." And the third was, "The whole purpose of learning has shifted in a way that I think also impacts the way that they're developing."

There was broad acceptance that metacognition was not only developmental, but also could be affected by the learning experience. However, the lack of a curriculum or formal process of intervention was identified by interview Subject C who said: "I don't know that there is an intentional curriculum that is woven through the developmental stages that we teach across the academic lifespan." In terms of professional development, Subject G felt: "including it in teacher education is super important." Subject H saw metacognition transcending curriculum, indicating that teaching metacognitive thinking should be a core principle of education. "Learning how you learn and learning how to connect with your work is what education should be about … Connection, metacognition, and engagement (need) to be at the top of everybody's list in education. Not the bottom, the top."

5.4.4 Evaluation

Whether metacognition should be graded initially appeared to reveal a real split between practices. Some professors, like Subject F, believed strongly that metacognition should be evaluated. For her, this was done through a writing assignment on a student's metacognition, stating, "Papers will be graded. There will be a rubric and there will be expectations, and they'll be graded on what they write." She cited the needs of the teacher saying, "If you're just teaching about metacognition, you have no way of knowing if they get it, do they really get it? It's an abstract concept, so it's nothing they can touch so we have to make it touchable, experienceable (Subject F.)." Others, like Subject C, also felt: "Don't you want students to know where they stand." However, she struggled over the idea of who should be giving the grade:

> Is it my grade or is it their evaluation of their metacognition with an expert guide? Can you fail at metacognition? Is it a direct assessment or an indirect assessment? Because my research and training would say it has to be both.

Other professors took the opposite stance, like Subject E: "I don't think you can take a test on metacognition." However, she did not rule out an informal assessment in a conversation: "I would have a conversation about how students use metacognition, how they use their self-awareness in becoming better students or whatever their goals are." Subject G stated: "No, I would never grade it … I'm very averse to grading. I think it diminishes whatever's been accomplished." Subject B described it this way:

"Feedback, not evaluate," sarcastically indicating that she would never say, "Doing a good job there, sport. I give you an A in metacognition… I would never do that."

5.4.5 *Questions*

Questions were also found to be a central component of metacognitive teaching at PAL. Most, like Subject H, identified questioning students as the first step of their process: "The beginning is just kind of simply getting to know a student. Asking them questions." These questions were identified as being of a highly specific nature. "I think questions are very important. Not questions like, Da-data-da-data. What-dayahdo? What about this? You know. But really questions." (Subject H) Subject B described herself as being: "Very deliberate and intentional about what I say to them, what question I might insert." Subject C described the questioning process as: "asking the student a question to which he or she already knows the answer … but in asking the question, making the thought process illuminated for the student." Subject D specifically identified the importance of 'how' questions:

> The magic word is how. How much do you know about this? How much do you remember about that? How does this apply to your life? How are you going to do this? How are you going to remember that? How effective was it last time you used flashcards? All of those.

Subject D identified that the reason these "how" questions were so effective was that they identified evaluative processes that: "just bring it out there and address it explicitly." However, Subject D was not the only professor to overtly identify the importance of 'how' questions. Subject E also identified "how" questions as significant: "The questions have to do with how do I … You know, how do I take in information? How do I express information? How do I remember information? How do I react to my professors?".

Coding identified practical, self-reflective questioning occurring as a primary style across subjects. "What do you think about that, and how did you approach that, and why did you choose this over that, and what were your thoughts, what were your feelings, how did that affect you?" (Subject G) These kinds of questions highlighted a question strategy that focused on self-understanding and self-discovery. They suggest a deeper functional base to the questioning process than simple information seeking.

Subject H identified that these questions had an emotive and motivational dimension to them: "Just the questioning makes them think. Like, this person is interested in me." Subject F described: "It's not about comparing yourself to everybody else, and saying, am I better than them? It's like, what is the best that I can do?" Subject A described important motivational discussions being developed around the question: "How did you feel? … Everybody wants to feel better or feel good … Let's look at what you did that led to what made you feel so good, or what you think made you feel so good." Subject B described how they used questions to encourage problem-solving around feelings by asking: "What is in your way? What is gnawing at you today?" We start with that and clear that out of the way and then proceed with whatever work we're going to work on that day."

Subject D also identified "why" questions as important: "Because this is how we become aware of the unconscious patterns, mindsets, assumptions, language, and habits drawn from the past that influence processes now." Using questions to help uncover ideas and realities that the student may not be aware of, or be biased toward, was another identified theme. Subject B described how she used questions to open up a conversation to analyze a student's thinking: "I don't settle for the general statement of, "Well, that was fine." Instead, she would use questions to draw out details:

> What does that mean? What about that did you like? What about that? What exactly did that look like that worked? "Really doing their own task analysis or thought analysis, but (also) showing them how to do that."

Questioning was identified as an important and multidimensional aspect of these professors' approach to education.

5.4.6 Pedagogy Versus Praxis

Descriptions of teaching practices were contrast coded as statements about pedagogy or statements about praxis. Pedagogical statements referred to more standardized elements of teaching related to procedure, curriculum, or elements of practice. Praxis referred to elements of teaching that were related to individualized actions or approaches toward education that were student or situation specific. Praxis related codes were often expressed as stories about the professor's work with individual students or represented in the moment-to-moment teaching judgments that would not be standardized or expressible in a lesson plan or curriculum.

Pedagogy- and praxis-related statements were found throughout the interviews. For example, a statement like, "I assign them *How to Read a Book You Don't Want to Read*, which is a nine-minute YouTube thing, which is about chopping the book up and all this. Okay, now reflect on that, you know? Tell me about it with regards to you, specifically (Subject F)," would be coded pedagogy. Whereas a statement like, "I use at least that initial easing them in, sports conversation perhaps, to relax. It gives them practice talking to somebody who does not judge them," would be coded praxis as it is more focused on the needs of the student in the moment. This coding scheme helped to add a deeper dimension to participant descriptions about their teaching practices.

Contrast coding in this way revealed a very individualized educational practice at the PAL program. The educational experience of a typical PAL session was highly contingent on personal and situational variables. Learning conversations had a very clear and predictable pedagogical core with replicable goals and practices. However, coding made it clear that much of what a PAL professor was doing was a response to the real and immediate needs of the student. Through responses to their student's immediate needs, these professors would aim to improve their student's ability to respond to these challenges in the future.

5.4.7 Psychological Versus Neurological

Another finding identified that these educators strongly used components of psychology and neurology in their teaching of metacognition. Considering Dr. Webb's approach when founding the program, and the influence of former PAL professors such as Jane Adelizzi who was credited by interview Subject D as the person who in their opinion brought the practice of educational therapy to the East Coast, it was not surprising that coding identified strong themes related to psychotherapeutic approaches. While coding revealed a deep respect and understanding of neurology, it also revealed that for most PAL professors, neurological understanding was secondary to psychological understanding. Some subjects directly identified their approach as being psychotherapeutic in nature. For most professors, their interest in neurological information was strictly focused on how it practically informed their teaching practice. Subject E expressed that, "once it gets connected to learning, that's what's most interesting to me."

For me, this was quite surprising, because it was the revelation of my neurological profile, as revealed by the Wechsler Adult Intelligence Scale (WAIS), that had made such a profound impact on me personally. This experience led me to believe that knowledge of neurology was the most valuable source of metacognitive knowledge. However, this data caused me to re-evaluate and realize that I was slightly biased to the idea of the supremacy of neurological understanding. Analysis of the data revealed that metacognition was much more of an active process than a neurological mental state or operation occurring in a localizable area in the brain.

This realization caused me to reconceptualize metacognition as a cyclical and personal process of integrating an individual's various neurological skills and evaluating them in service of improving their development. This finding suggests that there is a perspective-shifting perceptual ability that underlies the process of metacognition that these professors help their students use. This ability to shift perspective promotes self-understanding and regulation, but students must be supported to integrate their abstract, non-perceptual cognitive functions like reason, analysis, or logic with their perceptual and experiential knowledge. "It is not just language," said Subject D. The role of the teacher in metacognitive work is helping their students to better integrate qualitative perceptions and sensations with the brain's cognitive abstract processes by directing the students' awareness of both.

To expand on Subject D's observation, metacognition is about more than language, it is about more than knowledge, it is about identifying and organizing the qualia of perception and experience with the reason of cognition and logic, thereby improving the individual's response to challenges in their environment. To help a student engage in this kind of integration, PAL professors attempt to be as respectful, nurturing, attentive, and responsive to the internal qualitative experiences of their students as they were to their depth of knowledge about the brain and learning strategies. This finding was most enlightening for me as the researcher. It revealed a personal bias toward neurology that had motivated much of my research up to this point. It revealed that, perhaps, my sensitivity and ability to understand and relate to the qualitative experiences of my students was more behind my effectiveness as a teacher than my depth of knowledge about the neurological underpinnings of brain function.

Neurology was shown to play more of a critical role in addressing problems with learning, i.e. metacognitive regulation, rather than simply explaining learning problems, i.e. metacognitive knowledge. Neurology was used as a tool of discussion by these professors to educate students about themselves, for the purposes of improving and explaining their self-regulatory strategies and problem behaviors. Similar to earlier stated examples where professors used phrases like, "you are doing it again," or "that is a problem to solve," neurological and psychological information were used to identify and label problems for discussion. Once identified in this way, professors could develop a student's understanding of how to address the issue in an abstract way that was less distorted by emotional interference. Rather than a simple explanation about what was negatively affecting the student's learning, neurological information was used to identify and address problems with learning in a more abstract and objective way, limiting emotional interference. Subject A described it this way: "When kids learn that it's something physiological or neurological or maybe adults too, that it sort of takes a burden off the identity of it."

However, these professors were also keenly aware that, for some students, this level of technical discussion does not resonate. For this reason, professors used neurological understanding as part of a broad constellation of topics identified as important in generating the self-understanding necessary to achieve better self-regulation. Along with identifying a slight preference for psychological over neurological approaches, this investigation identified a preference for presenting information that could be used more in service of building a student's metacognitive regulatory abilities rather than knowledge. Subject G explained it this way:

> These are theories. These aren't written in stone. I still think that relating behaviors back to the brain is a really good idea for students. Because it's foundational. It would be like explaining to an athlete how muscles work or explaining to a sick person who needs to improve their health how the body works."

Clearly, a neurological understanding was considered a very important part of the educational practices of PAL. However, these perspectives were tempered by practical concerns about the actual psychological situation of the student and other competing needs that may impact their self-regulation.

5.4.8 Conscious Versus Unconscious

Another contrasting code used was related to conscious and unconscious processes of metacognition. This code was generally related to the protocol question asking if the subjects found metacognition to be more conscious or unconscious. However, aspects of conscious and unconscious behavioral observation surfaced throughout the interviews. Again, this coding structure revealed unique patterns and overlapped with other codes. For example, some subjects felt metacognition was an important conscious activity that helped address implicit bias. "My personal practice of metacognition (is) to be constantly aware of my physical experience of the moment, to include my noticing of assumptions that I've made, and to really reflect on those." (Subject G) Several subjects identified that over time metacognitive capacity moved from being a conscious activity to an unconscious activity with practice: "It may become less conscious once the metacognitive user is in the habit of applying it." (Subject F).

This coding scheme was often embedded with statements that were identified with the professor's practice. Professors said a large part of what they were doing with students was helping to reveal aspects of thinking or behavior that were otherwise subconscious and hidden. Subject F described this as: "Just bringing it to his conscious level of awareness… then we clarify it." It was found that these professors all viewed metacognition as both a conscious and unconscious process. It was also found that helping to identify subconscious thoughts, problem behaviors, or areas of knowledge where a student lacks a complete understanding moved them into consciousness for investigation and discussion was a centrally important component of their job.

5.4.9 *Definition of Metacognition*

Several subjects referred to a feeling that the concept of metacognition itself was larger than its popular definition of thinking about thinking. Subject D went so far as to say: "It's not three words. It's not thinking about thinking. It's got to be more than that." It was found that for these professors, the concept of metacognition included many facets that transcended traditional concepts of learning. These facets included a conscious awareness of thoughts, conversation to clarify feelings and action, a reliance on memory to define and diagnose problems, and an ability to identify, comprehend, and evaluate perspectives that are different from our own.

One thing that was made very clear through this coding structure was the dichotomous nature of the concept of metacognition. While the vast majority of statements indicated that these professors identified metacognition as a process that a student actively engages in, a large number of statements were made that also identified metacognition as a feature of cognition, like vision. However, just as frequently, it seemed that professors were describing a process that needed to be practiced to be improved. Frequently, it was difficult to determine if the subject was referring to metacognition as a process to be practiced or a feature of mind that needed to be developed. This finding seems to indicate that terms and conceptual descriptions need to be reorganized to better delineate between the active, interactive, and intrinsic neurocognitive features of metacognition.

5.5 Narrative Analysis

After open, axial, selective, and contrast coding of interview subjects was completed, reflected upon, and written up for the professors' interviews, the same coding structure was applied to my personal reflections on metacognition. By applying the same structure of analysis, it became possible to identify similarities and differences between my approach and thinking with those of the various interview subjects. I also identified variations of thematic importance. For example, coding identified that I was highly interested in defining metacognition in a way that was more nuanced than Flavell's (1979) learning about learning statement. However, as a result of the work done through this study, I believe I have gained a deeper appreciation of the descriptive simplicity of Flavell's initial definition.

The investigation not only identified strong similarities between myself and these PAL professors but also interesting differences. For example, while themes of addressing anxieties with students through metacognition were ubiquitous across interviews, I placed heightened importance on the impact of trauma in producing these anxieties. This was probably due to my years of specialized work with traumatized students. Similarly, all professors delineated the importance of the metacognitive relationship, but only two, besides myself, identified having significant metacognitive relationships outside of their professional relationships with students. One was Subject C, who talked about the relationship they had with their mother. The other was Subject G, who identified having such a relationship with their husband, stating:

> I will have discussions when he'll say, "Well, I'm doing this and they're not getting it and they're not getting it." I say, "Oh, sounds like you might be overloading them a little bit too much. You should-"… through our conversations about the brain and our arguments about motivation, what causes motivation. I think he's really grown as a teacher.

This quote reminded me of the metacognitive relationship I have with my wife, and how our metacognitive conversations have helped improve our relationship and ability to support the other. Moreover, my narrative investigation found relationships with others support conversations of metacognitive insight that are important in work environments. Harri-Augstein and Thomas (1991) also recorded positive impacts in work environments using learning conversation in the management of employees, a phenomenon I spoke about directly in my narrative investigation.

5.6 Managing with Metacognition

Again, metacognition was how I kept the overwhelming demands related to running these programs under control. However, despite my success with the students, I struggled to explain the uniqueness of what I was doing to administrators, or even other educators outside the program. Administration was never interested in providing the resources to address the scheduling, planning, and protocol issues related to the program. I was left to solve these issues myself inside the classroom the best I could.

I toiled for years, believing I could craft the perfect program with limited support from an administration that was becoming increasingly concerned with testing and saving money. I became disheartened, and part of me felt I was wasting my time. I was engaged in what seemed like fruitless self-reflection, but again the solution to this problem appeared in the form of a teacher. The solution to this problem was Trish.

Trish was brought on as the co-teacher of the program the year after the classroom's student numbers surged past the state limit for substantially separate programs in the public schools. For the first time in my career, I had another teaching professional who was living the same situation I was. I had another teacher to talk to and bounce ideas off who could understand what I was talking about because she was there having the same unique experiences and dealing with the same unique challenges that I had been dealing with for years. It was empowering for me to finally know for sure that I could not only get another highly trained educator to understand and appreciate what I was doing, but that she actually wanted to take the things that I was doing and apply them herself.

Thanks to Trish, I came to realize that my disability was again holding me back. However, now it was not simply my communication difficulty that was the problem, it was the uniqueness of my situation. My formative educational experiences were much different from other teachers. Moreover, the daily work of my job was so different from most other educators that they simply had no frame of reference from which to relate to me. Plus, since I had taken to hiding my disability from other teachers and administrators, the best tool and mechanism that I had to help build a frame of reference between us was missing. This was the source of many of the problems and confusions that occurred when I spoke with administration.

Thanks to Trish, I had someone to share my troubles with, someone to ask me clarifying questions, someone to assist me in my own metacognitive process. Thanks to Trish, I came to realize, from a wider perspective, the importance of working with others metacognitively.

References

Artino, A. R., Jr. (2008). Promoting academic motivation and self-regulation: Practical guidelines for online instructors. *TechTrends: Linking Research and Practice to Improve Learning, 52*(3), 37–45.

Brownstein, M. (2019). Implicit bias. In E. N. Zalta (Ed.), *The Stanford Encyclopedia of Philosophy* (Fall 2019 ed.). https://plato.stanford.edu/archives/fall2019/entries/implicit-bias/

Dweck, C. (2013, March 1). *2013 Ridley Lecture: Carol Dweck on Student Mindsets.* Retrieved from https://youtu.be/eGnqgXmlTk4

Flavell, J. H. (1979). Metacognition and cognitive monitoring: A new area of cognitive development. *American Psychologist, 34*(10), 906–911. https://doi.org/10.1037/0003-066X.34.10.906

Gödel, K. (1992). *On formally undecidable propositions of Principia Mathematica and related Systems.* Courier Corporation.

Harri-Augstein, E. S., & Thomas, L. (1991). *Learning conversations: The self organized learning way to personal and organizational growth.* Routledge.

Hofstadter, D. (1979). *Gödel, Escher, Bach: An eternal golden braid*. Basic Books.
Kegan, R. (1982). *The evolving self: Problem and process in human development*. Harvard University Press.
Mezirow, J. (1975). *Education for perspective transformation: Women's reentry programs in community colleges*. Center for Adult Education Teachers College, Columbia University.
Mezirow, J. (1991). *Transformative dimensions of adult learning*. Jossey-Bass.
Minsky, M. (1988). Society of mind. Simon and Schuster.
Nelson, T. O. (1996). Consciousness and metacognition. *American Psychologist, 51*(2), 102–116. https://doi.org/10.1037/0003-066X.51.2.102
Penrose, R. (1989). *The emperor's new mind: Concerning computers, minds, and the laws of physics*. Oxford U. Press.
Pennini, S. W. (2006). College students with learning disabilities: A case study. (77) [Doctoral dissertation, Lesley]. https://digitalcommons.lesley.edu/education_dissertations/77
Tryggvason, M. T. (2009). Why is finnish teacher education successful? Some goals Finnish teacher educators have for their teaching. *European Journal of Teacher Education, 32*(4), 369–382.

Chapter 6
Analysis

> Thinking about thinking, It's a … seemingly simple, elegant … phrase.
>
> Elegance like you would use in physics. The most simple, the most meaningful kernel of it. (Subject B)

Subject B's statement about the elegance of metacognition well-frames this discussion. The simple definition of "thinking about thinking" (Flavell, 1979) captures an infinite complexity that is akin to the mathematical expression of relativity in physics, and yet somehow, to this point, has escaped meaningful mathematical expression. It is a statement that carries with it far-reaching practical implications for our understanding of learning. Much like the way relativity explains the motions produced by gravity, imbuing those who understand it with an unprecedented ability to influence and control the physical world, it is believed that metacognition unveils the features of learning in such a way that it imbues those that understand it with an unprecedented ability to control their mental world.

Metacognition describes a form of personal mindfulness that opens up a learner to higher levels of understanding and more complex behavioral choice. It enables learners to discover their own implicit mental traps, and the implicit bias created and reinforced repeatedly through interactions with others around them. Knowledge of metacognition also informs teachers' understanding, providing insight into which educational techniques will enable the student to develop a skill. By exploiting the brain's ability to identify its own neurocognitive features of learning, metacognitive educational approaches capitalize on the infinite human capacity to problem solve (Deutsch, 2011) and self-direct their own learning.

P. R. Hulbig, *The Pedagogy of Self-Authorship*,
https://doi.org/10.1007/978-3-031-41436-7_6

6.1 The PAL Approach

The PAL program's approach to metacognition is important because of its unique history. For over 50 years, the program has helped a demographic of college students who were at one time barred from participation because of the common belief that their learning disabilities made success in college unattainable. In many ways, PAL's approach is better designed to address the complex educational issues today because it is focused on helping individual students work through the varied demands of college. The PAL approach complements traditional educational formats, and has been shown to transform the educational experiences of students. PAL's metacognitive approach to learning addresses many challenges that traditional modern education finds intractable.

PAL professors are doing more than teaching content or learning strategies. They are providing their students with the tools, support, and opportunity to take control and direct their learning. They are teaching their students the processes necessary to author their own life narrative. It is a program that offers an immediate benefit to students in their college course work, and the long-term benefit of leading them to become actively involved in their world. It is an approach focused on instilling habits of self-directed learning by developing a personally motivating understanding of their learning that honestly represents the best use of the student's ability. It is an approach through which practitioners seek to teach students how to identify and achieve an optimal manifestation of themselves as a learner.

6.2 Learning Conversations

This study identified a core PAL approach to metacognitive education. This approach was specifically labeled by interview Subjects B and H as the learning conversation (Adelizzi & Goss, 1995; Fox, 2010; Harri-Augstein & Thomas, 1991; Pennini, 2006). These learning conversations were found to not only instruct metacognition but also build a student–teacher relationship capable of supporting the expansive development of a student's processes of understanding. Through learning conversations with their PAL professor, the student develops the ability to enact strategies to meet the demands of school and life. But what exactly are learning conversations, and how does one engage in a learning conversation with a student? (Adelizzi & Goss, 1995; Fox, 2010; Harri-Augstein & Thomas, 1991; Norris & Bullock, 2017; Pennini, 2006).

First, learning conversations are done predominantly between individuals or in small groups. These conversations require a high degree of intimacy and a freedom of expression. Students must not only feel safe to express their thoughts and identify their weaknesses, but they must also have the time and space to do so. Even in what has been traditionally considered a small group structure, the size and configuration may not be ideally suited to the depth and freedom of expression/exchange that is imperative to engage properly in this teaching style. Moreover, traditional classroom formats are poorly suited for these conversations to take place in. The very size of traditional classroom formats affects a student's ability to speak freely and engage in the level of raw self-investigation required by this educational approach. Plus, the management structure of the traditional classroom places constraints on a student's opportunity and ability to express themselves. Such constraints run counter to the goals of the learning conversation itself.

Massachusetts educational law 603 CMR 28.06(7) defines small group special education as eight students per certified teacher, with 12 being the legal limit with the support of an aide (Massachusetts Department of Elementary and Secondary Education, 2018). However, as a teacher who has managed many of these small group programs in a variety of Massachusetts public schools, my experience is that even a group of five students may be too many to have meaningful metacognitive conversations. The process is degraded not only by the natural time constraints produced by having more people involved in the conversation, but also the exponential extrapolation of social variables that occur when more people are brought into the process. Three of these social components, mentioned repeatedly across the interview process, were power, bias, and derogatory judgments.

Several professors in this investigation, and Webb (1972) herself, identified that a pronounced differential in power was an impediment to metacognitive teaching. Many investigations (Foy, 2018; Janis, 2008; Plous, 1993; Sapolsky, 2017) have shown that large differentials in power biased judgments (Janis, 2008; Plous, 1993) and impaired performance (Foy, 2018; Sapolsky, 2017). The negative effects of power differentials can range from individuals withholding information to only presenting information that they think the person in power wants to hear (Janis, 2008). Power differentials can cause individuals to try to judge what they think others want them to say, rather than focusing on the factors that are most relevant to them personally (Plous, 1993).

At its most elemental level, power is defined as one's capacity to alter another person's behavior, condition, or state of mind (Langner & Keltner, 2008). This is very close to the definition of education because the influence of power is built into the educational relationship. It is not possible to simply remove power from the educational relationship. In some cases, students desperately need their teacher, or professor, to get them to a point where they can gain power/control over themselves (Pennini, personal communication, December 4, 2020). Younger and less experienced students are more reliant on the judgments of others to develop their own (Foy, 2018; Plous, 1993). However, the negative influences of power on behavior and cognition can be invisible to both the student and the teacher. Through a metacognitive approach, the influences of power, both obvious and obscure, are identified with the students and open for honest discussion.

Metacognitive discussions about how power relationships affect learning are not done in a power vacuum, but rather with the intention of teaching how power can be understood and managed, just like any other factor that affects a student's learning. Power imbalances resulting from implicit bias can be most difficult to address because of their abstract nature (Foy, 2018; Sapolsky, 2017). As the number of individuals in a group increases, so do the number of influential and confounding factors that could affect a learning conversation (Adelizzi & Goss, 1995; Fox, 2010; Harri-Augstein & Thomas, 1991; Pennini, 2006) or degrade a student's metacognition. Differentials in power between students are frequently overlooked as a factor affecting metacognition and instruction.

Traditional approaches to education frame student behavioral expressions regarding power or judgmental bias as an issue of classroom management. However, at PAL behaviors are addressed through learning conversations rather than simply managed. For example, Subject G described, "If I have a conflict with a student, I will say to them, 'Help me think about this.' Help me understand what just happened here." Issues are discussed and investigated openly with the student. This is because while a teacher can learn to address the impact of their own power, bias, and judgment, their students will necessarily lack this knowledge and behavioral maturity. Learning conversations (Adelizzi & Goss, 1995; Fox, 2010; Harri-Augstein & Thomas, 1991; Pennini, 2006) impart this knowledge and aim to develop maturity and a knowledge of the educational power dynamic.

Students are generally not developmentally ready to address the impacts of power. They are likely unaware of the subtle influence implicit biases have on their behavior. As groups become larger, participants need to be more metacognitively aware, particularly of these influences, if such groups are going to function in a way that promotes the metacognition of each member of the group. When numbers become large, metacognitive learning conversations (Adelizzi & Goss, 1995; Fox, 2010; Harri-Augstein & Thomas, 1991; Pennini, 2006) simply become impossible. The conditions necessary to address deeper levels of metacognitive insights are stunted as the need for passive conformity and classroom management become more necessary to maintain cohesion.

Ideally, learning conversations at PAL (Pennini, 2006) start as highly personal, one-to-one conversations between a student and educator. As a student's ability to understand and use metacognition develops, it becomes possible for them to more effectively participate in larger group metacognitive discussions. Such group-level metacognitive discussions were identified by Webb (1989) as having many positive results. The most important result of small group metacognitive learning conversations (Adelizzi & Goss, 1995; Fox, 2010; Harri-Augstein & Thomas, 1991; Pennini, 2006) is that they develop a student's ability to engage in learning conversations with peers and may increase the likelihood that these kinds of conversation will occur outside of formal institutional educational constructs.

The PAL program has historically provided mentoring and leadership experiences to their students. It is hypothesized that developing a student's ability to engage in learning conversations with other students could be used to further harness and spread metacognitive learning techniques across a population, improving and developing peer support networks (Hulbig, 2019). However, even in small group situations, students and teachers must maintain the ability to drop into one-to-one learning conversations to accommodate the highly individualized ways of knowing diverse life circumstances dictate.

6.2.1 Structure of Learning Conversations

The structure of learning conversations (Adelizzi & Goss, 1995; Fox, 2010; Harri-Augstein & Thomas, 1991; Pennini, 2006) closely align with the main theoretical findings of this investigation, which will be described in detail later as the general model of metacognitive instruction. The structure of a learning conversation (Adelizzi & Goss, 1995; Fox, 2010; Harri-Augstein & Thomas, 1991; Pennini, 2006) has been defined through integrating ideas drawn from across interviews and narrative investigations. First, these learning conversations involve bringing ideas and realities into awareness for purposes of investigation. Subject F described it as, "Just bring it to his conscious level of awareness," and subject B detailed this process as, "They'll say something and then we'll take that apart and then they'll say something else and we'll diagram that sentence. Really doing their own task analysis or thought analysis, but showing them how to do that."

The second idea involves deeply connecting with a student and supporting their ability to stay connected with their world, accepting all its splendor and complexity. This view was best expressed by subject H when they said, "Metacognition is … about connection. Not only just a connection to yourself, but a connection between the two of us. Connection to the classes. How it connects deeply to your life … What works? … What will make you remember? What triggers something good, or bad? … connection to the world, and connection to the people around you."

Learning conversations (Adelizzi & Goss, 1995; Fox, 2010; Harri-Augstein & Thomas, 1991; Pennini, 2006) are personal interviews about the student's progress toward their goals. It requires a skilled intertwining of questioning and modeling on the part of the professor. It requires a student to look critically at themselves in a deep and non-superficial way. If these conversations are to be useful, they must touch on the emotional factors that impact the student's learning and the learning relationship itself. The common goal of the teacher is demonstrating to the student how to identify their problems and solve them. This will by its very nature necessitate deep listening and highly sensitive routines of self- evaluation.

Learning conversations begin by questioning. The questions take two forms. One type of question is information seeking. These are questions that allow the student to tell their story. They also reveal the students' definition of themselves. What their goals are, what they value, what they believe their strengths and weaknesses are. With careful listening, professors can identify patterns in their students' behavior and thinking that the student may not even be aware of, or are powerless to do anything about. This leads into the second form of questioning, which seeks to bring into consciousness those less defined areas and patterns of behavior for deeper practical discussion. This is the stage where 'how' questions become most important.

However, it is more than simply asking how a student does a certain task. Professors work with their students to construct a schema of the students' own concept of learning. Then, the professor uses the conversation to direct the students' attention to areas of self-development that have not yet been deeply considered or perhaps are blocked in some way. It is a process of closely listening and helping the student identify the weaknesses and strengths of their approach to the various demands of their life. Sometimes it is demonstrating or helping them develop an approach from scratch. Sometimes it is an examination of their fears or motivations. Sometimes it involves getting students to try something new. It is highly personal, and both requires and produces a close bond between the professor and the student.

6.2.2 Outcomes and Objectives of Learning Conversations

To the untrained eye, these learning conversations (Adelizzi & Goss, 1995; Fox, 2010; Harri-Augstein & Thomas, 1991; Pennini, 2006) may seem like simple conversations between a student and professor about their education. Perhaps even the students themselves may be unaware that they are deeply engaged in a learning experience. However, the professors are conscious and intentional about how they are directing conversation. "They think we're just chatting," mused subject B. "I'm very deliberate and intentional about what I say to them, what question I might insert, one may be a cheerful, jolly joking comment or labeling." Through these conversations, professors are helping to name and identify things the students do not have a name for, describe things they do not have a description for, and explain things they do not have an explanation for. When students realize that these are more than simple conversations, they become more intentional about the conversations too. I believe that this is where transformational learning occurs in the PAL program.

Students who understand their role in these learning conversations begin to use them to deeply reflect on themselves as learners, and use them to connect their goals and aspirations with actions. Learning conversations lead students to conceptualize learning as a process they not only have control over, but also can invite others into for support and development. Subject C described it as an "implicit curriculum that we're making explicit," and produces a student who "sees his learning as collaborative."

Success and failure are not conceptualized as definitive, but rather part of the process and data to use. The reality that failure is a potential is not hidden. The fact that success is frequently less assured than failure is open for discussion. However, PAL students are accepted when failure happens, and they are supported through the steps that come next. These are the crucial steps required to recoup, continue learning, and expand one's skills in ways that will reduce their risk of failure in the future.

More than this, failure and success both become framed as momentary conditions. Regardless of the outcome of events, these conversations demonstrate for the student how to think through the events of their life. These conversations focus on the processes of thinking and behaving that allow a person to stay connected to their work and the things that matter most to them. Students learn how to think about themselves and really look at and address the hardships and failures that impact them. Through learning conversations, PAL professors can demonstrate how students can reduce the frequency of their failures and learn how to overcome the problems of their lives as they arise in the future. Over time, these learning conversations become part of an internal dialogue that the student learns to have with themselves when facing the myriad of self-regulatory challenges of life (Harri-Augstein & Thomas, 1991).

Through learning conversations, PAL professors attempt to help students learn to see themselves and their power of self-control. It is a process that helps the professor see what kind of learner the student is, and communicate that knowledge to the student. Subject H described why the process of really trying to see your students for who they are is so powerful in the context of metacognition. It is because "when someone else sees you, you begin to see yourself." It is this process of seeing themselves as the professor sees them that enables the metacognitive student to become better able to think deeply about their thinking.

While most PAL professors said they did not think students should be formally graded on their metacognitive ability, all described using a process of evaluation in a constant and ongoing manner. The centrality of questioning procedures and the kinds of questions used made it clear that PAL professors are guiding their students through a process of evaluating their own evaluations. They are teaching and evaluating the techniques of evaluation with their students all the time and highlight for their students how these evaluations can deepen their understanding.

Discussions of learning preference and disabilities, while presented as knowledge, are being used to define features of the student's own learning so that they can better evaluate their abilities and take more effective actions. Rather than being an end point of instruction that attempts to objectify the students' knowledge into a number or normative average, PAL professors work with their students to help them both identify standards and learn how to effectively apply them in the evaluation of themselves.

This is an almost continuous process of evaluation, one that reflects upon nearly any level or type of activity the student engages in. Simply put, the PAL approach to evaluation is through evaluative demonstrations of self-evaluation. Progress can be measured by comparing the steps a student identified as important during planning, the steps actually taken, and the student's general level of success in achieving the goal.

Some PAL professors did formalize this process by having their students write papers reflecting on their metacognition. But even these classic pen and paper response essay forms of evaluation function differently than traditional forms of evaluation. These were largely mechanisms through which formal writing and research skills could be taught. Subject F stated, "Those papers will be graded. There will be a rubric and there will be expectations, and they'll be graded on what they write, yeah. Not so much how perfectly they articulated." Moreover, these written evaluations were extended and added to over time as the student developed more awareness of themselves and their learning. The paper becomes a source of data for future discussions about the student's metacognition, providing examples of the student's earlier level of ability in writing, self-conception, and reasoning. "Reflecting on it in writing," was identified by Subject F as important. "So if they can't discuss it with someone else, at least they could maybe journal it," indicating that writing may be used by an individual as a surrogate to the learning conversation.

Most professors performed this evaluative technique through questioning and interviewing their students. Some specifically identified student learning difficulties or anxiety around writing as the reason why they did not formalize the process. "I have a series of questions that I ask my students about the semester and I … I don't have them write out the answers … Usually they like it that I do the writing because then they can just think," said Subject E. The notes taken by the professors resulting from these meetings formed the data for future metacognitive discussions. "I have notes in my planner. We need to work on this today, because a student will want to talk to me all day about sports," said Subject B.

Another common theme echoed by all the professors was that metacognitive reasoning could be disrupted. Metacognition was described as a developmentally sensitive process. There was a general sense that metacognition could be disrupted by traditional, arbitrary grading systems. The skill of self-evaluation was one that must be nurtured and grown by the professor as opposed to introduced and evaluated. Findings suggest that metacognition could be disrupted or nurtured by emotional experience. A centerpiece of the PAL evaluative technique was to investigate with the student how emotions were affecting the student's ability to properly evaluate their experiences and take action.

In conclusion, the PAL evaluative technique is composed of four elements. The first is a constant and continuous evaluation of a student's skills of self-evaluation. This includes asking questions as to what the student intends to do and how they intend to do it. The second element involves setting plans for completion and execution. The third is a reflection on the actions actually taken by the student towards these ends. A fourth evaluative technique used at PAL is the summative report that is written at the end of each semester, where the professor attempts to gather an evaluative snapshot of their progress. These elements can be compared to make evaluative determinations of a student's progress that are informative for the professors, articulable to other professionals, and helpful in a way that is practical to the students, their parents, or anyone interested in the student's progress. However, perhaps the most important feature of PAL's evaluative procedure is that these evaluations are primarily intended to help give students the feedback they need to better reflect on events that have happened to them. Students become better at evaluating why what happened turned out happening as a result of their planning and execution. It is a form of evaluation that improves the student's ability to plan more sophisticated actions in the future.

6.3 Unique Solutions to Professional Development

The nature of the learning conversation (Adelizzi & Goss, 1995; Fox, 2010; Harri-Augstein & Thomas, 1991; Pennini, 2006) approach to metacognitive education practiced at PAL necessitates individualized and small group practices. The close interaction of the program's learning conversation (Pennini, 2006) places qualitatively different demands on the learning experience and requires a qualitatively different approach to program development. These approaches must be highly individualized and supportive of the unique needs of the students in the program. Professors entering the program will require practical face-to-face experience and specialized knowledge in learning, neurology, and psychology. However, there will remain gaps in their practice that will be difficult to develop professionally. This is because the program seeks to serve a neurologically diverse range of learners. This not only requires a detailed knowledge of numerous diagnostic categories and the best educational practices of addressing these student's learning needs, but also a conditional knowledge that comes from practice. PAL's interdisciplinary approach to learning makes the professional development needs of the program unique in many ways.

PAL professors deal with profiles more than curriculum, and circumstances more than subjects. For PAL professors to meaningfully approach their students, they must possess a diversity of experiences teaching atypical learners. By necessity, their approach must differ specifically and systematically depending on their students' presentation or profile. It is not what they teach, but how they teach it. Professionally, it is difficult to communicate such intricately conditional knowledge to new teachers or those that lack a wide diversity of educational experiences.

Programmatically capturing and enshrining in policy the practices of professionals who have mastered the art of teaching metacognition will require the collection of both data and an interpersonal transfer of knowledge and history. Care must be taken not to simply attempt to align the PAL model to better conform with traditional education paradigms that do not address transformation or self-directed learning. Rather than attempting to make PAL more commensurate with traditional approaches, it may be more fruitful for the program to clearly identify the best practices of their own educators and programs. To this end, it is suggested that PAL preserves and develops the program using a model that closely aligns with the learning conversation (Pennini, 2006). The processes of transferring and developing the program's professional practices could be modeled on PAL's own model. This would not only be instructive for new staff, but also the process could be adapted to identify and preserve metacognitive understanding, practices, and insights in a way that could be more broadly cataloged. Such a practice would enhance transfer through discussion, questioning, and modeling. It would also aggregate, communicate, and archive the specialized approaches developed in the service of their students and situations.

One way to bridge this divide was mentioned by interview Subject A, who felt there would be real value in hearing the stories of other professors. "What did she do that was successful … Just to hear people's little stories because those really stick for me, when people describe a kid and something that was effective." However, interprofessional communication is only going to be as successful as the ability of professors to communicate what they are seeing and what they are doing. For a program like Curry's PAL program, which has a legacy that is more than 50 years old, preserving the historical contributions of its professors becomes an important consideration.

Along with being the first college-level program for students with learning disabilities, PAL was also one of the first programs to develop, largely out of direct practice, a pedagogy for transformative learning. PAL's ability to collect and share student and situation-specific insights about metacognitive instruction will prove valuable to itself and other institutions endeavoring toward the same educational goals of transformative metacognitive education in the future. As professors retire, preserving their knowledge and communicating it to future generations of PAL professors will become increasingly powerful and important to the institution's metacognitive ability as a whole.

6.4 Power of Personal Narratives

When metacognition is practiced on an individual level, you need a frame of reference. That reference frame can be strengthened with the support of another person. When I came to realize that metacognition was deeply tied to supportive relationships, it led me to more deeply value the people in my life who were willing to engage in this style of thinking with me. It was the support that others offered my thinking and self-regulatory processes that enabled me to better achieve my professional goals and more strongly stand for my core ideas and principles.

I now realize that metacognition has a developmental piece to it that is only recoverable through our historical narrative. This extends to our ability to explain our understanding to others. So much practical understanding comes from raw experience and how we choose to perceive it.

Metacognition prepares and allows the mind to think through raw experiences from different perspectives. The metacognitive perspective of another person can further deepen and expand this process when they understand how your thinking came to develop. However, this is a perspective they can only gain from thoughtful, meaningfull discussion with you. Through a process of explaining yourself, you come to know yourself. By allowing another person into your metacognitive practice, you can share and connect your experience and perspective in such a way that it produces new knowledge you can use. In conclusion, it is my belief that the practical practice of constructing a personal narrative of one's own understanding of themselves allows for an ever deepening capacity for metacognition, which can become transformative when supported by others who are willing to support its engagement.

References

Adelizzi, J. U., & Goss, D. B. (Eds.). (1995). *A closer look: Perspectives and reflections on college students with learning disabilities*. Curry College.

Deutsch, D. (2011). *The beginning of infinity: Explanations that transform the world*. Penguin Books.

Flavell, J. H. (1979). Metacognition and cognitive monitoring: A new area of cognitive development. *American Psychologist, 34*(10), 906–911. https://doi.org/10.1037/0003-066X.34.10.906

Fox, L. (Ed.). (2010). *Changing lives through metacognitive relationships: LD/ADHD and college success*. Curry College.

Foy, S. L. (2018). Challenges from and beyond symptomatology: Stereotype threat in young adults with ADHD. *Journal of Attention Disorders, 22*(3), 309–320.

Harri-Augstein, E. S., & Thomas, L. (1991). *Learning conversations: The self organized learning way to personal and organizational growth.* Routledge.

Janis, I. L. (2008). Groupthink. *IEEE Engineering Management Review, 36*(1), 36.

Langner, C. A., & Keltner, D. (2008). Social power and emotional experience: Actor and partner effects within dyadic interactions. *Journal of Experimental Social Psychology, 44*(3), 848–856.

Massachusetts Department of Elementary and Secondary Education. (2018). *603 CMR 28.00.* Retrieved from: https://www.doe.mass.edu/lawsregs/603cmr28.html?section=06

Norris, E. M., & Bullock, I. (2017). A 'Learning conversation' as a style of feedback. *MedEdPublish, 6*(156), 156.

Pennini, S. W. (2006). *College students with learning disabilities: A case study* [Doctoral dissertation, Lesley]. https://digitalcommons.lesley.edu/education_dissertations/77

Plous, S. (1993). *The psychology of judgment and decision making.* Temple University Press.

Sapolsky, R. M. (2017). *Behave: The biology of humans at our best and worst.* Penguin.

Webb, G. M. (1972). Building a sense of worth. *Academic Therapy, 8*(1), 41–49.

Webb, G. (1989). *Tuning in to learning.* Waltham.

Part III
Integration

Chapter 7
General Theory of Metacognitive Instruction

When the insights of these professors were compared and contrasted with my early insights and research, certain common traits of metacognitive teaching came to light. These will be outlined in this section as the general theory of metacognitive instruction (GTMI). It is believed that these are the core and most generally applicable methods of metacognitive instruction. There are central commonalities like the finding that rather than mastery of subject matter, the greater goal was the desire to teach a thinking process that could enable a student to achieve deeper investigational abilities and more self-control. Subject C described it as, "I don't want to give them things to do and tell them to do it… I want to teach them what they could do, and how they could do it. So that when they come to a new situation, they can say to themselves, 'What could I do and how would I do it?'"

Certain themes and ideas were identified across interview subjects, my reflections, and the diverse literature of metacognition. These themes are hypothesized to be elemental components of a metacognitive instruction that are separable from other aspects of pedagogy and are grounded in neuropsychological developmental phenomena. These are elements of a learning process that supersede subject knowledge formation. Subject knowledge can be thought of as the vital medium through which we teach a deeper understanding of the routines, processes, and behaviors that improve learning and personal performance. The self-regulatory aspects of metacognition require active involvement in a task, goal, or situation.

The GTMI are elements of instruction that are structured around what was found to be the central goal of metacognitive education, self-authorship. This process of metacognitive self-authorship depends on an internal cognitive process that is self-similar to the interactive practices employed by both the learner and a teacher. It is a process that balances the need for developmental support and the development of understanding, using prediction and data driven discussions of behavior. The GTMI can be thought of as the essential components of an education that develops a student's ability to act, even in areas of personal difficulty.

P. R. Hulbig, *The Pedagogy of Self-Authorship*,
https://doi.org/10.1007/978-3-031-41436-7_7

7.1 Self-authorship

A cursory look at the most general problems that affect learning reveals a set of problems that are not within a teacher's or curriculum's power to address adequately. These are problems that occur within a student. They are caused when a student lacks an awareness or knowledge of something. It could result from organic issues, or internal manners of thinking that make understanding hard for them. They may be missing information because of disruptions during learning or environmental impacts. Additionally, if a student does not feel capable, they may give up. Furthermore, a student may limit their behavior or their expulsion of cognitive energy because of habitual or socially constructed limits. These problems are categorically the subjective experiential problems of the learner. While teachers and administrators can devise educational structures to support the learner, they can never truly be sure the learner has committed themselves to addressing these problems. The subjective issues that affect an individual's learning tend to be particularly intractable to large, public institutions.

Subjective issues, however, can be addressed directly through metacognition. When a student can identify the issues that affect their learning and development, they become empowered to address those issues. By directly attempting to address those things that stand in the way of their learning and development, students become more academically capable because they are now involved in a process of self-authorship.

Kegan (1996) defines self-authorship as a stage of human development that occurs when an individual achieves a level of personal awareness and self-control that enables them to consciously take responsibility and control over their development and its expression. The broad array of skills that are harnessed through metacognition support an individual's educational development, academic attainment, and ability to self-direct their own learning, making the attainment of self-authorship possible. Conceptually, self-authorship provides a powerful and personal motivational reason to learn and practice reflective metacognition. It connects the process of metacognition with its product. Self-authorship requires a willful, metacognitive effort and a willful, metacognitive effort produces self-authorship. It is a cyclical, integrative, cognitive activity where students learn new skills and integrate them into their daily practice. This integrating of cognition consists of three interacting processes. These are the processes of identification, sense making order, and evaluation. This trio of cognitive skills seem to sit at the base of any educational model or personal learning strategy.

7.2 Identification and Sense Making Order

Identification is the logical first step of any cognitive process. It is fundamental. To learn anything, a student must become adept at identifying a subject and its important features. Metacognitive learning seeks to identify the important features of a student's way of knowing. This is achieved through ever more nuanced variations of two questions: How do I understand the subject/task at hand? And how successful am I at it? The first question seeks to identify what is known, and the second question seeks to evaluate its practicality. Through this investigative process of identifying and evaluating, the need for order develops. As one brings order to both the process and product, new understandings can be identified. Different kinds of order can be identified through the use of discussions, notes, planners, calendars, lists, organizers, and these can be used to guide, manage, define, or relate to the task/subject at hand.

Sense making order is a unique quality. Using order, organize and make sense of both our external and internal environments. Sense making order need not be symbolic in nature, just meaningful. For example, we may place things in designated places, or color code things to produce order in our visual environment. Order has this quality that makes things more easily understandable, accessible, and functional. Internally, our brains can briefly construct feelings, sounds, images, sensations, and other mental constructs to simulate aspects of our external perception. These mental constructs organize our internal environments the way that designating a place or using color codes orders our external environment.

Order also seems to be fundamentally tied to identification. It is an abstract quality that can be qualitative, like an arrangement of colors, or quantitative, like a numerical counting pattern. Order is fundamentally involved with learning by making information more understandable, accessible, and functional.

When order occurs randomly in nature, it leads to stunningly complex and creative physical systems like the water cycle, galaxies, or living organisms. Even an abstract ordering of expressions as "something" and "nothing" allows programmers to produce rich and complex computational systems. Understanding is tightly bound to this quality of order. Sense making ordering supports learning by presenting information in ways that make it understandable and functional. How order is made possible through an extrapolation of the ability to make identifications is not well understood, but what is clear is that identifying and ordering are as fundamental to learning as memory. They are even more important to metacognitive learning, which seeks to help students address the more ambiguous and shifting subject matter of self-authorship.

While order eases the difficulty of identification, order and identification are linked in a way that does more than allow one to enhance the other. Ordered identifications make new identifications within that order possible, and new meta-identifications. On a personal metacognitive level, it helps students see things about themselves that they never noticed and discover choices they did not believe they had. This relationship between identification and order suggests a mental phenomenon at their base. This would be a fundamental phenomenon that binds aspects of perception to cognitions, making future perceptions more easily identifiable and cognitions capable of producing tools of thought (Vygotsky, 1934).

Tools of thought (Vygotsky, 1934) are ordered systems of thinking that organize and bestow practical powers on the intellect. Metacognitive thinking allows the learner to experience a transcendence of these systems and tools of thought. For example, one of the most useful systems of organization at the mind's disposal is the process of language. Not only does language enable interactions between people that support complex levels of interpersonal organization, but language confers the ability to internalize communication, making an internal dialogue possible. With the development of an internal dialogue, intrapersonal organization can occur. However, language is doing more than increasing an individual's power of thought. It is also a tool that contributes to behavioral self-control.

As stated, internally generated sensory experiences are transitory and brief. The amount of time the brain can perform any kind of internal representation without external stimulus is constrained by time. Whatever the brain represents is degraded by the constant ebb and flow of distractions within the mind. For example, we know from investigations of non-meditators that focused awareness, without an object of focus, quickly decays (Holzel et al., 2011). The brain cannot throw up an internal vision for much more than a fleeting second, and attempts to reflect on that vision can often more quickly distort it. But language, by design, produces quick, information-dense inputs that can regulate the rapid flow of thought and direct attention as it wanes. Once one understands how language enables behavior to be directed, one can use it to better regulate their actions. Not only with self-talk, but with written notes, agendas, calendars, and through communication with other individuals. Language is a tool of thought that improves one's metacognitive ability to use and exploit its own abilities. It facilitates identification and ordering, and so by necessity fosters deeper levels of understanding and more complex behavior.

Students can improve their understanding of anything they set their attention to. Conscious attention has a power that leads to more nuanced identifications. When this ability is turned back on itself, it begins to identify the many dimensions of the self. The better a student understands the self that they are constructing, the more sophisticated they will be at organizing themselves. The more organized a student's understanding of themselves becomes, the more choices they will find available to them, as choices come out of a cognitive organizational structure that produces multiple behavioral possibilities. As students come to better identify the details that make up who they are, they become better at organizing themselves and productively integrating with their environment. A lack of productive behavior by a student, by this model, would be attributable to a lack of understanding about the self or the situation the self is embedded within.

7.3 Behavior Modification and Metacognition

Classical models of behavior modification can be successful in the short term, supporting an individual in regulating a behavior. The weakness is over the long term. In one sense, behavior modification plans order behavioral situations and identify behavioral consequences more clearly, making it easier to choose correct courses of action in the situation being modified. However, classical behaviorism also treats the mind like a black box, so the metacognitive understanding that promotes the transference of behaviors to new situations does not always happen. This results in the student going back to doing similar maladaptive behaviors when the rewards or other environmental features of the behavior plan are lifted. However, by adding the element of metacognitive knowledge and self-reflection, long-term, intentional behavior change can occur. One can also see how the opposite can occur in systems that do not include a behaviorally modifying focus, but rather only seek to address cognitive elements of behavior change, like traditional psychodynamic approaches. Here a knowledge of the behavior is developed without an active element. There is no impetus to use the knowledge to produce detailed strategies of behavior change. This results in a student who can speak deeply about their self-regulatory problems, but remains powerless to do anything about them.

Through supported use of metacognition, the student can come to understand the component tools of behavior modification and self-reflection. More than this, they learn to use them to aid in their own personal process of self-authorship. This is why the most successful forms of behavior modification have been found to involve bringing the student into the process with behavior contracts and collaborative problem-solving (Greene, 2009). Through metacognition, students can learn to modify their own behavior. They both learn and develop the ways that allow them to address or work around the constraints placed upon them by their internal or external environments.

7.4 Metacognitive Teaching Interactions

A teacher of metacognition will work to improve their student's ability to identify tools of thought and the aspects of their behavior that affect goal achievement. The process requires students to make choices and then reflect on the outcome of those choices. Questions become very important, opening a channel through which a dialogue about the task can occur. Modeling similarly opens a channel that shows how to move orderly through the task. Regardless of the channel, the process of identifying, organizing, and building an understanding remains a primary learning structure, whether the focus is on the student or their course work.

For learning to become self-directed, it must be self-conscious, self-aware, and reflective. From self-consciousness comes a level of self-control. Mistakes refine this process. Teachers support and refine the ability of the student to identify and address the specific points in a process where mistakes can occur. Being aware of the mistakes that can occur in a task has the effect of producing more successful self-regulated behavior. Identifying mistakes paves the way for ordered behaviors that can be employed to avoid the identified mistake. Ordered behaviors can be turned into lists of procedures that make the behaviors easier to complete and communicate to others. These proceduralized adaptive behaviors can over time become internalized and subconscious. Moreover, organizing mistakes into categories serves in the identification of correct choices, which can be used to build a conceptual organization that can improve the execution of the identified positive behaviors in a variety of situations.

Understanding is developed through sitting with a problem and allowing yourself to experience the problem. This ability to sit with a problem is an issue with intentional, consciously focused attention. To address the problem of a student's shifting attention, teachers create tasks to bring their student's mind back to the issue or ideas relevant to their development of understanding. Skilled teachers can create and mediate learning experiences (Feurstien et al., 1980) in ways that enable their students to experience and solve problems that would occur so subtly in a student's life that they would not otherwise notice them or be able to identify the discernable order they make. While such a constructed learning experience can take virtually any form, the core of that experience will be an experiment hypothisized to help the student identify a problem and all of its salient components. Discussion and verbal feedback are powerful mechanisms for error-correcting this process. By saying something, the teacher can tap into an underlying natural heuristic of human communication, and that is the desire to respond to an identified problem.

Questions powerfully compel a response in most learners, and when carefully choreographed, questions can focus the student's conscious awareness on a component of a problem that they may not yet be aware of. We may not be aware of something for two reasons. First, it may be we have not yet had a conscious experience of it. Maybe we have never seen it before. Maybe, it was never taught to us, or no one ever mentioned it. This even includes experiences that may happen all around us, like the growth of a specific wild plant in our environment. Such a plant may grow relatively unnoticed by the conscious mind for years in the very environment where we live. Although we may look at it every day, its existence blends into the background scenery. Noticing its existence starts the process of understanding. Identification, as explained, is the first step, and it is the step that is repeated over and over, producing order, knowledge, and understanding.

The teacher's first step in instruction is to identify, then facilitate communication of what has been identified. In metacognitive instruction, the first step starts with helping the student to communicate what they identify as their most important characteristics. The teacher's role is to give the student a forum to identify themselves to themselves. Through question and response, the teacher strives to build the student's ability to project that communication more clearly. Often, this takes the form of restating what the student has said back to them. For example, a teacher might say to a student, "I heard you say X," restating what the student said. "Does this mean Y," highlighting ways that the statement could be interpreted by a receiver of this information.

This kind of back-and-forth exchange builds a student's ability to communicate their understanding, and creates a space to safely contemplate other ways they could be interpreted or misinterpreted. The broad goal of developing self-authorship will require an investigation of the student's goals and responsibilities as well as an evaluation of how well they are achieving their goals and addressing their responsibilities. As a student becomes more metacognitively aware, they will refine their communication, bringing in written and visual models to enhance the process. To do lists, calendars, and journals are our records of intended courses of action and important sources of data for reflective discussion. The metacognitive teacher is there to support their student in identifying and articulating what has been identified. Helping a student identify to a teacher the internal and external impediments to their learning will better enable that teacher to support the student, and better enable the student to access the help and support they need in the future.

Over time, as the student learns to better work with their metacognitive teacher, they come to realize the importance of identifying where breakdowns in their knowledge, communication, and task execution occur. A skilled metacognitive teacher will help keep their student aware and focused on both the internal and external points of difficulty when pursuing a goal. Internal points of difficulty may have to do with self-communications about task difficulty, self-confidence, or motivation. External points may have to do with factors like how well the student is communicating with others about their expectations or even how to avoid an argument. Many different types of internal and external factors can come to bear. They are interrelated in a multitude of ways, requiring a teacher to be metacognitive and flexible enough to understand when to avoid or switch approaches to keep learning moving forward. This line of thought suggests a teacher's skill set and a student's needs can be incompatible. It may require another person to step in and work with the student. However, it also suggests that a teacher can work to identify the concise and precise methods of communication, whether they be spoken, written, visual, or mixed media, that will assist the student in identifying their strengths and weaknesses in learning and performance.

Sometimes a student's descriptions of themselves have become so rigidly aligned with definitions attributed to them by parents, peers, professionals, or culture that they have lost sight of the reality that they are more complex than any definition or diagnosis or role they may be playing. For example, there are students with ADHD who take their diagnosis to literally mean they have little to no control over their attention, so they make little to no attempt to focus their attention. A strong metacognitive teacher would identify these false beliefs and help this student reframe their self-definition in a way that is more growth-oriented and hopeful.

The ability to define an identification leads to a natural kind of closure. After an understanding is achieved, it is natural for a student to feel they have explained everything. At these points, the metacognitive teacher's role is to not only praise and reward the student for their accomplishments, but also remind them that this is not the end of the learning process. A student's new understanding represents a growth in their knowledge. It is an understanding they can use to attack new problems and work toward new goals to achieve new growth, which will lead to new understandings that have not yet been identified but are now possible because of the achieved understanding.

Students need to learn that communications they have about themselves, that they may use to explain themselves, are not themselves. Even the representations produced by their senses cannot express the infinite relationships of a simple object they may see every day. Like that plant in your environment that you never noticed before, once you have identified and defined it, you begin a chain of identifications that will come to be linked to your perception and knowledge about that plant. For example, once identified, a plant can be understood by its name, taxonomy, growth cycle, adaptations, cell structure, chemical makeup, medicinal or nutrition value, history, and even highly personal facts like its beauty or if it provokes an allergic reaction. There is an infinite quality to the human capacity for understanding, and part of the metacognitive teacher's job is helping the student realize this capacity about himself and others.

A truly metacognitive education strives toward opening up a student to a manner of thinking that leads to the active pursuit of improving their skills of understanding. Because of the infinite variation in skill, ability, and disability, it is a task that is never fully completed, and may plateau or decline if obstacles toward it become too great. There is an elegant universal design to metacognitive education. It is able to sincerely incorporate scientific methodologies into one's approach toward self-investigation, opening up a cognitive process of seemingly infinite depth that leads to the development of the ultimate integration of an individual and their environment, called self-authorship.

Metacognitive self-examination is linked to scientific methodology in a profound way. It hones an individual's natural skills of collecting personal data points that can be compared, contrasted, or researched to assist the development of skills that deepen self-understanding, promoting the development of new knowledge, skills, and regulation. These are the natural skills that make understanding and discovery possible. A metacognitive teacher draws these skills out of their students by creating a learning experience where setting goals and executing the behaviors needed for goal attainment are directly identified and organized to produce more effective behavior. Students learn to use metacognition to build understanding of who they are and what they need to do to gain control of their internal and external environments in a way that promotes learning and development.

7.5 Environmental and Emotional Impacts

The final critical element of the GTMI is the relationship of metacognition to emotional qualia. Starting with Hart's (1965) investigation of the feeling of knowing, an aspect of metacognition has been found to be bound to a class of cognitive experiences called qualia (Chalmers, 1996). These are non-computational (Penrose, 1989) aspects at the visceral level of experience. They are qualitative aspects like the redness of a rose, the warmth of the sun, or a feeling you get when you may or may not understand something. Emotional qualia are the sensory experience of emotion. They are very highly tuned to situations in the environment, and represent the viscerally felt emotional quality of the experience. Interestingly, metacognition, despite its cognitive nature, seems to be very interconnected with this visceral level of perceptual experience.

The impact of emotion on metacognition is much more significant than is presently appreciated, both in its positive and negative dimensions. Present research (Sapolsky, 2017) has been primarily focused on the negative impact of emotion and the destructive impact traumatic events can have on thinking generally. In this study, emotional qualia were identified repeatedly as an impediment to the development of metacognition.

There were just as many statements that indicated that a large piece of metacognitive questioning involved helping students identify positive emotional relationships. "I have met many students that may not be doing well, but when they hit something that they feel good about (they become capable of things) they didn't think they could do." Subject A felt that identifying what brought a student positive emotion was a foundational element of her approach. "Let's look at what you did that led to what made you feel so good, or what you think made you feel so good. I think that's a good opening."

There is a qualitative, felt aspect to metacognition that is sensitive to emotional experience. To teach metacognition, one must know the impact of emotion. Teachers must study the effects of emotion on their students and be ready to both harness and blunt the effects of these emotions in a transparent, thoughtful way. Emotions can be identified, ordered, and made sense of in a way that they enhance the metacognitive capacity of students as well as restrict them. A metacognitive teacher must be aware of how emotional experiences and trauma can limit a student's ability to reason, or even engage, metacognitively, but they must also be aware that emotional experiences of hope and curiosity expand it.

The student–teacher relationship has historically been identified as an important feature of education. A strong student–teacher relationship is particularly important to address the emotional undercurrents that underpin the act of self-regulation and metacognitive learning. Weak student–teacher relationships may strain under the emotional burden of self-reflection, or lack the personal investment needed to find and resolve difficult problems. The visceral feeling of emotions can deter us from having certain thoughts, engaging in certain behaviors, and sustaining in certain situations. A big part of metacognitive education is examining why these specific thoughts, behaviors, and situations are difficult and how they affect student learning.

Metacognition is a process that allows us to identify different modalities of thought. It allows us to evaluate and order those modalities in a way that identifies some as being disruptive or disabling and others as being more supportive and enabling. The goal of every teacher of metacognition is to develop a relationship with their student that peaks their honest and active engagement in the developmental processes of their learning, and enables them to be an honest editor of their life.

Depression and anxiety are examples of two common disruptive and disabling modes of thought that must be addressed through metacognitive education. However, only the student will be able to directly address the internal evocations of these experiences. The experience of disruptive qualia explains why imparting metacognitive insight was not always achieved by all students, even with the support of a PAL professor. "I have students that are still flailing in the same ways that they were flailing at the beginning (Subject A)." A teacher of metacognition will only be as successful as their ability to get their student to orient their attention toward identifying and understanding the qualia of their cognitive experiences, which could be painful and frightening for them, but also enjoyable and empowering.

7.6 Metacognition Evaluative Technique

The evaluation of metacognition is necessarily unlike traditional standardized testing metrics. Traditional, standards-based and statistic-driven assessments have certainly been applied to the evaluation of a student's knowledge of metacognition. Evaluative questions about the subject, like Schraw and Dennison's (1994) Metacognitive Awareness Inventory (MAI) instrument, have been used toward this end. However, regardless of whether the evaluation is a Likert Scale, multiple choice, sophisticated open response, or other such common evaluative techniques, only one aspect of metacognition is actually being evaluated, metacognitive knowledge. Such evaluation techniques do not measure the regulatory aspects of metacognition, which are highly conditional and situation dependent.

Traditional mechanisms of assessment are fundamentally unfit to fully evaluate metacognitive ability because they are fixed in time and cannot take into account the situational or subjective features of self regulation. The temporal weakness of any kind of one-and-done testing technique could be blunted by the use of formative testing or by using a testing regiment that tracks the growth of knowledge over time. While these approaches greatly improve the validity of traditional testing results, they still fail to address the subjective regulatory aspects of metacognition.

Metacognitive evaluation requires integrating information and action. For a full evaluation of metacognition, traditional assessment techniques must be integrated with the subjective lived experience of the student during the entire process, even during the assessment itself. By integrating the collection of objective and subjective information metacognitively, both the student and the teacher can make far more nuanced and actionable evaluations.

Metacognition is as much of a skill as a subject. There is an active quality to metacognitive evaluations that is missing from assignments generally. For example, I could test you on all the aspects of skateboarding, but there could be a significant differential between what you know about skateboarding and what you can actually do on a skateboard. Skills are frequently introduced and evaluated in a form that has been so abstracted from real life that they provide the student with no practical ability to effectively perform the skill, despite having tested competently. Inversely, a student could end up in a situation like mine where they are assessed as far less capable than they actually are. For proper metacognitive evaluation to take place, a third node of evaluation must be integrated, and this is the students' own subjective evaluation. This three-point evaluative architecture includes the student and develops a student's ability to evaluate themselves. This three-node system allows the teacher to better understand the student's learning to build better lessons that can better target and stimulate student learning. It enables administrators to make more informed and helpful institutional decisions about student needs.

Metacognition integrates disparate modes of thinking and perception, knowledge and regulation, objective and subjective, conscious and subconscious, emotion and cognition. Standards are still necessary to evaluate the achievement of self-regulatory objectives and the quality of metacognitive knowledge. Part of these standards will necessarily be derived from the insights of another more skilled educator or individual. However, regardless of their skill, they will only be able to evaluate behavioral observations of their student's regulatory ability and awareness. Students will necessarily need help identifying subconscious influences on their thinking or behavior that impair their ability to evaluate.

Despite this, students are the ones in the best position to evaluate the subjective qualities of their own learning and express how they experience those qualities. For this reason, the metacognitive evaluation process requires the student's honest participation. The approach is to have the student repeatedly ask themselves, "how do I describe myself and my learning" at that critical recursion point in the learning cycle. The professor's job is to promote deep reflection, supporting the student in identifying deep truths that can be taken into the future to support their problem-solving. The ability to be part of their own evaluation is critical to developing the student's ability to evaluate their own management of external demands and their internal management of emotions and cognitions.

To develop a student's accurate self-evaluative ability, lessons are derived from the student's own actions. The teacher supports self-evaluation that is student-centered and nurturing of the fundamental human drive toward problem-solving and creativity. Students learn to evaluate themselves through engagement with their processes of learning, acquiring increasingly more self-control over their learning. Teachers devise experiences, create lessons, and help students to identify and bring what is being learned under their control, supporting their students in the areas that tax or require improved self-control so they can identify and address impediments to their achievement of greater self-efficacy.

7.7 Overview of GTMI

The general theory of metacognitive instruction (GTMI) provides a clear educational structure that is simple enough to be communicated and practiced by students, while allowing teachers, professors, and educational professionals a way to conceptualize the very complex and multifaceted work of metacognitive instruction. This description of metacognitive teaching can be used both to guide the development of metacognitive lessons and to evaluate their effectiveness. Its elements can be found throughout the educational literature, but are being presented here as a way to separate the elements of metacognitive teaching from other more subject or skill-driven modes of education. It is done to clarify what is meant by metacognitive instruction, so that its elements can be better integrated into other educational structures. The basic structure is as follows:

1. Goal
   (a) Self-authorship and self-directed learning

2. Procedures
   (a) Cyclical identification and ordering routines
      (i) Identify a problem, goal, or task to address
      (ii) Compose a plan or hypothesis to solve the problem or achieve the goal
         1. Discussion and questioning
         2. Modeling
         3. Structured tasks
         4. Mediated experiences
      (iii) Execute steps
      (iv) Evaluate the outcome
      (v) Identify a new goal, problem or experience to address
   (b) Key procedures
      (i) Make choices and reflect on the results
      (ii) Develop greater awareness and self-control through practice and reflection
      (iii) Identify and address environmental and emotional impacts on thinking and behavior
3. Evaluation
   (a) Integration of three domains
      (i) Objective assessment
      (ii) Teacher observation and critique
      (iii) Subjective student measures.

Metacognition can be appreciated and understood by all ages and aptitude levels. It can add structure to ambiguous learning situations and provide meaningful direction for the student and teacher while working together. By consciously turning the reflective element of learning back upon the learning process itself, a deeper understanding of one's own processes of learning becomes possible, producing a capacity for greater behavioral control and complexity.

References

Chalmers, D. J. (1996). *The conscious mind: In search of a fundamental theory*. Oxford University press. https://antilogicalism.com/wp-content/uploads/2019/04/conscious-mind.pdf

Feuerstein, R., Ya'acov Rand, Hoffman, M. B., & Miller, R. (1980). *Instrumental enrichment: An intervention program for cognitive modifiability*. University Park Press.

Greene, R. W. (2009). *Lost at school: Why our kids with behavioral challenges are falling Through the cracks and how we can help them*. Simon and Schuster.

Hart, J. (1965). Memory and the feeling-of-knowing experience. *Journal of Educational Psychology*, 56(4), 208–216. Retrieved from https://doi.org/10.1037/h0022263

Hölzel, B. K., Lazar, S. W., Gard, T., Schuman-Olivier, Z., Vago, D. R., & Ott, U. (2011). How does mindfulness meditation work? Proposing mechanisms of action from a conceptual and neural perspective. *Perspectives on Psychological Science, 6*(6), 537–559.

Penrose, R. (1989). *The emperor's new mind: Concerning computers, minds, and the laws of physics*: Oxford U. Press.

Sapolsky, R. M. (2017). *Behave: The biology of humans at our best and worst*. Penguin.

Schraw, G., & Dennison, R. S. (1994). *Metacognitive awareness inventory*. Contemporary Educational Psychology.

Vygotsky, L. S. (1934). *Thinking and Speech*, Retrieved September 9, 2019. from: https://www.marxists.org/archive/vygotsky/works/words/Thinking-and-Speech.pdf

Chapter 8
To Be Neurodivergent

The last subject I wish to cover in this book is the important role metacognition has to play in building a neurodiversity movement based on principles of health and resiliency. More people than ever are standing up to express their support for neurodiversity, and thanks to the work of advocates like Temple Grandin, television stars like Whoopee Goldberg, and business leaders like Bill Gates, there is not only greater awareness of the issue but a greater respect too. However, there is a problem facing the neurodiversity movement. It is a problem with conceptualization and a bias that is so widespread, the only way it can possibly be addressed is through the kind of thoughtful discussion-based practice outlined here.

The neurodiversity movement comes framed as a political movement, but there is no polarized opposition to it. It is not that kind of political movement. The goal of this movement is not power, it is a movement for support. It is a movement of people who need help and would like to help others in need. Unfortunately, offering help to people does not receive as much support as it should these days because offering help is now so often equated with government spending. Because of this, people who would generally get behind a movement like this feel they must respectfully deny their support because they cannot support any more government spending no matter how much it helps. This is the present political reality of the neurodiversity movement.

I believe if the neurodiversity movement is going to be truly successful, it will need to focus its efforts on helping others develop the resiliency necessary to be a neurodivergent thinker. But even as I write these words, I am sure they are incorrectly expressing my meaning to most who read them. This is because I know the logical error inherent in the wording, the potentially obscuring bias, which I can even identify for you as the assumptions of a medical model of disability. This is disheartening. Because the truth that I am trying to give words to is, in fact, an expression of neurodivergent thinking. Statistically speaking this means that if the readership of this book is a normative sample of the U.S. population, probably two-thirds of people reading this will not interpret what I am trying to say the way I mean it, and roughly

P. R. Hulbig, *The Pedagogy of Self-Authorship*,
https://doi.org/10.1007/978-3-031-41436-7_8

a third may even be offended, with ever smaller fractions of the population being more offended than the others.

Interestingly, my only hope of rectifying this transference problem with communication, represented in my meaning of the phrase, "the resiliency necessary to be a divergent thinker," is to present it in a metacognitive way that points out the differing interpretations. Rather than charging into an objective review of the literature or a personal narrative as I have done in earlier chapters, I am going to try to demonstrate an internal dialogue using metacognition as my problem-solving approach.

While I can only be sure of what I know, I can be pretty sure that there are other ways of knowing. My neurology has made this reality glaringly obvious to me. Plus, I have been diagnosed by professionals as not always being aware of specific other ways of knowing that other people are plainly aware of in the domains of language. I know I make mistakes both in interpretation and expression, and for this reason I must be hypervigilant in situations involving language. I have learned through years of trial and error that this breakdown occurs at what I conceptualize as the edges of expression. That stage where the words and the ideas come together in a meaningful way for those who hear them.

What I have found is that when others reach this liminal space between words and meanings, there is some underlying logic that leads them to coalesce around certain words for the expression of certain ideas and not others. Sometimes I can work this logic backwards, and see why it was formulated that way, but other times it just seems to be a biological predisposition a majority of people have. I am part of a subset of the population for which this biological predisposition is not so readily available. However, I am far from the worst at this kind of reasoning, as there are ever smaller fractions of people in my diagnostic grouping that demonstrate ever more difficulty making these connections with language.

But back to the phrase, "the resiliency necessary to be a divergent thinker." When you think about someone who expresses the neurological differences that they experience, as I have just done in the preceding paragraph, it is easy to think that the resiliency being spoken of is the resilience related to the grit needed to soldier through the neurological challenges presented by my learning disability. And while I would agree that if you have an identified disability, you will need tremendous resiliency to deal with the challenges of your neurology, do not underestimate this challenge simply because it is not the kind of resilience I am talking about here. Your neurological challenges are not simple challenges, and come in two forms, ones that can be noticed by keen observers, and ones that are far more subtle, like the issue outlined above. They may be ones that only you can observe. Developing this kind of resiliency should be part of every healthcare and educational program because this is the kind of resiliency that is necessary to survive as a person who has a weakness. This is definitely a very important form of resilience in its own respect, but if you interpreted the phrase this way, you would have missed its real meaning, and perhaps you would have ended up contorting the rest of this chapter to fit that perception of meaning.

Not all resiliency is the same. I believe the resilience needed to confront one's biology is actually an easier form of resilience to develop than "the resiliency necessary to be a divergent thinker." I believe this is because when you start to lean into your weaknesses, you will see growth, and it is the ability to see your own growth that promotes healing. This is why neurological conditions that involve some form of neglect, repression, or disassociation are so difficult to contend with. You have to become aware that there are perceptions that are occuring that you do not perceive, or forms of thinking that include information that you can only access in a secondhand, abstract way. When I communicate, I have to be aware of these errors in my perception and how they present, but through this I gain greater levels of self-regulation and control. Although I am performing activities differently than most, I can achieve the same results.

It is the ability to really experience the feeling of improvement, which can be so empowering that it pushes you on, helping you improve and helping you to become more resilient as you learn to work with and around your weaknesses. But this important form of resiliency can be impaired, damaged, or destroyed by the actions of others, and these are the things a divergent thinker must learn how to recover from. Unlike your biology, you may not be able to see steady improvement in these interactions, or even be able to predict when they are coming. Your only recourse is to build a kind of social resilience that will shield your consciousness from damage.

This resiliency to the cruelty of others is a confusing mix of angry tenacity and compassion. A compassion that allows you to rationally detach from the toxic emotions their behavior can conjure in you. The anger will help keep you focused on whatever goal you have for yourself. Sometimes you have to fight to make a dream real, but it must be tempered by compassion for those very same people whose callous lack of insight into their own thinking makes their ability to conceptualize someone else's thinking difficult for them. Those undiagnosed minds move so quickly to mental scaffolds like hierarchy, and then place themselves at its apex. However, it would be a gross overgeneralization to attribute this mindset simply to the undiagnosed neurotypical mind. In my experience, it is just as likely that a person with an atypical neurological presentation will be just as prejudiced, and express their prejudice in much the same way, and this gets closer to what I am trying to express.

The reason there are just as many non-neurotypical people harboring ill feelings and prejudice against those with neurological disabilities as there are neurotypicals harboring prejudice is because these groupings are groupings of people, and people have a hard time accepting differences. Our common primate propensity for tribalism and fear of the unknown identify us as part of the human species. This quality of tribalism is a common human trait that becomes particularly acute for about one-third of the population, and considerably more intense for certain smaller fractions of this group.

Another common feature of being human is thinking differently than everyone else does, to a lesser or greater degree. There is absolutely no doubt that this is the case. However, we have devised ways we can categorize similarities and differences we see in the human mind, and presently there does not seem to be a way to avoid it or even any other way to do it other than the way we do it. However, this system of classification is based on the absolutely false assumption that people think the same, and you can label these people with the same categorical label. Maybe a case could be made for identical twins but even here, the neuroplastic effects of experience will ensure there will be differences over time. One twin will focus more time on some things than the other, building skills and synaptic connections that the other will not have.

Being able to categorize similar kinds of thinking makes it easier for us to discuss and think about the neurological function of certain groups of people who demonstrate certain similar qualities. But this does not erase the fundamental fact that no two minds think the same thoughts or function in a perfect synchrony in response to a similar stimulus. Each experience is uniquely processed and experienced by you and every neurological ability that you have is uniquely yours.

While experience makes us different and develops our unique skill set, exposure to new experiences is not always a good thing. Some experiences can cause damage, be it genetic, traumatic, physical, or mental. Maybe you were born with it. Maybe you were injured. Maybe someone or something hurt you in a way that floods your system with a fear that steals your personality from time to time. In all cases, the damage suffered leaves you changed. You will never recover fully. The healing process will still leave behind permanent scars and sometimes those scars will change the way you have to do things. In the case of physical trauma, the damage may change the way you move. In mental trauma, the damage may change the movement of your thoughts. With neurological or genetic damage, you may have to contend with both.

But in the healing process, we can gain back lost skills. We can feel ourselves get stronger as we recover, and we can take charge of our recovery to further improve the outcome of our healing. This does not change the fact there could be a level of damage that is irrecoverable, but this does not mean your healing stops. Healing can continue until you find the way to live without the irrecoverable damage getting in the way. Healing includes workarounds, supports, even prosthetics that allow you to be the person you desire to be. This ability "to be" is a certain behavioral mindset that reflects not just on the damage but also on the process of recovery. It's a mindset that does not look away from the damage but also does not wallow in it. A mindset that is able to sincerely ask the question, "What can I do?".

"What are my strengths?"

"What are my weaknesses?"

"How do I enhance my strengths and work with my weaknesses?"

In the process of healing, we learn. We learn that we can move ourselves forward. How effectively we can learn from our healing experience will determine how we regulate ourselves toward healing in the future. Perhaps the most detrimental thing that can happen to a person is to incur damage to their ability to engage in the reflective thinking needed to learn from their healing. This is a post-traumatic inability to see the need to see healing, that leaves you trapped into perceiving only the damage, and only able to speak of yourself in relation to the damage. For many this causes them to seize on a label for their damage, a label that for them defines a limit they cannot cross.

This is a horrifying mindset to experience and equally horrifying to watch another person struggle with. From a third-person metacognitive perspective, you can see that the problem is more than cyclical, it is built into the processing of information itself. You will not see it if you remain in the first-person subjective state of consciousness. You will see the cycle, but the force that leads that cycle back to focus on the damage will not be seen because it is not there to be seen. It is not experienced in that way.

It is your frame. It is how you identify it, how you problematize it through a lens of damage and weakness. This lens allows a barely perceptible self-fulfilling prophecy to occur, compelling your behavior toward actions that will justify what you already believed. It protects you from thinking about the hard reality of your situation, and prevents you from changing your behavior to promote your healing and growth.

I have seen this mindset manifest across disability categories, personality types, races, and genders. It is a mindset born from tragedy, pain, and sorrow. For a long time, doctors, philosophers, and scientists have contemplated why some people go one way and some go the other. What is becoming clear to me is that it is trauma and a lack of the resiliency needed to be neurodivergent. A resiliency that can identify and accept what is needed to heal rather than implode. It is the awareness of the healing process that supports and amplifies your ability to heal. We have a responsibility to ourselves and everyone around us to orient ourselves toward healing and the healing of others. Such an orientation can lead us to calm our anxieties and bring harmony and healing to those in our families, communities, and societies.

It is important for individuals to realize how trauma can cause them to create behavioral routines and ways of doing things that can prevent them from healing and prevent them from being themselves. Serious trauma can cause serious distortions of thinking that can cause people to engage in behaviors that make it more likely that the trauma that so injured them will happen again. However, it is equally important for all people to realize that societies are the creation of our collective behaviors and have inadvertently encoded this destructive mindset of trauma into our social systems.

In America, the social manifestation of this traumatized mindset is all around us. We have created systems that specialize in treatment, but not healing. These are amazingly effective systems of damage diagnosis and identification bolstered by advanced forms of treatment. But after the acute phase of damage is addressed, there are few social systems in America that focus on long-term healing, and even those that do approach their role through the medicalized lens of offering treatment rather than supporting healing. Particularly in the field of education, there is an almost post-traumatic bureaucratic desire to avoid any responsibility for supporting healing. Despite the mounting evidence from the field of neuroplasticity, many refuse to accept the role that learning and education play in promoting healing. While they will use a medical model for diagnosis, they will refuse to see healing, and use terms like progress and achievement in a way that obscures the relationship.

Despite the attempts of numerous activists, parents, and teachers, Individualized Education Programs (IEPs) continue to be conceived as a mechanism to identify the damage and administer school-based treatments, leading to educational services only being offered in relation to the damage. It's a system that works on a medical model of handing out labels for damage and none for healing. In special education today, regardless of what a student has overcome, regardless of the hurdles they have successfully managed, they will still leave their educational program with a label that will define them diagnostically by their limitations for the rest of their lives. Imagine how differently education would function if we had a special education system that had terms to identify different kinds and levels of healing? How different would the educational experience be if your IEPs all truly identified their students through their strengths and level of healing? Upon leaving school rather than a diagnosis, you would leave with labels like "highly resilient," "creative," or "knows everything about cows."

The ability to face persistent experiences of dehumanizing medicalization, judgments of inferiority, and just straight cruelty is the resiliency that is necessary to be a divergent thinker. Most of us with a level of neurological difference reject it, try to hide it, refuse to accept these traits that are part of ourselves. We want to join in with society, so this means hiding, rejecting, or medicalizing our difference to a point that it is not part of you. Sometimes this is a healthy way to conceive your disability as if it is something separate from you. Something you can abstract from yourself, even imagine yourself talking to, as if it were something separate from you. This is a particularly powerful approach to anxiety. But all too often this is not what happens. The label is merely accepted at face value and then put, metaphorically, on a shelf and never really examined in any other way than like a specimen in a jar. As long as you only conceptualize your disability in a third-person abstract way, you will never personalize it or accept its role in your subjective experience. You will be as trapped in your healing process as those whose traumas have left them trapped in similarly styled self-fulfilling prophecy cycles of fear and despair.

Jim Sinclair, a founding member of the Autism Network International (ANI) described autism like this on his blog:

> Autism isn't something a person *has*, or a 'shell' that a person is trapped inside. There's no normal child hidden behind autism.
>
> Autism is a way of being.

The same is true for all of us with neurological differences. I have spent years of my life thinking about my medical condition, studying it so that I could emerge from my shell of dyslexia as a healed person. But what I have found is there was no healed person, there was only damaged old me. A person just trying to get a handle on my weaknesses and express my strengths in a way that enables me to see my growth and transform into the person I most desire to be. While my differences were identified as symptoms of an underlying medical condition, they were really a simple manifestation of my individual differences and the differences in the way I have to function, which most other people do not have to contend with.

Advances in technology have shown me that differences in my ability to read and write were merely socially imposed barriers. Today there are computer programs, word processors, and apps that have allowed me to perform at a doctoral level, but they have not cured the underlying condition. However, my weaknesses have allowed me to grow. I believe these technologies that have been invented to support memory, planning, and communication will ultimately have the same effect that technologies that supported physical handicaps like ramps, curb cuts, and universally designed products have had for the fight for physical disability rights during the 1970s.

During the civil rights movement, those with physical impairments could make a powerful case that cultural ideas of disability were a social construction that societies had overlaid upon individuals with impairment. The fact was many of the intractable problems of the "physically disabled" were dealt with by simply acknowledging their different needs and rebuilding the structures of our social world with that in mind. We realized that physically changing the way we construct our bathrooms, buildings, and cities could bring new levels of productivity and inclusion to our society, leading to a better standard of living for all. I suggest that all that is needed to deal with the many problems related to "neurological disability" is to simply construct a new mental environment in our families, schools, communities, and society. This would be a construction that would uplift even more than standards of living, it would uplift our standards of being.

Medicalized attitudes must assume their proper role in the identification and treatment of damage. Once the medical intervention is finished, a healing model that promotes a person's ability to grow beyond the confines of disability must be adopted lest we find ourselves using the medical model to justify practices that either expressly or subtly lead to unnecessary exclusion and isolation of individuals with disabilities.

Greater acceptance of neurodiversity is a social movement that must innovate in ways that break down stereotypes and critically reframe the conditions of the disabled. In the United States, disability rights were bolstered by the Civil Rights Act of 1964, which made discrimination against individuals based on race, religion, sex, or disability illegal. Later bills, like the Rehabilitation Act of 1973, further protected workers from discrimination based on disability, and the Education for All Handicapped Children's Act of 1975[1] guaranteed educational access. A powerful reason why the disability movement could make such tremendous gains was that activists could offer real, tangible alternatives to many of the social conventions that historically led to exclusion and oppression. Innovations like the dropped curb (Goldsmith, 1963), ramps, door handles, and handrails were easy to implement, life-changing for the disabled, and required minimum buy-in from the public, who often saw these inclusive designs as improving their quality of life as well. These solutions inspired a universal design movement that continues to produce innovations that support and uplift the performance and social participation of those with disabilities while improving life for everyone.

For myself, I can tell you it never really registered that I had a problem until middle school. Before middle school, it didn't really seem like a problem. I couldn't read, so I went with this group of other kids that couldn't read. This was really not so different from the kids who <u>could</u> read really well, who had their own group, and the kids that were average readers had their group. Sure I went to a group for handwriting with some different kids outside of my usual class, but we were all working on writing. Everything was very task specific in elementary school. But in middle school, that

[1] This bill has since been updated and is now called the Individuals with Disabilities Education Act.

changed. We were clearly segregated. Everyone knew it and the fact that both they and us called our class the "retard room" made it clear we were not there to learn a skill like everyone else in school, we were there because we couldn't.

No one ever explained why we were in that room. Reasons were left to be inferred. I personally inferred the worst, which turns out to be pretty common for people with these kinds of experience. I did not know what special education meant. The acronym SPED was just another insulting term people used to describe you.

It is almost comical when you think about how the language around neurological disability has evolved. The word idiot has been in use since the ancient Greeks, who pronounced it idiōtēs, and interpreted the word more to mean you were from a common or lower social position. Over time, an idiot came to be defined as someone who was uneducated or ignorant. However, this all changed in the early 1900s, when the new field of psychometric testing was kicked off by Alfred Binet and his student Theodore Simon. The Binet-Simon scale would assess students in 30 categories of competency so that weaknesses could be targeted with instruction. But soon psychologists, who did not understand Binet's vision for the test but likely thought they did, began applying it in a more medical and less educational way. Psychologists like William Stern started averaging categorical skills to produce a number they described as the Intelligence Quotient. This was an idea that fit more easily than the true idea Binet was trying to express. It was a simpler idea that already fit with the common beliefs of psychologists, eugenicists, and segregationists of the day. With wide support, Stern was able to approach the annual meeting of the American Association for the Study of the Feeble-Minded on May 18, 1910 and propose that the term idiot be used as the descriptive term for those who scored the lowest (0–25) on these kinds of test.

Along with medicalizing the word idiot, this act also stripped the word of its historically social connotation, now suggesting a more clinical inborn defect than a social one. This was also reflected in a change in the way the test was used. Rather than using the test to identify and deliver educational support, the test became routinely used to make placement decisions. These decisions did the opposite of what Binet intended, funneling resources and skilled teachers to the highest-scoring students and segregating the lowest scorers into poorly staffed and funded classrooms. Moreover, this testing was used to justify their exclusion from mainstream public education altogether. The medicalization of the word idiot also birthed new words like imbeciles, whose development was considered higher than an idiot, and morons, who were a class of people higher than imbeciles (Huey et al., 1912). Ultimately, all these words entered the common vernacular. Today, despite no longer using these terms as the scientific descriptors of a neurological condition, they continue to be used as insults.

It is important to understand that a word that was originally used to identify a person of low social standing eventually became the clinical designation for a person who lacked the intelligence to be considered a person. What is more interesting is that the psychological community saw this cruel irony and tried to rectify the problem by using a more accurate descriptor, something that did not carry the social baggage of the word idiot. A word developed by scientists and not eugenicists. A word that would denote the reality of learning and intelligence as mutable and not fixed … retarded. Today, one can see this same bastardization of the word "special," which was the newer word used to replace the word retarded in professional spheres and in education. Clearly, the problem here is not in the word but the meaning that people think the word identifies.

There is fear and hatred here. An unwillingness to face the tough realities of how the brain works, and how what it produces can be lost. For this reason, we also fail to look at how we can use what the brain produces for healing and broader social gains. It is a collective unwillingness to face those who do not have the luxury of living in that reality. You hear it when politicians rail against welfare bums and the homeless. You hear it in the voices of the exasperated special education teachers who have run out of diagnostic tricks to support their students' impairment. You hear it from parents or relatives who have simply had it with your shit.

They don't mean it. They are scared, and that fear prevents them from seeing how scary it is for you, the actual person who suffers from the condition that makes them recoil. But there is a solution that I believe will work for them and enable them to identify these biases and self-fulfilling prophecies they harbor, even though these forces may be working just beneath the level of their conscious perception.

The problem today is a division between the haves and have nots that is so vast that even those with the same disability do not see themselves in the same desperate category. Those in the most desperate standard deviations of their category of diagnosis can barely achieve respect from their peers simply because their struggles, which are, ironically, the same basic struggles their peers experience, have become framed through the lens of disability, making what should be similarities seem alien to them.

No matter how I attempt to describe it, there is going to be some people who will be incapable of understanding what is being expressed. Probably they will come from backgrounds of privilege that never had to face deep adversity or daily abuse. They will probably be white or black or brown. Most likely they will be a man, or a woman, or trans. As expected, they are old boomer types or young zoomer types. You probably know the type. They're rich or poor or somewhere in between. You know how they think because all of those people think the same way. I hope you see that this whole line of argument expresses the problem.

What needs to be done is to engage these people in a conversation that helps them identify who they are, what they believe, and what they want this world to look like. Help them identify the best qualities in themselves, their strengths, and highest aspirations. Discuss with them how they can use these strengths to work around or cancel out their weaknesses. What you will find is that they are not so different. You will find they want a better future, and you can help them think about how to put it together. Help them with the planning and the difficult work that comes with self-transformation, because I believe that this is the deep goal of the neurodiversity movement.

This book has been written to provide a road map for producing the tools of self-transformation. The scientific evidence that self-transformation is possible is overwhelming. The processes and pedagogy that can promote this transformation are already well researched and can be tied to much deeper processes of neuropsychological function. The process of learning and self-transformation is integrative, and you can see it across scientific literature. But if you can take this information and integrate it into your life, your transformation will affect those around you in your family and community. If you share this knowledge, you will empower others, regardless of their damage or disability, to heal and develop a uniquely powerful form of resilience that can enable the ability *to be* in the face of both open and implicit oppression. You will be able to accept and preserve the best parts of who you are and develop into the person you would like to be, even though your natural neurological diversity has caused you to think differently, a quality that we all share.

References

Goldsmith, S. (1963). *Designing for the disabled*. Rutledge.

Huey, E. B. (1912). *Backward and Feeble-minded Children: Clincial Studies in the Psychology of Defectives, with a Syllabus for the Clinical Examination and Testing of Children*. Warwick and York, Incorporated. www.jstor.org/tc/accept?origin=%2Fstable%2Fpdf%2F993583.pdf&is_image=False

Uncited References

Bench, C., Frith, C. D., Grasby, P. M., Friston, K. J., Paulesu, E., Frackowiak, R. S. J., & Dolan, R. J. (1993). Investigations of the functional anatomy of attention using the Stroop test. *Neuropsychologia, 31*(9), 907–922.

Bethune, B., & Doidge, N. (2015). How your brain heals itself. *Maclean's, 128*(4), 40. https://www.macleans.ca/society/health/how-your-brain-heals-itself/

Bruner, J. S. (2009). *Actual minds, possible worlds*. Harvard University Press.

Carey, S. (2000). The origin of concepts. *Journal of Cognition and Development, 1*(1), 37–41.

Cotman, C. W., & Berchtold, N. C. (2002). Exercise: A behavioral intervention to enhance brain health and plasticity. *Trends in Neurosciences, 25*(6), 295–301.

Diamond, J. M. (2006). *The third chimpanzee*. HarperCollins.

Dignath, C., Buettner, G., & Langfeldt, H. P. (2008). How can primary school students learn self-regulated learning strategies most effectively? A meta-analysis on self-regulation training programmes. *Educational Research Review, 3*(2), 101–129.

Doidge, N. (2007). *The brain that changes itself: Stories of personal triumph from the frontiers of brain science*. Penguin.

Eagleman, D. (2022). *Livewired, the inside story of the ever-changing brain*. Pantheon.

Haier, R. J. (2009). Neuro-intelligence, neuro-metrics and the next phase of brain imaging studies. *Intelligence, 37*, 121–123.

Hughes, J. R. (2010). A review of savant syndrome and its possible relationship to epilepsy. *Epilepsy & Behavior, 17*(2), 147–152. https://doi.org/10.1016/j.yebeh.2009.12.014.

Livingston, E. M., Siegel, L. S., & Ribary, U. (2018). Developmental dyslexia: Emotional impact and consequences. *Australian Journal of Learning Difficulties, 23*(2), 107–135.

McWhinney, S. R., Tremblay, A., Boe, S. G., & Bardouille, T. (2018). The impact of goal-oriented task design on neurofeedback learning for brain–computer interface control. *Medical & Biological Engineering & Computing, 56*(2), 201–210

Oberman, L. M., & Ramachandran, V. S. (2008). Reflections on the mirror neuron system: Their evolutionary functions beyond motor representation. In *Mirror neuron systems* (pp. 39–59). Humana Press. https://doi.org/10.1007/978-1-59745-479-7_2

Piore, A. (2013). When brain damage unlocks genius. *Popular Science.* https://www.popsci.com/science/article/2013-02/when-brain-damage-unlocks-geniuswithin/

Snyder, A., Bahramali, H., Hawker, T., & Mitchell, D. J. (2006). Savant-like numerosity skills revealed in normal people by magnetic pulses. *Perception, 35*(6), 837–845. https://doi.org/10.1068/p5539

Snyder, A. W., Mulcahy, E., Taylor, J. L., Mitchell, D. J., Sachdev, P., & Gandevia, S. C. (2003). Savant-like skills exposed in normal people by suppressing the left fronto-temporal lobe. *Journal of Integrative Neuroscience, 2*(02), 149–158. https://doi.org/10.1142/S0219635203000287

Statistic Brain Research Institute. (2018, July 23). https://www.statisticbrain.com/gym-membership-statistics/

Veenman, M. V. J., Prins, F. J., & Elshout, J. J. (2002). Initial inductive learning in a complex computer simulated environment: The role of metacognitive skills and intellectual ability. *Computers in Human Behavior, 18*(3), 327–341. https://doi.org/10.1016/S0747-5632(01)00143-9

Printed in the USA
CPSIA information can be obtained
at www.ICGtesting.com
LVHW021941130124
768905LV00004B/41

9 783031 414350